EssexWorks.

For a better quality of life

SAf

25 - 1 - 12

25 · 2 · 12

17 · 3 - 12

Please return this book on or before the date shown above. To renew go to www.essex.gov.uk/libraries, ring 0845 603 7628 or go to any Essex library.

Essex County Council

CELEBRITY HOTEL

CELEBRITY HOTEL

*True Inside Gossip, Scandal
and Intrigue*

Neil Kirby

As told to Paul James

Book Guild Publishing
Sussex, England

First published in Great Britain in 2010 by
The Book Guild Ltd
Pavilion View,
19 New Road,
Brighton,
BN1 1UF

Typeset in Garamond by Ellipsis Books Ltd, Glasgow

Printed in Great Britain by CPI Antony Rowe

A catalogue record for this book is available from The British Library.

ISBN 978 1 84624 441 4

Dedicated to:
my darling wife, Wendy,
our children, Nicola, Neil junior and David,
grandchildren, Katie and Ben
and my mum and dad, Kathleen and George Kirby.

Contents

1

Manager of Life

That energy which makes a child hard to manage is the energy which afterwards makes him a manager of life.

Henry Ward Beecher, *Proverbs from a Plymouth Pulpit*

The door to apartment number four opened a mere couple of inches, not quite far enough for me to gain entry to the darkened room. A chambermaid beside me in the corridor was becoming hysterical as I placed my full body weight against the door and pushed. An unknown heavy object was barricading the room, and each thrust simply resulted in a dull thud. I pushed again, even more vigorously. Thud. And again. Thud. Had I known that with each heave I was hitting against a man's head, I would have used less force.

The man was dead. The very thought that I had killed him by continually hammering the solid wooden door against his head, even though unintentionally, filled me with terror. My heart was pounding when the police called me for questioning, and I watched in disbelief as ambulance men also carried out the body of a woman from this luxury suite of the Grosvenor House Hotel in London's prestigious Park Lane.

My relief was intense when an autopsy eventually revealed that the man had died two days earlier from a drug overdose. It had been a suicide pact with his wife, although medics managed to save her life. As General Manager of such a large hotel, dealing with death was not an uncommon experience for me; on average four men a year were found dead as a result of over-indulgence, but it was the only occasion when I faced being arrested for manslaughter.

At the time I should have been organising a lunch for Princess Diana, and arranging for a new bed to be constructed to bear the weight of Luciano

Pavarotti, but instead I sat in my office with a stiff drink. As the prospect of a prison cell mercifully receded, it was a moment for heartfelt contemplation. Here I was at arguably one of the city's most distinguished addresses – a luxury hotel in fashionable Mayfair designed by Sir Edwin Lutyens in 1927, then the epitome of Edwardian elegance overlooking the 360-acre Hyde Park. For the first twenty-eight years of my working life the Grosvenor House Hotel was to bring me into daily contact with some of the most beguiling people in the world.

As one of the largest and most luxurious hotels in London, and the first to be built on Park Lane, Grosvenor House was a Mecca for royalty, aristocrats, Hollywood film stars, mega-rich sheikhs, and wealthy eccentrics. One day I could be escorting the Prince of Wales into dinner, the next sitting on Lauren Bacall's suitcase while she zipped it up. Whether searching for Natalie Wood's lost jewels, mopping up after an incontinent duchess or running errands for Dame Margot Fonteyn, it was a unique world that I loved. Yet, with the simple opening of a door, I could have lost it all.

Hotels are awarded five stars for a reason: they provide an impeccable service, often above and beyond the call of duty. For the staff no two days are ever alike, and employees have had to adapt to the ever-increasing demands of today's guests who, in general, have become younger, wealthier, with higher expectations. If they have the money, they insist on the best, whether it is in standard of room, range of facilities, or quality of food. Many wear £100,000 watches, have shoes handmade at over a £3,000 a pair, and I have even seen guests with diamond-studded mobile phones. Invariably I have been asked to obtain theatre tickets for shows that are almost impossible to get, or tickets for the tennis at Wimbledon or the Henley Regatta at £1,500 each. Once I had to arrange for an Aston Martin car to be delivered to a guest, just for the weekend so that he could impress his new girlfriend. In 1993 the Grosvenor House laid claim to London's first £1 million hotel bill, paid by the Qatari Royal Family.

Gone are the days of palm court orchestras and sedate afternoon teas in the lounge; today it is plasma-screen TVs, high-speed internet and Wi-Fi access, civil partnership ceremonies and gay wedding receptions. Guests are now just as likely to ask the receptionist for contraceptives as to request directions to the nearest cinema. At the Ritz-Carlton, South Beach, Florida, a breastfeeding mother recently asked the concierge for cold iceberg lettuce leaves to relieve the nipple pain she was experiencing. More incredibly, a guest at the Beverley Hills Hotel called for the concierge to find him replacement parts for his AK-47 assault rifle. Some requests just have to be declined.

In any hotel, one also has to deal with the idiosyncrasies of your fellow employees. When I worked as a valet, the staff toilets were on alternate floors. Our room had a small old-fashioned sink with a nine-inch draining-board all the way around it and my immediate boss, Mr Dick Smith, used to relieve himself in the sink rather than go up to another floor. Because of the draining-board, he could not reach the sink directly but would aim instead at a plate so that his urine ricocheted in the direction of the plug-hole. Whenever I went to the sink to fill up a kettle, the smell was atrocious. Mr Smith had been there forty years! When he wasn't around, I used to put ammonia down to disinfect it.

If there is any advice to a would-be hotelier, it is *always expect the unexpected*. In January 2008 an agitated guest at a Tasmanian hotel brought a box to reception which had been delivered to him earlier in the evening by a courier. After signing for the package, the man opened it in his room only to discover a single human eyeball staring back. The foam cold-box marked 'Live human organs for transplant' had been wrongly delivered to the hotel and was intended for a local hospital where an operation was due to take place. The guest returned the box to the hotel reception desk. I think I would have fainted if I had been that receptionist.

Celebrity guests often spring the most surprises. When golfer Tiger Woods played in the 2006 Open Championship at the Royal Liverpool Course at Hoylake that July, he did not just book himself a room at the luxurious Victorian Hillbark Hotel, or even their magnificent executive suite, but took over the entire hotel for five nights at a cost of £140,000 ($240,000), thus ensuring his privacy. This, however, was insignificant when compared to his wedding in 2004 when he booked all 110 bedrooms at the Sandy Lane Hotel in Barbados, spending a reputed $1.5 million, with some rooms costing up to $9,000 a night each.

When Angelina Jolie and Brad Pitt booked the whole Burning Shore boutique hotel on Long Beach, Namibia, for a holiday in April 2006, consisting of just seven rooms and five suites, it seemed unremarkable in comparison, and when you work with such lifestyles on a daily basis, what might seem exceptional to others eventually becomes commonplace to the staff. As Manager of a five-star hotel I almost took it for granted if guests wanted the wallpaper changed in their room, or arrangements needed to be made for their private jet.

When I first began working at the Grosvenor House at the age of fifteen and a half, washing up in the basement kitchens, life was very different. We were kept below ground like moles at all times, and no one who worked in the basement area was ever allowed 'above stairs'. Any of the staff found using guests' entrances or exits were instantly dismissed and we certainly never came into contact with the guests themselves. Not until I later began training as a valet in the summer of 1969 was I allowed even a glimpse of the opulence above me.

I will never forget the first time I saw the hotel lobby. Until that moment, the most glamorous scene I had witnessed was a party at an RAF barracks in Germany. Pressing my nose against the mess window pane, I saw my father and his colleagues looking so smart in their uniforms, while my mother danced the can-can. She had once been a professional dancer and as she danced gaily, clearly having such fun, I thought that it was the most enchanting sight I had ever seen. It remained with me for years, especially when times were tough, this vision of my mother dancing as if she hadn't a care in the world. In reality it was just a social gathering of servicemen and women in a bleak wooden hut, but to me as a young child it was as mesmerizing as if it had been a ball at the Ritz.

Now all around me were magnificent chandeliers, marble floors, and rich customers everywhere. And I mean seriously rich. Staff were in abundance here too. There were sixteen doormen at Grosvenor House, all wearing top hats, and because quite a number of them were ex-guards many sported large handlebar moustaches. The uniform of the twenty-four pageboys was black with numerous buttons in two rows, just like the character Buttons in *Cinderella*. Furthermore, the pageboys wore little pillbox hats, embossed with the words 'Grosvenor House Hotel' in gold, and had white gloves, one of which sat on their shoulder under a gold epaulette, a tradition of pageboys. They all worked under the head Hall Porter.

There were seven guest lifts, each manned, offering a fantastic service. When the lifts were on the top floor, for example, the doors would open and the liftman would say: 'Going down, Sir,' or 'Madam' as appropriate. Many times I would hear them say to a customer: 'It has just started to rain outside, Madam. May I suggest that you need an umbrella?' Everywhere the service and attention to detail were as immaculate as the surroundings.

The Grosvenor House has two and a half miles of staff corridors, which extend under Park Lane. It resembles an ants' nest. There was a small army of staff working 'below stairs': 112 chefs, 48 maintenance staff, 10 carpenters, 2 printers in the hotel's own print room producing all the menus and hotel literature, 2 french-polishers, 22 painters, 10 men in the goods bay and stores, 40 people washing up and cleaning floors, plus an additional 8 chefs in the staff canteen, 4 security personnel for the staff entrance, 12 staff in the laundry room, 5 plumbers, 4 audio-visual technicians, a health and safety officer, a tailor just for staff uniforms, and 4 staff in the hotel's upholstery department.

In the hotel above were yet more employees, including some 40 receptionists, 44 valets, 24 pageboys, 24 housekeepers, 125 maids, 25 bathroom cleaners, 12 carpet vacuumers, 8 lift operators, 18 luggage men and 12 pool staff. With three restaurants, a large ballroom, and the Great Room that could entertain thousands of people at one function, there was another army of kitchen porters, waiters, silver polishers and so on. Altogether around two thousand people worked at the Grosvenor House to see to all the guests' needs and ensure the smooth day-to-day running of the business.

Grosvenor House was a far cry from the bleak RAF barracks on the Wirral, where I was born on 15 November 1952. My father was stationed at West Kirby in the north-west of England, where life was tough. Being based at the barracks meant that we had no home of our own, and I was one of four children. Even if this was hailed as the 'new Elizabethan era', with a young Queen on the throne, it must have been a struggle for my parents to bring us up. No silver spoon or deep-pile carpets. Shortly after my birth we were transferred to the RAF base at Bruggen in Germany, where I was to spend the first four years of my life.

Weighing a mighty eleven pounds when I was born, I looked like a baby gorilla and, as I developed, I kept falling flat on my face, squashing my nose, which did little to improve my appearance. Doctors diagnosed that I had bow legs and I had to suffer a very painful operation to correct the condition. My legs were broken, stretched and straightened. After the surgery, my legs had to remain in plaster from ankle to groin for two whole years. This would seem a very long time for an adult, but for an energetic two-year-old it felt like an eternity. Unable to walk properly, let alone run or jump, play was severely restricted. Every six months the plaster was removed and I had to have my legs replastered. Sores inevitably developed and to ease the chronic itching my mother gave me knitting needles so that I could scratch my legs, but it was unsatisfactory. To add to my plight, with my legs totally encased in plaster, going to the lavatory in the normal way proved impossible. My father constructed a special table so that I could sit on the toilet with my legs stretched straight out in front of me. I still have that table today, as a grim reminder.

Children can be extremely cruel to others who are different and I soon found myself a target for bullies. Because my legs were in plaster, I could walk only very stiffly, like a zombie in one of the horror films that were popular at the time. One day I sneaked out of the house and headed for the local playground, but it was not long before two German boys, aged eleven or twelve, pushed me over in the sand and stole my toy Dinky car. As I was still under four years of age, it was an extremely frightening experience as the boys were so much bigger than me. Fortunately my brothers came to my rescue and chased my tormentors away, but the incident made such an impression on me that I remember it vividly and it gave me a lifelong abhorrence of bullies. When I eventually entered the hotel business, I refused to tolerate the bullying that I frequently encountered.

After two tedious years, the plaster was permanently removed and I hoped that my restrictions were over. Alas, no. Special boots that extended halfway up the calves of my legs had to be made. Other children continually made fun of me and now I was tormented with mental bullying rather than physical. I had to endure those boots for twelve interminable months before finally experiencing freedom.

Born in 1912, the same year that the *Titanic* sank, my father decided in 1957 that it was time for him to leave the RAF and we moved back to England. He was then aged forty-six, was the undefeated UK boxing champion of all the armed forces, but had no actual job and, having lived in various barracks wherever he happened to be stationed, now had no home either. There must have been thousands of ex-servicemen in a similar situation at that time, despite having served their country and putting their lives at risk. Initially we settled in Wolverhampton, but, as there was no work of any description available in the Midlands, my father's money quickly dwindled as he struggled to support his family.

Hearing that jobs were more plentiful in the south of England, my parents decided to head towards London and so we moved to Battersea Park. It was a huge gamble, with no money and no home, and it was one that did not pay off. My father was unable to find work and the only option was for my mother, sister, two brothers and I to go into what was then called 'a halfway house'. It was an awful time for us all. Hundreds of people lived in the building and every meal was like the workhouse scene from *Oliver Twist*. There were rows and rows of benches with wooden tables, where the women and children sat to eat. Men were not permitted to stay at the house and my father was only allowed to visit us once a day, but never at meal times. There were no private bedrooms, only large dormitories containing several families at a time. None of us had any privacy whatsoever and it was a degrading situation for adults and children alike.

All adult males were expected to find a job within a maximum timescale of six months. This was intended as 'shock treatment' to force them to obtain employment. The situation inevitably caused friction between my parents and arguments were frequent. With scarcely any money for food, my mother used to try and fatten us up with bread and dripping, and cheap but filling dishes such as shepherd's pie and bread pudding. Still we would wake in the night with terrible hunger pains.

If one of us became ill with a common childhood illness, such as whooping cough or German measles, my mother would lock us all in the same room together. That way, we all suffered the same illnesses simultaneously and recovered from them in the shortest possible time. Living in such appalling conditions we also endured the indignity and misery of head lice, and on one occasion I discovered a gigantic rat, almost the size of a small cat, in our dormitory. The caretaker killed it with a broom.

The situation that we found ourselves in was a shock to the whole family. One minute we had been leading a wonderful life in the Royal Air Force, with very good food, and the next we were living in absolute poverty and degradation. My parents had been so happy in Germany too. What a contrast to our life in Battersea Park, where my mother rarely smiled and my father was living away from us in a dingy bed-and-breakfast, trying desperately to find work.

After six months of such terrible conditions, my mother was at the end of her tether. Desperate to improve our situation, she made the heart-rending decision to walk away from her four children. It was an attempt to bring our plight to the attention of the authorities, so that we might be given a proper place to live. The four of us cried incessantly; the feeling of abandonment was total. After just two days my mother returned, unable to be parted from us any longer, but her drastic action had worked. We were moved to an inappropriately named block called 'Magnolia Mansions', consisting of one hundred flats backing on to a glucose factory, but at least it meant that the family could be reunited.

My father finally managed to find work in a bar and life took on some semblance of normality. By now, however, I had an additional brother, which meant that our family had increased to seven. As the rooms were very small, we were given two adjacent flats instead to ease the burden, but even so there was no real privacy. When I began to be attracted to the opposite sex, as a typical high-spirited boy I started pleasuring myself for the first time. One day my father walked in on me. I tried to hide my state of arousal under the bedclothes, but it was highly embarrassing and I longed for some space to myself.

Even though we had two flats, neither of them had a bathroom. Every Friday my father would march us in military fashion down the high street to the public baths. With a towel tucked underneath our arm and a bar of soap in hand, everyone must have known where we were heading. We had very little money and could not afford the luxury of shampoo, but it was great to at least feel clean again. The baths were enormous, with hundreds of cubicles, every one containing a deep Victorian bath with chunky taps. We would each enter a cubicle and after a while my father would shout, 'Are you OK, Philip?' and pause for a reply. 'Michael?' Pause. 'Sandra?' Pause. 'Neil?' It was not quite *The Waltons*, but almost.

One family occupying two neighbouring flats was not the most convenient way to live, and we were always going in and out of them both throughout the day. To make access simple, we used to hang the keys on a piece of string on the inside of the doors so that we could easily reach them through the letterbox. One evening my parents went out for a drink and an opportunist burglar could not believe his luck, finding door keys attached to string. He entered the flat where my ten-year-old sister, Sandra, was sleeping. She woke up and saw the man; they said 'Hello' to each other and the man fled, taking with him some of our few prized possessions. My father was particularly upset at the loss of a wall clock that he had been awarded during his highly successful boxing career.

Two months later the burglar returned, this time to our second flat. Once again he pulled the key through the letterbox, but on this occasion my father was waiting for him. Like a wise old fox, my father had hoped that the burglar might return to the scene of the crime. We heard a commotion and ran in to the hallway to find my father, dressed in boxer shorts and vest, and the burglar lying unconscious on the floor. As soon as the burglar had opened the door, my father, still endowed with a great physique, had grabbed him by the neck and thrown an uppercut under his jaw. If only the thief had read the inscription on the clock he had stolen, he would have seen 'Imperial Services Boxing Champion'. My father was considered a hero, and the police patted him on the back for giving the villain no more than he deserved. Today my father would probably have been arrested by the police for GBH and sued by the burglar. I always thought of my father whenever we had boxing matches at Grosvenor House, and a full-size ring would be set up in the Great Room while rich guests dined at tables around it. How different the surroundings would have been when he was a boxer.

In 1960 we were given the opportunity to move across London to a new council estate in West Norwood. It was clean, well maintained, with striped lawns and no graffiti. Crime was unheard of and, not only could you safely leave your key hanging on a piece of string, you could even leave your door unlocked. There seemed to be acres and acres for children to play and have fun, and I made many new friends. It was as if my life had suddenly changed from black-and-white to colour. I joined the Cubs, knocking on doors during bob-a-job week to undertake small tasks, and loved every moment. I collected all the badges and became a 'sixer' with two yellow stripes.

I started primary school at the age of eight, and being dyslexic I found the work a struggle and achieved very poor test results. I had not told my parents, but I was going deaf and could not hear the teacher properly. Eventually, when they realised that something must be wrong with me, I was taken to see a doctor. My ears were syringed and within a week I was rushed into hospital to have my tonsils and adenoids removed. As the children's ward was full, I was placed in a private room beside a lovely gentleman, but he was dying. 'Don't worry,' my mother said, 'when you have your tonsils out, you'll have ice cream every day.' I had none. As I was not in the children's ward, they forgot all about me. It was such a disappointment and at the age of eight I had already learnt that life can be very hard at times.

Perhaps it helped me to appreciate the good times so much more. The darker the night, the brighter the stars.

At least now I had a lot of friends, and one day a group of us went to play hide-and-seek in some nearby stables. They were adjacent to a Nestlé's ice cream factory and, exuberant, dare-devil young kids that we were, we decided to walk across the pitched corrugated-iron roof of the stables. There was a low parapet wall around the edge of the roof, separating it from the flat wired-glass roof of the factory and, as I was at the rear of the party, I was looking ahead towards my friends and did not notice the wall. I stepped on to the glass roof and fell fifty feet on to the factory floor below.

Blood seemed to be everywhere, pouring from a gash under my arm, and I was all alone. Fearing the worst, my so-called friends had fled and not one of them summoned help. Being a Sunday, the factory was closed. With nobody around, I was crying my eyes out and feared that I would be locked in until Monday morning. I eventually found a ladies' toilet and tried to clean myself up, and then made my way up a flight of stairs to where I could see a window. It looked out on to the play area where I lived, but some old rusty bars across prevented my escape. I was bleeding heavily and trapped.

There was nothing for it but to squeeze through the bars, where I then dropped some thirty feet on to the yard below, and somehow made it home to my mother. Horrified, she took me into the bathroom to try and clean up the blood, but when she looked under my arm she fainted. Both the broken glass and the wire running through it had caused terrible lacerations as I had crashed through the factory roof. My father rushed me to hospital, where it took some four hours to clean the injury and remove all the particles of rust that had entered the wound as I squeezed through the iron window bars. I then needed thirty-two stitches in my arm, and still have the scars to this day. By some miracle, I had no broken bones.

I left primary school, and the Cubs, at the age of eleven and moved on to Kingsdale School in Dulwich. It was a very modernistic building that had been opened just five years earlier. Its architect, Leslie Martin, had previously designed the Royal Festival Hall, and Kingsdale characterised 1950s architecture. The classrooms were separated by very narrow corridors, without windows, which over the years became a haven for bullies, and the school eventually gained a reputation for antisocial behaviour. By the 1990s it had deteriorated to such an extent, both architecturally and academically, that the whole school was given a multi-million pound transformation, resulting in a contemporary building that is now the pride of the area.

I was very excited about going to Kingsdale, and my mother was so proud when she saw me in the school uniform, with my little satchel, cap, shorts and smart blazer with its badge depicting the school motto: 'FACOMNIA AD DEI GLORIAM' (Everything for the Glory of God). I boarded the train for the one-stop journey and then walked the final mile to the school itself. I entered through the gates and into the school for the first time. 'Go home,' I was told, 'School doesn't start until tomorrow!' In her enthusiasm, my poor mother had sent me a day early.

I loved being at that school. I became the cross-country running champion for my age group and eventually went on to become South London and London Cross Country Champion. Running was a sport that I adored and for two years took part in the All England Cross-Country Championships in Sheffield and Derby, and the South London and London Mile for athletics. I also began playing football in the playground and found that it was a sport that came naturally to me, especially because of the speed and stamina required.

Within three months of my joining the school team, football scouts asked to sign me up as a youth player. Both Crystal Palace and Charlton Athletic wanted to sign me and, although Crystal Palace was my local ground, I opted for Charlton Athletic. I was so excited on the day of my first match as ball boy, coming out of the tunnel with the First Team players. The team colours were white sleeves with red body, and so their signature song was 'When the red, red robin comes bob, bob, bobbin' along' because of our red chests. Although I enjoyed playing in the youth team, the distance from home proved to be too far, requiring two changes of train and a journey time of one-and-a-half hours. The travel never worried me, and helped me to become streetwise, but as I was still only twelve years old it seemed sensible not to continue. As Crystal Palace still wanted me, I was released from my contract with Charlton Athletic. With Crystal Palace I was able to play football at great venues, was selected to play for Surrey Schoolboys, and even played in one final at Highbury. After only ten minutes on the pitch, I headed in a goal. What a marvellous feeling that was! Our team won 3–2.

At home, my mother unexpectedly became pregnant at the age of forty-four with her sixth child, my brother Stephen. It was a shock to the whole family, and the financial hardship continued. I wore clothes handed down from my elder brothers, and nearly every Saturday we visited jumble sales, while my mother scanned shop noticeboards looking for bargains. The fact that she smoked fifty cigarettes a day did not help matters, and on Saturday evenings she would spend the housekeeping money at bingo, forever hoping for that elusive big win. I felt very sorry for my father, with another child on the way and consequently one more mouth to feed. He worked seven days a week, so we saw little of him, and his only treat was to take an empty bottle to the off-licence on a Saturday night and have it filled with cheap wine out of a barrel. On the way home, he would buy a packet of winkles from the mobile fishmonger.

One Saturday evening two louts in their mid-twenties ventured on to our estate, with leather jackets and scooters. I was playing quietly with a tennis racquet and ball, when the two bullies approached, pushed me away roughly and threw my ball over a fence. My mother was just setting off on her way to bingo and saw what had happened. She was a tough cookie, and without a moment's hesitation slapped one of them hard across the face. 'Hit anyone, hit a woman,' she challenged. The stunned thug did nothing.

At that moment my father returned from the off-licence with his weekly treat of wine and winkles, I immediately told him what had gone on.

'Which one of you threw my son's ball over the fence?' he demanded.

'*I did*. What are *you* going to do about it?' replied one, aggressively.

My father remained very calm. 'Why don't you and I step on to the grass and discuss it like men?' he said.

With that, my father walked on to the grass, took off his jacket and handed it to me with his bag of treats.

'Hold this, son,' he said, 'I won't be long.'

By now, thirty or forty people of all age groups had gathered to watch. These two bullies had intimidated the community for a long time, and word had spread like wildfire around the estate. I knew that my father was an ex-boxing champion, but he had retired from the sport before I was born, so I had never actually seen him fight. He was only five foot nine and the bully was six foot two, and I was concerned that my father would end up getting hurt. He raised his hands and took up a boxer's stance.

'Why don't you hit me first, as you have such a big mouth?' he taunted the lout.

He took a swing at my father, who just leaned back gracefully. The punch missed his chin by half an inch. Suddenly it was if I were watching everything in slow motion. My father threw a left, followed through quickly with a right, then a left, each punch reaching its target under the jaw. The lout fell backwards on to the ground like a sack of potatoes. He had been knocked out completely. The crowd stood in stunned silence. My father turned to me, took his jacket and bag, and then said to the other bully, 'Pick up your friend, and never come back here again.'

Everyone had their mouths open in disbelief, and we just turned and walked up the road towards home. It would have been the icing on the cake if it had been into the sunset, like a scene from a John Wayne movie. My father was treated as a hero and the bullies never returned.

My own boxing career was less successful. I started boxing while at Kingsdale School and had no problems adapting to a new sport. In those days the maximum number of rounds was three, and I won all of the short fights amongst my contemporaries.

'I hear you've taken up boxing,' said my father casually one day from the kitchen, 'and that you're the so-called champion of your age group too.'

'That's right.'

'Do you want to be a boxer?'

'I don't really know.'

'Well, we'll soon find out.'

In a cupboard under our stairs there was always an old trunk, and none of us had ever known what it contained. My father opened it and took out a pair of leather sparring gloves, which were large, flat padded gloves. Back in the kitchen, my father decided that it was time to give me a sparring session, but after barely fifteen minutes he shouted, 'Stop! Stop! Stop!'

'But why, Dad?'

'You'll *never* make a boxer. There's not enough reach or power. Pack it up now.'

There were not many times in my life when I took my parents' advice, but I did on this occasion. It was the end of my fighting career. When boxer Chris Eubank stayed at Grosvenor House, even if he was outspoken, I was not prepared to challenge him.

Despite being a boxer, my father was a very kind and charitable person. Every Sunday he would take time to visit a local man who was suffering from multiple sclerosis. Wheelchair bound, the man could neither speak

13

nor eat, and could only manage to take sustenance through a straw. My father would look after him for a few hours to enable the man's wife to go out, and always took along a Guinness for the man to enjoy. Although my father often asked me to accompany him on these visits, I was nervous about seeing someone who was so ill. One day, however, I plucked up the courage.

My father had often told me that the couple had a son in his mid-twenties, something of a rebel, who could never accept that his father was dying. My father had never met this son, who was rarely at home, but we had not been there long when the son suddenly walked in. When he saw us, his jaw practically touched the floor. He was the bully that my father had knocked unconscious. We all looked at each other, but not a word was ever said about the incident.

'Thank you for coming to see my father,' he said nervously and shook us both by the hand.

Each time my father visited his friend after that, the son was always there to greet him. I like to think that my father's punch brought him to his senses, and maybe he realised that there is good in the world. I joined my father at the funeral when the man died a year later.

Like practically every school in times past and present, Kingsdale had its own bully. Everyone feared him, and I was no exception. The school was designed in a square, with a courtyard in the middle that we had to cross to reach our classrooms. One day I was walking across the courtyard for my next lesson when the bully pushed against me, his shoulder bumping mine.

Although he was a year older than me, I was not going to be bullied by anyone, and instinctively I said, 'I hope that was an accident?'

'No, it wasn't,' he said bluntly, 'What are *you* going to do about it?'

The words were so familiar.

My mind flashed straight back to my father. Even though he had told me that I would never make a boxer, I had learned from him. Once he had advised, 'If you are ever confronted and need to protect yourself, there is only one effective place to punch that will render your opponent helpless. Hit him straight up under the jawbone, as hard as you can.'

In my mind's eye I could see my father, and I turned to face my aggressor and punched him straight under the jaw. It had the desired effect. I was never aware of him bullying anyone else again, and I unexpectedly found myself something of a hero at the school.

Life soon began to take a turn for the better. In 1967 we moved a few miles south into a brand-new council house on the Roundshaw Estate in Wallington. The terraced house had four bedrooms and its own garden. Now a built-up area of Greater London, in the 1960s it was still a rural area, with hills in the distance and cows in fields. I had never seen so much grass. There were now six children to feed, and my parents still had a financial struggle, but at least our surroundings had improved. I took on a paper round to help out, for which I was paid twelve shillings and sixpence (63p) a week for delivering morning papers, and one pound a week for the evening newspaper round. It was the first money that I had earned and it felt good.

I had no interest in academic work at school and just wanted to be a professional footballer. Frequently I would bunk off school because I hated the lessons, which got me into terrible trouble at home, but shortly before my fifteenth birthday I was approached by Crystal Palace. They wanted me to sign an apprentice professional contract and join them on a two months' trial basis. It seemed like a dream come true, and I was allowed to leave school and play football full time. All too quickly, the bubble burst. I soon realised that I was just not good enough to play professionally and I was released from the contract. I was extremely disappointed and downhearted.

Reality kicked in. I had no qualifications and no job. The future began to look very bleak for a fifteen-year-old living on a council estate. My father was working at the time for Advance Laundry (later merged into the Sunlight Laundry) of Camberwell, which had a contract with the Grosvenor House Hotel in Park Lane, and he was able to get me a job at the hotel doing the washing-up. With its 452 bedrooms and 160 private apartments, the Great Room alone seating up to 2,000 people in one sitting, and additional ballroom seating for another 500, plus over 2,000 full-time staff and 600 casual staff employed on a daily basis, there were an awful lot of plates for me to wash.

One day I was in the basement, washing up with another member of staff, when a very smart man walked through the kitchen, dressed immaculately in a white shirt and a navy-blue suit with a crisp white handkerchief in his top pocket. When he had gone, I nudged my friend at the sink.

'Who was that man there?'

'He's the General Manager of the hotel.'

'*That's* what I want to be one day.'

Suddenly I had a goal in life.

2

Low Pay, Long Hours . . . and the Importance of Being Tipped

He who would climb the ladder must start at the bottom.
English proverb

After only six weeks of washing up at Grosvenor House I was promoted to the laundry room. This entailed counting all the dirty sheets and linen sent down the linen chute from the floors above. The paraphernalia we used to find in the sheets was unbelievable, ranging from bras and knickers to vibrators. All items had to be sorted, packed into wicker baskets and entered into a ledger categorising them by type. This book was then handed to the Head Linen Keeper at the end of each day. All linen was collected by an outside company and returned clean twenty-four hours later. I found the job so boring that in the end I could not be bothered to count everything.

The food for the guests was naturally of the highest standard, and the staff had more than their fair share too. At four o'clock every afternoon, my colleague Paul and I would sneak along the corridors to the Pastry Department. As soon as the chef turned his back, we would steal some cakes and hide in part of the large boiler house where nobody could see us. We then savoured our ill-gotten gains at our leisure.

The staff canteen was divided into two rooms: one for the uniformed staff, the other for the rest of us. Like the big country houses centuries ago, there was a definite pecking order below stairs. Although I had no choice in the matter, I actually enjoyed being with the non-uniformed staff. Many were from Jamaica and the West Indies and I used to sit for hours listening to the way they spoke, with phrases such as 'You razz glad!' They used to tell stories of how they came over on boats to seek their fortune in England.

17

One was called 'Mr Gordon', another 'Mr Christmas', although these were not their real names. On arriving by boat, one saw an advert for Gordon's Gin and so decided to call himself 'Mr Gordon'; the other arrived on Christmas Day. There were many more that did the same and we only ever knew them by their adopted names, although their wage packets always bore their correct titles.

In the staff locker rooms during breaks they used to play dominoes, and you could hear their voices down the many miles of corridors, often shouting 'You razz glad!' They were good fun and extremely hard workers, but inevitably there were episodes of racism. I always tried to stand up for them if they were ever taunted about their colour, especially when the culprits were the arrogant chefs who felt that they were superior to everyone else in the hotel. Fortunately this attitude has begun to change slightly, but I have encountered many hotels over the years where the chefs are the most feared members of staff and the present culture of aggressive celebrity chefs swearing on television has not been a positive step.

I was very streetwise when I was young and a tough lad for my age, but my upbringing had taught me to detest any form of bullying and, as I moved up the ladder of success, I have never tolerated it in any of my kitchens. I have never forgotten the guys I worked with in the basement and in later life at the Grosvenor House I always told the staff that everyone should be considered equal. All have a different part to play and no single person is more important than any other in the team. When I worked in the basement we may have been called the 'moles' of the hotel, not even allowed to see the chandeliers above, but those behind the scenes are at the very core of the hotel.

Grosvenor House had its own football team in the Catering League, which included all the other hotels on Park Lane, plus the nearby Playboy Club. One day the Grosvenor House team was short of its usual players and I was seconded to play. Little did they know that I had been quite a good footballer in the past and I soon found myself promoted to their star player. As a general rule, after the match you would go back to the opposition's hotel for drinks and sandwiches. On one occasion we went to the staff canteen of the Playboy Club and were allowed to go upstairs and see the roulette tables. It was the first time that I had seen the famous bunny girls in uniform. Wow! They were absolutely stunning in their sexy outfits of high-heeled shoes, fishnet tights, black leotard, bunny-rabbit ears and fluffy white tail. I was a hot-blooded youth of sixteen and every time we played against the Playboy Club, I made absolutely certain that I turned up for that particular game.

At the end of the 1968 football season, the Grosvenor House football team was second in the Catering League, and the Hilton Hotel on Park Lane was in top position. Our team was to play the Hilton's at Highbury in the final. We had just three weeks to get ready for the match and extra training was needed. As Hyde Park was just across the road from Grosvenor House, we used to train there. To reach it, we walked through a subway which was the haunt of beggars and people who slept rough. Some of the team used to taunt them, but I always gave them what little change I could afford. I could not forget the hardship my own family had suffered, when we had no food or money, and I knew that many were beggars through no fault of their own but through unfortunate circumstances. It irked me too that vast amounts of food were thrown away by the hotel on a daily basis, mostly from banquets, when these wretched people on the streets were starving. The chef used to over-order and prepare far in excess of what was actually required in the function rooms. As a result, the staff were never short of food and management often lived like lords, with smoked salmon and caviar. Sometimes I wished that I could smuggle food out for the beggars, but I could not afford to risk losing my job.

On the day of the match at Highbury, the hotel manager put on a lunch in one of the function rooms before we departed, but I could not eat much. I was tense and excited as it was a big event and only my second time of being there as a player. The atmosphere was electric with two thousand supporters for both teams. Our strip was all white and the Hilton played in blue, and on this occasion I was back in defence. It was a warm sunny day and the pitch was as hard as rock. Five minutes into the match, the goalkeeper took a long, high kick. The ball dropped down in front of me, just by the halfway line; I turned to do a high back pass to the goalkeeper, not realising that he was off his goal line. The ball went beautifully over his head and into the back of the net. An own goal. Our supporters went completely silent, apart from Arthur, our football team manager. He was late out of the dressing rooms and, thinking I had scored for Grosvenor House, he began jumping up and down with joy. Once it dawned on him what I had done, his language became unrepeatable. The game finally finished with a score of 2-2 after extra time and, as it was getting late, the hotel and catering officials decided to share the trophy. We all went back to the dressing room for champagne and my faux pas was soon forgiven.

After nine months of working in the Linen Rooms, I was offered the position of trainee valet. At the time I had no idea what a valet actually did and, so as not to show my ignorance at work, I had to ask my father at home. 'A valet cleans shoes and presses clothes,' he said. 'He's a gentleman's gentleman.' I liked the idea. The pay was ten pounds and ten shillings a week (£10.50), and I saw it as an opportunity towards one day getting into that navy-blue suit.

On my first day as a trainee valet I was given a uniform of black trousers with a gold band up the outside of the leg, white shirt, black tie, and a waistcoat with yellow-and-black horizontal stripes on the front, a black back and sleeves. We had to be immaculately turned out, with crisp creases in our trousers, shoes spit-and-polished like the military, clean white shirt, black socks, with face and hair completely groomed. I worked hard all night making sure that everything was perfect, put on my uniform in the staff locker room, and then walked up the stairs to the hotel lobby for the very first time. The mole had emerged. For the second time in my short life it was like changing from a black-and-white film to colour.

I looked around at all the splendour and was in awe, as if I had been transported to another world. Suddenly someone tapped me on the shoulder. It was the Personnel Manager with the Head Valet, Mr Dick Smith. We made our way up in the staff lift to the sixth floor. None of the staff, except the General Manager, were permitted to use the guest lifts at any time. To do so resulted in instant dismissal.

There were eight floors in the hotel and each had a valet service. One shift started at 7 a.m. and finished at 3 p.m., the other from 3 p.m. to 11 p.m., seven days a week. An all-round valet service was provided for the customer, and I was shown around a selection of bedrooms and suites by Mr Smith. I could not believe how big they were. Some of the rooms were larger than our whole council house, which slept eight people.

All heads of department in the hotel had to be addressed by their surname, and Mr Smith proved to be a very kind man who took me under his wing very quickly and soon began treating me like a son rather than an employee. Dick Smith had been at Grosvenor House for over forty years and therefore had tremendous knowledge and experience. At the end of my shift I used to make him a cup of tea, and, while I was mopping the valet service floor, he would be drinking his tea and telling me stories of the many stars that had stayed at the Grosvenor House during his time, and he had much to tell.

He also taught me how to provide the best service for the guests. If trousers sent for pressing had a small hole in the crotch, he insisted that we darned it, even if guests were unaware. If shirts that we ironed had a button missing, he showed me how to sew on a new one. I also learned from him how to shorten or lengthen a pair of new trousers for a guest if necessary. My skills in all areas began to improve under his guidance.

The first thing he taught me was how to spit-and-polish shoes. In a five-star hotel it was not just a matter of rubbing polish over the shoes, but a whole procedure had to be followed.

'Firstly, the laces have to be tied in to a bow,' he told me.

'Why do that?'

'It is for the benefit of the customer. If the laces were not tied when the shoes were cleaned you would certainly get polish on the laces, and the guests would then get polish all over their fingers,' he explained gently.

After tying the shoelaces, the next stage was to put a hand in the shoe, turn it over and ensure that there was no dirt on the soles, or mud on the instep. After this, the shoe was turned over and polish applied first to the top of the shoe. This was done by wrapping a rag around the index finger and dipping it into the polish, which was then applied all over the shoe, including the groove formed between the sole and the upper. The shoe was left for between ten and fifteen minutes, after which a little cold water was poured into the lid. The index finger was again wrapped in the rag, dipped into the water, then on to the front of the shoe, back into the polish, then water, and finally polish. The shoe was left for a further fifteen minutes before being buffed with a silk rag.

The valet service also included ironing clothes, which was another skill I had to learn. Again, there was a precise system for pressing a suit. An old electric kettle was used to create steam. The lid would be taken off, a piece of cloth cut to the correct size would then be placed over the space, and the lid was then hammered back into position to obtain a really tight fit. This ensured that steam only came out of the spout. The suit would then be steamed from the inside before being pressed with a former tailor's iron, weighing 5 pounds (2.25 kg). It was not very sophisticated, but it worked well.

When we pressed a gentleman's suit, we began by hanging the trousers upside down, placing a clip on the bottom of one trouser leg at a time, and applied steam to the *inside* of the trousers, including the crotch. This could often result in the most awful smell. Some had yellow stains on the inside, which we knew meant piss on the pocket lining! All garments gave off different aromas and eventually we were able to identify who each belonged to simply by the smell. We knew who'd had a curry for dinner too.

Next we applied steam to the outside of the trousers, finishing the operation by hand-pressing them. Regular ironing boards were not used, but a specially padded table measuring 6 feet by 4 (75 x 120 cm). The tailor's iron we used had very little heat control. A rag would be dipped into a bucket of water and rung out to remove the excess, which would then be placed over the garment. Pressing the heavy iron over the clothes resulted in the most fantastic effect. The operation may be considered old-fashioned, but it produced the sharpest creases you have ever seen. We were jokingly told that, if you did the job properly, you could cut yourself on the creases. Finally, we pressed the top of the trousers, pulled out the pockets and ironed those as well. After the trousers, we moved on to the jacket doing the lining first, and the lapels always had to be 'rolled', never pressed flat as it would leave a crease.

On many occasions we found money in pockets when we were pressing suits. Mr Smith told me that I was to inform him personally if I found any cash or wallets, and he insisted that all notes were ironed flat. Now that *is* service. I was never totally sure whether the guests always received their money back, as clothes and shoes were returned to guests only by Mr Smith. As a trainee I was certainly never allowed to take anything back to a room and, for all my respect and affection for the Head Valet, it galled me that he got all the tips for the work that we had done. I never knew how much he actually received. One day I happened to memorise the serial number on a ten-shilling note as I ironed it. At the end of every week Mr Smith used to give me ten shillings as my share of the tips, and that particular week he gave me the ten-shilling note with the serial number that I had pressed!

Tips formed part of the salary for everyone working in hospitality and some staff really benefited from them and ended up with second homes in Spain simply through the tips they received. At that time it was one of the excuses for managements to offer low wages. Realising that Mr Smith was taking advantage of the guests, when I discovered several notes in a pocket, I felt no qualms about peeling one off a roll and keeping it for myself. These guests were incredibly rich and I certainly wasn't. It was probably just one note less for Mr Smith. Little did he realise that, as far as tips were concerned, he taught me to be as crafty as him. Sometimes if I found some twenty-pound notes in a pocket, I would take one or two for myself and replace them with five-pound notes. That way the guest was less likely to notice that any money was missing. Dick Smith knew all the tricks of the trade and, if a guest was not actually in the room when he returned items, he would leave a note saying 'Have pressed suit <u>and</u> repaired it.' This guaranteed Dick a large tip the next day.

There was a whole ritual regarding tips at the hotel. Guests arriving by car or taxi were met by the doorman. He raised his hat, bowed, and greeted them with 'Good morning. Welcome to the Grosvenor House.' Nine times out of ten he would receive a tip. The luggage porter would stand to the left of the doorman to take guests to reception and collect luggage. He would then wait and watch for the guests to go up to their room, after which time he would follow with the bags and knock on the door. The luggage did not arrive until the guests were safely in their room. Why? So that he would receive a tip from them. Once the luggage porter had his tip, he would inform the valet service that the guests had arrived and whether or not they were good tippers. The valet would then knock on the door and introduce himself to the guests. We used to offer to unpack the cases and hang up clothes, and asked them to leave any shoes outside their door at night for cleaning. This was a complimentary service; however, the custom of tipping gave the staff an extra incentive. We would also collect any laundry or dry-cleaning, providing a same-day service, and would undertake any hand-pressing that was required. Once I had my tip, I would then inform room service and so the ritual continued.

For the departure of guests, Mr Smith taught me how to pack cases with everything wrapped in tissue paper. It was quite an art and, lo and behold, you received a tip for this service too. I quickly realised that for providing the most efficient service, you always received a good tip in return. Fifty per cent of my income actually came from the tips and I have often wondered how much Mr Smith pocketed. As far as tips were concerned, the richest uniformed staff on Park Lane were, first, the hall porter – nowadays often called the concierge – next the valets, and then the doormen. Some doormen actually used to have the inside of their tail jackets strengthened, and also pockets enlarged, to hold their cash tips. They could triple their salary, which would equate to £1,200 a week in today's monetary values.

Grosvenor House attracted the seriously wealthy, including one of the richest men in the world, the 28th Sultan of Brunei, Omar Ali Saifuddien III, who used to book all seventy-eight bedrooms on the fifth floor. Half the rooms were for storage, with the beds taken out so that when the Sultan's entourage went shopping, there was somewhere to put the many items bought. On one occasion this included fifty children's bicycles. They would visit Harrods, Selfridges and the shops in Bond Street and bring back vast quantities of goods, which would later be shipped back to Brunei.

The Sultan had his own security people, who were all ex-Gurkhas. Whenever the Sultan came out of his suites on the fifth floor, the whole entourage would line the corridor, wearing their traditional clothes and small hats peculiar to that part of the world, and all would bow to His Royal Highness. It was just like a scene from *The King and I*. The Sultan had several wives, but we were never allowed to go near them.

There was tremendous jealousy around the hotel of the staff who worked on the fifth floor because of the enormous tips they received. I worked on the sixth floor at the time receiving modest tips, but little did I know then that twenty-five years later one member of staff would receive a tip from the Sultan of Brunei amounting to £75,000. When the Sultan's son, Prince George, stayed in 1990 I was asked to gather the staff who had attended to him and they were given a £138,000 tip. This was divided amongst the forty or so staff members and the cash was placed in brown envelopes with their names on. The fifteen chambermaids each received £2,000; the six butlers were given £5,000 each and so on. From the two concierges to the assistant manager, everybody received their share. The only problem was, the next time the Sultan and his family came to stay, *everybody* wanted to work for them! Three of our waiting staff actually became so popular with the Sultan that he wanted to take them back to Brunei with him. Consequently his private secretary contacted the General Manager of the day, and many years later they are still working for the Sultan, with stories of fantastic pay and a chauffeur-driven car each day. The only setback is that no alcohol is allowed.

After three or four months I was practically fully trained as a valet and one Sunday was left alone on the 3 to 11 p.m. shift that nobody else wanted to do. I was only just sixteen, and one of the housekeepers asked me to take an ironing board up to her room on the top floor. She was twenty-eight, very beautiful, and when she opened the door to me was wearing nothing but a negligee. She asked me to place the ironing board in the corner of the room, and as I did so she put her arms around my waist, swung me round and began undoing my uniform. I'll let you use your imagination as to what happened next, but I was receiving tuition in more ways than one at Grosvenor House. I was so shocked at being unexpectedly seduced and too frightened to ever go back to her room again

In the late 1960s, tough days with long hours were expected of all hotel staff. In addition to my regular duties as a valet I had to clean the mirrors in all the suites, and also all the chandeliers by hand because the chambermaids were not allowed to work on ladders above a certain height. If any guest required valet, maid, or room service, there were buttons for them to press in the rooms, including the bathrooms. The buttons were arranged in clusters of three and a light would come on outside in the corridor beside the hotel room door when one was pressed, and would also trigger a light in the appropriate service room. I will always remember that they were blue for waiters, orange for valets, and green for maids, and each of the eight floors had permanent staff to provide these services. On each floor there were four vertical corridors, arranged in the shape of a squared letter 'A', which contained seventy-eight guest rooms.

When a light came on in one of the service rooms, it would indicate whether service was required in corridor one, two, three or four. We would then go to the appropriate corridor, look to see which room had a light illuminated, turn it off by springing the light back, and knock on the door to see what the customer wanted. It was a brilliant service and, unlike today, there were no telephones to worry about.

The service provided at Grosvenor House was second to none. We had our own silver-polishing department in the basement, where all the silver was cleaned daily. It was so shiny that you could literally see your face in it, and there was many a time when I used a teapot to check whether my hair was tidy. Breakfasts would be served in the guests' rooms on silver trays every morning. Staff prepared the tea, coffee and toast on each floor, but fully cooked breakfasts would be sent up from the main kitchen in the basement. There were six dumbwaiters for this facility – small lifts for conveying trays of food between floors. The breakfasts were delivered on an impeccably presented trolley covered with a pure-white linen cloth. The waiter would offer to draw back the curtains and pour the tea or coffee; the toast would always be hot, the eggs runny, and guests would always receive their daily newspaper with the breakfast. All the waiters had black tails, white wing collars and black bow ties. Customers couldn't help but tip.

The wine list in the rooms comprised of more than a thousand wines, and I have never seen a wine cellar bigger than the one at Grosvenor House, not even at the vineyards that I visited later in life. There were two main cellars: one was refrigerated for storing white wines and champagnes so that they were ready for drinking at the correct temperature; the other was for red wines, ports, cognacs, fortified wines, spirits and liqueurs. The movement of alcohol was amazing and was all delivered to the 'city' below ground in a massive lorry, handled by eight loading-bay staff. There were three small fork-lift trucks, designed specifically for Grosvenor House, and the staff used to sit side-saddle on the back as the wine was transported in two gigantic lifts to the relevant store. The wine was picked up on pallets by the fork-lift trucks and transported along corridors to the wine cellar. As hundreds of thousands of pounds' worth of goods were taken into the hotel this way, security had to be very tight.

My eyes were opened when I started to get to know regular guests. One week some would be at the hotel with their wives, the next they were with their mistresses. Most of the men were titled and often members of the aristocracy, invariably in their sixties, with stunning mistresses thirty or forty years younger than themselves. Money and title can be quite an attraction to some girls. When the mistresses were out of the way, we would casually say to the men, 'Madam not with you this week, Sir?' They used to wink and say, 'She's away. Here's a little something for being so diplomatic.' We were delighted that they shared their wealth with us.

One of the regulars at the hotel was Sir Sean Connery, at the time having just become famous for his film role as James Bond. He was certainly very charming, but as a true Scotsman very mean with his tips. Unbeknown to him, I decided to get my own back. Autograph hunters were everywhere, and journalists were always wandering the corridors trying to find his room, so whenever someone said to me, 'If you tell us where Sean Connery is, we'll look after you,' and pressed half-a-crown into my hand, I pointed them in the right direction. I needed the money, but never told anyone about my actions as hotels can be rife with gossip and back-stabbing. A more generous Scotsman among our guests was Sir Jackie Stewart. As the years went by I got to know him very well. He is a very kind and loving family man and indirectly helped me enormously in my career. His attention to detail was second to none and he told me that you need to have this attribute to become a good General Manager. I was to find this out later on.

As money was very tight and I had an urge to see something of the world, I began taking on more and more overtime. I would start my first shift at seven in the morning, finishing at three in the afternoon when I would go to Hyde Park and kick a football around. I returned to the hotel at six o'clock to work 'in back' – in banqueting – washing up until two in the morning, then back at work at seven as valet. I was actually working a hundred hours a week. Instead of going home, my mate Paul and I decided that it would be easier to hide in the hotel and sleep over. Grosvenor House had a private gentlemen's club and we used to go through underground tunnels to the other side of the basement, along corridors upstairs and sleep on sofas in the club.

At night the hotel used to have fire patrol officers who had to insert keys at certain fire points around the hotel to prove they had checked that everything was in order. One night we were woken with a tap on the shoulder and bright lights from the nightwatchmen's torches shone glaringly into our faces. The next day we were reported to management, who quickly discovered that we were working sixteen to twenty-hour days and immediately put a stop to it. 'You are doing far too many hours,' Mr Smith told me, 'You will get tired very quickly.'

I explained that I was thinking of travelling to Europe and so needed the money. To my relief he said that the hotel management did not want to lose me and were impressed with my attitude and hard work. He told me that a job had become available for a full-time valet in the South Block, the apartment side of the hotel, and this would mean a larger basic salary and hopefully bigger tips. Everything in hotels seemed to come back to tips. Consequently I accepted the job.

Instead of being a trainee I was now a full-time valet, one of only four in the South Block which had eight floors and twenty apartments per floor. I was climbing the ladder, but soon realised that I now had to get used to a very different type of clientele. There was also fervent self-imposed segregation between the 'hotel staff' in the North Block and the 'apartment staff' in the South Block, and suddenly I found that I was caught in the North/South divide.

3

Hospitality Was His Forte

The interval between the decay of the old and the formation and the establishment of the new, constitutes a period of transition, which must always necessarily be one of uncertainty.

John C. Calhoun, *A Disquisition on Government* (1850)

I looked just like a giant bumblebee. My new valet's uniform was extremely smart, but its distinguished black-and-yellow striped waistcoat really made me stand out. I was now part of a team that were generally considered to be the best valets in London and I felt absolutely on top of the world. Unbeknown to me, however, there were changes behind the scenes at the hotel that could cause my world to collapse and the job to end before it had even begun. For the moment though, I was just enjoying being a bumble bee.

The Grosvenor House was unique amongst London hotels in that it consisted of two completely separate buildings. The North Block was the main hotel, at that time having 452 deluxe guest rooms which customers rented on a nightly basis, as with any hotel. The neighbouring South Block contained 160 private apartments, which were leased on a yearly contract to people who wanted to use the Grosvenor House as their London base, and so had a semi-permanent clientele.

The Dorchester and Savoy hotels were very envious of us, as their buildings did not allow them to offer the same residential facilities. There is a famous painting of the Grosvenor House Hotel in its early days when a road ran between the North and South blocks. Later it was discovered that planning permission had not been obtained for the road, and so the original owners employed Sir Edwin Lutyens to design a colonnade to link the two buildings, which is still a feature of Grosvenor House today and a landmark on Park Lane.

The Grosvenor House has had a glorious past and its foundations go deep into the site of a former royal residence. The hotel now covers an area where Gloucester House once stood, the London home of King George III's younger brother, Prince William Henry, Earl of Connaught, Duke of Gloucester and Edinburgh. The Prince died at Gloucester House in August 1805, and the building was purchased for £20,000 by Robert Grosvenor, 2nd Earl Grosvenor and 1st Marquess of Westminster. He transformed the building to his own taste and renamed it Grosvenor House after his family. The Grosvenors did much to develop the areas of Mayfair and Belgravia in London – many streets and squares still bear their various family titles – and in 1998 Robert Grosvenor was immortalised with a statue in Belgrave Square. Somewhat ironically in my opinion, on its base is carved a quote from John Ruskin: 'When we build let us think we build for ever.'

When I started work at the Grosvenor House Hotel, the large detached house that Robert Grosvenor knew had not actually lasted for ever. Just as he himself had developed and transformed whole areas of London, demolishing and rebuilding, so the former Gloucester House was itself demolished in 1927. In its place rose the Grosvenor House Hotel, which took two years to build, opening its doors in 1929 to serve the first transatlantic cruise passengers. Even then it was aimed at a wealthy clientele.

Just as Robert Grosvenor clearly had a vision for the house and was a man who tried to improve his surroundings, so successive owners of the Grosvenor House Hotel have each made their mark on the building. One of the biggest transformations in its entire history came just as I was about to progress in my career as a full-time valet. Such was the turmoil surrounding us that I genuinely wondered if my days at the hotel were numbered.

When I joined the staff in 1967, Grosvenor House was owned by a company called Trust Houses. They were not what you might call 'hands on' and really had not got a clue about how the hotel was being run. General managers could live a lavish lifestyle at the hotel's expense. Some forced the staff to press their clothes and clean their shoes; they entertained their families as if they were royalty, ate in the restaurant daily, ordered champagne to be served in their rooms, and really abused their position. One General Manager even had two apartments knocked into one to give himself more imposing accommodation. Often the General Manager's requirements had to be put before the needs of the guests.

The Grosvenor House had a staff bar. I think it was the only hotel in

London to have one at the time. Pints of beer were half price, and it was the equivalent of our local pub, somewhere we could sit and relax and chew the fat. One evening the staff bar was buzzing with gossip, and rumours abounded that the Grosvenor House was about to be taken over. The General Manager had informed his heads of department, and piece by piece details filtered down to those of us working in the bowels of the hotel. None of us knew what this meant for the future of the Grosvenor House or our jobs.

It was not long before all was revealed in the national newspapers. The Trust Houses Group was merging with Forte Holdings Limited, forming a company that would eventually become the world-renowned Trusthouse Forte. Although staff members were concerned about how the takeover would affect us as individuals, we had no idea at the time of the drama being played out behind the scenes in the boardroom.

Trust Houses was a long-established company, founded by the 4th Earl Grey in 1904, to redevelop the now redundant coaching inns of England. In the days when horse and carriage was the only form of transport, coaching inns had been essential overnight accommodation for anyone travelling on a long journey and were a thriving industry, as they provided dinner, bed and breakfast. Once the railways were developed in the 1840s and journeys became much quicker, it spelled disaster for these hostelries. Many became very run down or went out of business altogether, while others tried to make up for the lost revenue by promoting the sale of alcoholic drinks. This was seen in some quarters as encouraging drunkenness and lewd behaviour, and inns began to get a poor reputation.

Earl Grey established Public Home Trust Companies in every county of England, getting financial backing from prominent landowners to purchase and restore inns to their original status, where food and lodgings were the main focus rather than the sale of alcohol. They became what we would now consider to be 'hotels' rather than 'pubs', and were known as 'Trust Houses'. In the early years of the twentieth century the company had around a hundred hotels, which more than doubled in the 1930s, acquiring some of the country's oldest establishments with some dating back over four hundred years. Even then, they were recognized for the quality of service, the high standard of cleanliness, and for providing good food. They acquired the Grosvenor House as the jewel in their crown in 1963.

With the merger of Trust Houses and Forte Holdings Limited, Lord

Crowther was company chairman and Sir Charles Forte was on the board of directors. Lord Crowther said at the time that it was a marriage made in heaven as 'Trust Houses was a hotel company that had gone into catering, and Forte a catering company that had gone into hotels'. But it was not long before there was a clash of personalities and a big internal battle over the chairmanship of the company. Lord Crowther had said verbally that he would stand down as chairman after one year, and Sir Charles Forte would succeed him, but nothing was put in writing. A year passed and it then became blatantly clear that Lord Crowther had absolutely no intention of standing down and the animosity became personal. 'I'll ruin him! I'll ruin him! I'll ruin that bloody man!' Crowther once shouted.

Charles Forte was a self-made man, who had started with nothing more than a single milk bar in 1934 and, as a shrewd businessman prepared to take risks, became the owner of some of the country's most successful eating establishments by the 1950s, including the Variety Fare chain of restaurants, Slaters, the Kardomah cafés, Quality Inn, the Criterion in Piccadilly Circus, London's premiere society restaurant Quaglino's, and the famous Café Royal in Regent Street. Lord Crowther was of the old school, educated at Cambridge, he once edited *The Economist* and was seen by many as being autocratic and bureaucratic. He was not prepared to take the same financial chances on ventures as Charles Forte and the two men were in conflict over the direction that the company should take. There was further acrimony following a takeover bid by Allied Breweries, which Lord Crowther supported but Sir Charles Forte rejected and defeated.

Lord Crowther died very suddenly from a heart attack while getting off a plane at Heathrow Airport in February 1972. Sir Charles Forte was now independent and at the helm of Trusthouse Forte. Quickly buying 34 more hotels, including the Strand Palace and the Regent Palace in London and others in New York, his name was now becoming as well known for hotels as it was for catering. In 1982, during Margaret Thatcher's premiership, he was given a peerage and became Baron Forte.

When Charles Forte took over the reins at the Grosvenor House Hotel, many changes were put in place. My first experience of the new regime was not a positive one. Under Trust Houses' ownership all full-time staff received a Christmas bonus every year of one week's extra wages. I was then earning £10.10 shillings a week, so received £21 at Christmas, but as soon as Charles

Forte took over, the bonus was taken away from us. This was not an impressive start from the staff point of view.

The Fortes did a tour of the hotel, meeting the various managers and obviously worked out where changes could be made. Very quickly they brought in a new General Manager whose job was sadly to make cutbacks and economies. This was referred to euphemistically as 'centralisation of departments'. Where we originally had 46 valets in the hotel, and 25 valets on the apartment side, soon there were many redundancies and it went down to just 8 valets in the hotel and 4 for the apartments. A dozen valets now had to do the work that seventy men had formerly done, and Head Valet Dick Smith took early retirement. Pageboys went from in excess of twenty to just six; the hotel's print shop closed and all the printing began to be undertaken by an outside firm; french-polishers and painters vanished; liftmen were made redundant as the lifts became fully automatic.

Room-service waiters and waitresses in both blocks halved from forty to twenty, and waiters that had been based on each of the floors were moved down to the basement and three automatic lifts were installed so that room service trays and trolleys could be got to the floors more quickly.

At the beginning some forty or fifty staff a week lost their jobs, and around four or five hundred staff went in the first six months. Morale was low, as nobody knew if their job would be the next to go. I was nervous that my career would come to a swift end. I was a valet and knew that I could easily have been dispensed with. Each day in the bar we would hear that another person we knew had been made redundant. It always seemed to be below stairs where the majority of cuts were made rather than the white-collar workers upstairs, so we were scared.

With the reduction in staff, customer service inevitably reduced too. Those of us that remained began to take less care with the guests' needs; we were just concerned about keeping our jobs. It was not only the lower orders that were in danger; heads of department were also being fired left, right and centre. Some had worked there for twenty or thirty years. Absolutely no one's job was safe and it was a very anxious time. Ultimately the number of full-time staff fell from 2,000 to 1,200.

It took us several years to build the service standards back up again and in the meantime we lost many regular guests to Claridges, the Connaught, the Ritz, and to smaller luxury hotels which still offered the same level of personal service. Regular guests had come to know the valets, the butlers, the liftmen, the concierges, the receptionists, all by name, and hated the lack of continuity that now existed, as familiar faces on the staff disappeared. When waiters and valets were actually based on each floor, guests came into contact with them daily and appreciated a friendly greeting. In many areas at Grosvenor House the standard of service declined and, even when I became General Manager many years later, it was never possible to restore the original level that guests had once enjoyed. The days when staff spent their entire careers at the hotel, working their way from lowly positions and up through the ranks to be heads of department, never returned. I was the last of that generation.

Long term I could see what Trusthouse Forte were doing. They had to make staff cuts and put the money saved on salaries into refurbishing the whole hotel, which was in dire need of updating by this time. Some of the bedrooms had become very outdated and shabby, having received little attention since the 1960s. Furniture was past its best; carpets were becoming threadbare; lifts needed maintenance; there was no air-conditioning; buttons that guests pressed for room service were worn out; and, all in all, the hotel did seem past its sell-by date. Some areas of the hotel had really changed very little since the Grosvenor House had a post-war refit in the early 1950s.

New technology of the day was introduced with a modern telephone network and paging systems; security was upgraded; the latest fire alarms and smoke detectors were installed. Ceilings in many of the rooms and corridors actually had to be lowered by about two feet to disguise all the extra wiring. Air-conditioning was introduced, with individual units in each room, which was certainly much needed. When London was hot in the summer, everybody had complained about heat, especially as the clientele began to change and many Arabs stayed with us who were used to superior air-conditioning facilities. We were already losing custom to the Dorchester, and the newly built Inn on the Park, simply because they had air-conditioning.

The billing system was another area that the Fortes updated. In the days before computers, there were miles of tubing everywhere throughout the hotel for sending bills to reception by a vacuum system. So to send a bill from the valet service after I had pressed a suit, I would write a docket for £2, place it in the tube, and by suction it would go immediately to reception. This would then be added to the customer's final bill. The same happened if a resident guest ate in the restaurant, had a drink in the bar, made a telephone call or ordered refreshments in the lounge. Hundreds of these vouchers an hour could arrive at reception to be sorted.

During the refurbishment the tubing was taken out – there must have been hundreds of miles of it as it ran throughout the entire hotel. Although it was a very efficient system for its time, there was a huge potential for error and a massive amount of revenue was lost. Between 8 and 10 a.m. each day, when many guests were checking out, four or five hundred receipts could come down the chute and receptionists had a difficult task keeping up with the amount of paperwork. As guests used to book on a 'room rate only' basis, everything else, including breakfast, was billed separately. So if the bill for breakfast came down the tube after a guest had checked out, then it was money lost. If ten people checked out before their breakfast bills arrived, the money lost began to add up and there could be a big enquiry by the management, as the hotel had to write this money off. Sometimes there could be a blockage of paper in the tubes and so the bills reached reception too late or not at all.

Similar tubing systems still exist today, especially in major supermarkets for sending cash to tills. A few years ago one well-known chain was losing a lot of money, many hundreds of thousands of pounds, but could not find out how the theft was taking place. The canny thief had intercepted the tube system where it passed through the gents' toilets, having discovered that it was hidden in the false ceiling. He lifted up part of the ceiling and when he heard money whooshing through the tube, siphoned off some cash for himself. Inevitably he was eventually caught when one day he failed to replace the ceiling tile properly. He received a prison sentence, but you have to give him marks for ingenuity.

Determined not to lose any money myself, I always sent my bills to reception promptly and would sometimes bypass the tube and take the docket to reception by hand. The receptionists would smile because they knew very well that I was on commission and so had a vested interest. In other areas of the hotel, staff were not as always as well organized. With beverages, for example, they might forget to charge a guest for a bottle of wine, and sometimes could not be bothered to fill out a docket at all. It was no skin off their nose and it was the hotel that lost out. Occasionally guests would be honest and point out that a bottle of wine was missing – from their final bill; others were less scrupulous and kept quiet about any discrepancy in their favour. I would estimate that around £2,000 a week, maybe more, was lost in revenue because of lapses in the billing procedure.

As the years went by we changed from tubes to an index-card system, with all the guests' details written by hand, then on to computerisation. Registration cards had got larger and larger, as they contained so many details, and computers made life much easier. Paradoxically, if computers crash today we now go back to the oldest system of all – we have to *ask* guests what room rate they are on, if they had breakfast or any extras such as mini-bar, and we post them a receipt. It is crazy really. And with no computer system, we cannot take a credit-card payment without resorting to a paper slip.

All the alterations and modernisation of Grosvenor House took about seven years to complete. It was like working on a building site at times, and keeping the dust under control was an ongoing problem. Although one floor would be worked on at a time and was out of use to guests, the floors above and below would still be covered in dust. Just as quickly as rooms were cleaned, the dust returned. Sometimes lifts would be out of action while the new ones were installed; the installation of new piping could occasionally lead to leaks to the rooms below or a sudden power cut. Little wonder that some guests found alternative accommodation.

Not everything, to my mind, was an improvement. Beautiful chandeliers were removed, thrown away, and replaced with round modern light fittings; ornate cornices were ripped out; even the service buttons with their blue, orange and green lights were eventually taken away from the outside of each apartment. Polished parquet wooden floors in the corridors and the magnificent black-and-white marble floor in the main lobby disappeared under wall-to-wall carpeting. Sadly, gripper rods fixing carpets to the floors ruined the original surfaces underneath. Where the hotel management failed at this time was in not keeping the staff involved and informed. If we on the shop floor had been consulted, maybe many of the needless changes might not have been made.

Some of the alterations were done in the name of fashion. Ironically, years later chandeliers were put back in to the hotel, wood panelling was restored, the marble floor in the lobby was renewed, and much of the hotel was returned to how it had originally been. As Jean Cocteau famously said, we should forgive fashion everything – it dies so young. Like so many things in life, fashion in interior design often goes full circle. What is out of date to one generation comes back into vogue with the next.

Just as the Fortes refurbished the whole hotel block in the 1970s, so the apartments received a makeover too, making them much grander than before. Ironically, whereas chandeliers and cornicing were removed from the hotel during the refit, magnificent new crystal chandeliers and cornicing were installed in the apartments. Lord Forte's daughter, Olga Polizzi, and her design team introduced stunning wallpapers, impressive curtaining, antique mirrors and furnishings, with around £100,000 being spent on refurbishing a single apartment.

Ultimately, after seven years of upheaval, we came out the other side with a superior hotel. The rooms were much more luxurious than they had been before, and many more amenities were available for customers. Staff were also better trained, which naturally improved the service for guests, and with fewer staff this meant more tips for those of us that remained. In fact Trusthouse Forte's training was considered second to none. They had their own training school at Colebrooke in Devon, where staff could go on management courses. It was exactly like a real hotel, except that it was not open to the public. Staff members were able to spend two or three days there, and came out with a lot more knowledge about the hospitality industry and their whole attitude lifted a gear. In 1982 Grosvenor House won the Hotel of the Year Award under Lord Forte's leadership and became the flagship of the company. It was their biggest earner in the group with sales of nearly £55 million a year, and profits of around £20 million a year, eclipsing the nearby Cumberland Hotel, which made annual profits of just £9 million at the time.

When Lord Forte first took over the hotel and dined with his guests, he did not feel that the food or service was up to scratch, so he created a new restaurant called 90 Park Lane. It had originally been a gentleman's club and later a branch of the National Westminster Bank (NatWest) at Grosvenor House for the guests' use. A great deal of effort went into the conversion and it was beautifully decorated with wood panelling on the walls. One of the hotel chefs ran it and, although it was not an immediate success, the chef worked hard and the restaurant was awarded a Michelin star. When he eventually left, the Michelin star went with him, as is the custom. The famous chef Nico Ladenis was brought in, making us the first hotel to have a celebrity chef. He was not always the easiest person to work with and, like many top chefs, could be very demanding. The restaurant was leased to him for three years rent-free, with the Grosvenor House taking ten per cent of the profit. New kitchens were installed, the restaurant was refurbished to his taste, and the name was changed to Nico at Ninety. The whole project became Lord Forte's pride and joy. He dined there regularly for lunch, and his guests were frequently royalty, members of the aristocracy, and the leading politicians of the day including Prime Minister Margaret Thatcher.

The clientele changed as a result of the Grosvenor's new image and facilities, with many more American guests, plus we began to attract more corporate business such as multi-national banks and large firms of accountants. It was not that Grosvenor House or Trusthouse Forte wanted to lose the old-style customers but they had left us, particularly during the upheaval of the renovations. Because of the new technology, and the introduction of computers by this time, the hotel became much more appealing to businessmen and we began to cater particularly for their needs. A Crown Club floor was introduced, for example, which gave them the ability to book in upstairs on the eighth floor without having to queue down in reception.

All hotels were in competition and each introduced quirky additions like this to steal custom from others. There was always a sense of triumph if we had been able to attract a company away from the Savoy or the Dorchester. We almost waved a flag up in the air if we had taken a thousand room nights from a rival hotel. In hindsight, Trusthouse Forte did the right thing to change the mix of clientele and move the business forward, and once everything had settled down into a new routine we became much more efficient and streamlined. I lamented the departure from the days when there were thousands of staff and all the guests' needs could be personally attended to, but realistically I can see that from a commercial point of view the cuts had to be made. The businessman of the day was not interested in knowing staff members by name.

Another noticeable change was that guests would check in to attend a function in the Great Room or the ballroom, and would stay just for that one night only and by the next morning would be gone. There was a high probability that they would never stay with us again, and so we had no opportunity to get to know them. The rapport that we used to have with regular guests was disappearing.

I have no idea exactly how much Trusthouse Forte spent on the reconstruction and modernisation but when, later in life, I became a Projects Manager at Grosvenor House, I refurbished the reception area, which took two years to do, and that alone cost £5 million. I oversaw the conversion of 86 Park Lane from twenty apartments into conference rooms, and that was a further £4 million; so in the early 1970s they must have spent £8 million to £10 million on updating the hotel. It was a great deal of money in those days.

Although I bemoaned the loss of the Christmas bonus, the Forte family were very generous once established at Grosvenor House. They gave us a pension fund so that we could contribute towards our retirement, and they supported it by giving us a set amount each year to boost it. Then they brought out the Trusthouse Forte Gold Card, which was originally for guests, but later they gave one to all the staff which entitled us to a thirty per cent discount at any of their 850 hotels throughout the world, at Lillywhites, the sporting goods store, Little Chef and Happy Eater restaurants . . . in fact at all the businesses that they owned. As a runner, this enabled me to go to Lillywhites and buy my running kit at a reduced cost. They also introduced a Share Option Scheme for employees, which I opted in to, and when they lost the company in 1996, I cashed in my shares and received around £7,000. So they were very good to the staff.

I learned a lot from the Fortes, and eventually became much closer to them than I ever expected. In fact, I ended up as Rocco Forte's private valet in the late 1970s and he became my running partner in many marathons from 1982 onwards. I first saw the family when they originally came to look at the Grosvenor House Hotel before taking it over. Although I was working down in the basement, I happened to come out of the Timekeeping Office upstairs as they pulled up outside in a Bentley. A small man with a moustache got out, looking extremely dapper, who I discovered was Sir Charles Forte. A taller man with jet-black hair and glasses was with him, and that turned out to be his son, Rocco. That was the first time that I saw them, but I was then in much too lowly a position to actually speak to them.

The Trusthouse Forte board made its base at Grosvenor House, all their secretaries moved in to the first floor of the apartment block, and the whole empire was run from there. For about 15 years this was their headquarters, which kept us all on our toes, as they were on the spot and so were aware of everything that was going on in the hotel. Because of this, the Fortes probably showed a greater degree of interest in the day-to-day running of Grosvenor House than in any of their other hotels at the time.

The secretaries used to eat in the staff canteen with the rest of us, and inevitably they would hear the gossip. Maybe someone had got drunk on duty, or stolen some bottles of wine, maybe even held a party in their room on the previous evening. This was immediately reported back to the board of directors, and some staff found themselves fired quite swiftly as a result. It was difficult for any General Manager to survive, because if they stepped out of line for a second it would get straight back to the board, and they would be out of a job.

My first real conversation with one of the Forte family came quite unexpectedly a few years later. Rocco Forte was then Personnel Director for Trusthouse Forte, and one day his secretary summoned me to his office. He asked me if I would like to go to his house in Belgravia and become his private valet. I immediately agreed and we jumped into the little Mini car that he had at the time (he did not have a private chauffeur like his father) and he drove me down Park Lane, weaving in and out of the traffic, to Lowndes Place in Belgravia. Here Rocco had a small bachelor house, and his father lived opposite in a mansion. Rocco asked me to press all his clothes, clean his shoes, and undertake general valet duties, for which I would receive an additional monthly wage. I departed with my own key to his front door.

After I had been working privately for Rocco for about a year, in addition to my full-time job at Grosvenor House, I came into contact with his mother, Irene, Lady Forte. Initially I got a call from Lord Forte's PA, Jean Chalmers, asking if I would start pressing suits at his house as well. I arrived at Charles Forte's mansion as instructed and rang the doorbell at the staff entrance. It was exactly like the popular television series *Upstairs, Downstairs*; in fact the house was almost identical to the fictional 165 Eaton Place. Unlike the television programme, however, with its strict class divisions, many a time I would encounter Lady Forte in the hall mopping the floor, dressed in her finery, with gold rings encrusted with diamonds on her fingers as she mopped. 'Morning, Neil,' she would say, 'I can clean the floors better than the staff, so I might as well do it myself!'

A small room was set aside with steam irons for my work, and Lord Forte's suits were there ready for pressing. I seldom saw the man himself, and if he was at home I just received a simple greeting. He would rarely stand and talk, as Rocco or Lady Forte did, but he was always very polite. I was particularly impressed by his clothes. His suits were immaculate, the shoes were always handmade, ties were woven from the best silk – he was flawless in his dress.

Rocco held a dinner party at his own house one evening and I was employed to serve the canapés and pour champagne. I could not help noticing a striking painting on the wall, so I asked Rocco what it was. 'It's a Lowry,' he said. 'My father gave it to me as a birthday present.'

From then onwards, whenever I went to press Lord Forte's suits, I could see that he had at least a dozen Lowrys on his own walls, and I came to admire the artist's work as a result. I bought some pictures as soon as I could afford them, although mine are sadly only copies.

On a less happy occasion I was taken to one side by the Fortes' head of security and was informed that various items, ranging from jewellery to linen sheets, were going missing from Rocco's house. A hidden camera was placed in a room and it was not long before a live-in nanny was caught on film stealing personal possessions. Apparently she was taking them to a pawn shop and obtaining cash. Once the pawn shop was traced by security, most of the items were recovered. It was worrying for a time because, even though Rocco had complete trust in me, security seemed to consider that it was either her or me who was the culprit. Fortunately the camera caught the nanny out – she was arrested and obviously lost her job at the Fortes'.

I enjoyed working privately for the Fortes, as not only did I have a growing family and needed the extra income to pay for a mortgage, but I came to admire their business ethics and way of working. Even when I progressed to other jobs within the hotel, and into management, I still continued pressing their suits. The down-side was that, once I became private valet to Lord Forte and Rocco, other members of staff became quite jealous of me. Colleagues would feel that they had to watch what they said to me, just in case I reported back to my bosses in the way that the secretaries in the staff canteen did.

Lord Forte and Rocco always spoke to any staff that they met within the hotel, which I felt was a pleasant touch, and if Lord Forte passed the General Manager in the lobby I would hear him say, 'Morning, Mr Murkett, how are the figures? And the occupancy? Mmm, could do better I think . . .' He was ever the businessman, and always very astute. Streetwise too perhaps, as he had come from nothing, but I think that is why I admired him. As I learned more about Lord Forte's life, he became a real inspiration to me.

His has been called one of the greatest business success stories of the twentieth century. Born in the tiny mountain village of Mortale between Naples and Rome (now called Monforte in his honour) he moved to Scotland with his family as a young child, and his father opened an ice cream parlour in Dumfries. Following in his father's footsteps, Charles Forte started a small business of his own selling ice creams and coffee in a milk bar when he was in his early twenties. Business flourished and soon he owned five milk bars, and began to expand into the wider catering industry, each deal becoming more ambitious as he bought up any company he could connected with hospitality and leisure. His acquisitions were as diverse as Terry's Chocolates, a major brewery, the publishing firm of Sidgwick & Jackson, and he even had a stake in the *Catholic Herald* newspaper, although hotels and catering remained his priority. Ultimately he ended up with an international chain of hotels and restaurants and became one of the world's most successful entrepreneurs, with a multi-billion-pound empire. When other hoteliers are forgotten, the name of Forte is still known worldwide.

Even when the Fortes owned the Grosvenor House, they were still acquiring more luxury hotels – the George V, the Plaza Athénée and Hôtel de la Tremoille in Paris; the Ritz in Madrid; the Westbury in New York; the Sandy Lane in Barbados . . . Quality and service were the two overriding principles on which the Fortes worked. Above all, the Fortes were kind people who cared about their staff. If you have a happy and well-trained staff, then you are able to offer excellent service, and if the hotels have quality fixtures and fittings, then you have the key to success in the hospitality business.

Lord Forte died at his London home in February 2007 aged 98, and I was privileged to be invited to his memorial service at Westminster Cathedral on 1 May that year. There must have been nearly 1,500 people there, and all around me were faces I knew: the Duchess of Norfolk, the Duke of Marlborough, the Earl of Gainsborough, Viscountess Hambledon, Lord Charles Churchill, Baroness Thatcher, Lord and Lady Rothschild, Sir Jackie Stewart, even the 'Forces Sweetheart' – Dame Vera Lynn. Many I had served at Grosvenor House. In typical Forte style, staff from all the old hotels had been invited too, from housekeepers to chambermaids – nobody had been forgotten. I had a chat with Rocco Forte and his sister

Olga Polizzi Shawcross. At the service Rocco spoke warmly about his father and told the story of the time his mother had her American Express card stolen. Lord Forte had said that he would not report it to the police, as the thieves would certainly spend far less on the card than she had been spending.

Everyone admired the fact that Charles Forte was intrinsically an honest man, and people took their hat off to him for what he had achieved in his life. And he never forgot his humble roots, each year making a return visit with his family to the small Italian village where he was born, and each Christmas sending every household there a hamper of food. In the hospitality business, Lord Forte was really considered royalty. Whenever he arrived at Grosvenor House in a chauffeur-driven black Bentley – always a *black* Bentley – everybody knew him and guests would greet him affectionately.

After the service we went back to the Mandarin Oriental Hyde Park, a property that Lord Forte used to own when it was still called the Hyde Park Hotel. Lady Forte was in a wheelchair and looked very frail, which was sad to see, as I always remember her mopping floors in her glad rags. Sir Rocco was naturally very sombre, but he and his wife, Aliai, were charming to us. Their children looked stunning – one of the sons is named Charles, in honour of his grandfather Lord Forte. All around us the family shared stories. About how, despite his great wealth, Lord Forte never took money for granted. Although he owned magnificent boats and cars, he would say, 'Think how many cups of tea have had to be sold to buy them.' About how he would occasionally buy companies that he did not really want, simply because he felt sorry for the struggling owner or he wanted to return a favour. And I heard many examples of his humour. He was small in stature and, on receiving his knighthood in 1970, he declared himself to be 'the shortest knight of the year'.

Lord Forte's legacy still continues and in some ways his employees have a special bond. The Forte Club has now been established for former members of staff, with annual reunions at the renowned Brown's Hotel – once the favourite haunt of Agatha Christie.

I have often been asked if I always wanted to run my own establishment, but the idea of owning a hotel did not actually come into my mind until the mid 1980s. I had come from nothing, had been washing-up and counting the sheets, and had the goal of becoming General Manager at Grosvenor House. Then suddenly, just as Charles Forte had the vision whilst running a small milk bar that he could expand, I began to feel that it would be nice to run a place of my own. At the time, I never thought that I would have either the courage or the capital to make that leap. Maybe I should just have taken a leaf out of Charles Forte's book and risked everything sooner than I did. But when Trusthouse Forte took over the Grosvenor House in 1970, I was just excited that I had been promoted to a full-time valet in the apartment side of the business. Another door had opened up for me.

4

You May Have Done It for Money

Be the business never so painful, you may have it done for money.
Thomas Fuller, *Gnomologia*

I knocked on the door of Robert Wagner's apartment. There was no answer from the American film and TV star, so I let myself in with the master key to collect some clothes that he wanted laundered. No sooner had I entered than his beautiful wife, actress Natalie Wood, walked out of the bathroom completely naked. I decided not to put in a complaint to the management! She just stood and looked at me, completely unperturbed, and I knew then that I was going to enjoy my promotion to the South Block

Within the hospitality industry the word 'luxury' meant providing an impeccable service, complying with the guests' requests twenty-four hours a day. A 'first class' service was considered similar, but with restrictions. What the Grosvenor House offered guests in the apartments was luxury, and as a result we tended to get the more affluent type of clientele who were prepared to pay for the very best. Many were titled, such as Lords Astor, Wilton, Burghley, Grade and Spencer-Churchill; some were Broadway and Hollywood stars; others just eccentric millionaires.

The motivation for many people working at Grosvenor House was greed and money. Jealousy developed between the two blocks quite simply because the basic wage was higher on the apartment side (about £14 a week) and tipping was much greater too. Apartment valets had far more clothes to press, for example, hence more tips. Also we received fifty per cent commission on everything we ironed. The charge was £2 to press a gentleman's two-piece suit, more if it was a three-piece, and we received half of that amount. It was added to our wages and so we were taxed on it, but it nevertheless boosted our income. The laundry and dry-cleaning would go to an

45

outside contractor, but we still received ten per cent commission from that at the end of the week. Consequently we rigorously checked with residents whether they needed any clothes laundered and practically ironed anything that moved. If the opportunity was there, we grabbed it with both hands. I really didn't care what people thought about me; we worked very hard to earn our money and the hotel did well out of us too, so I could see no harm in it.

As the years went on, apartment valets came amongst the highest earners at Grosvenor House, with a bigger annual income than even the General Manager simply because of the commission and tips that we received. The top four earners, in order, were:

1. Head Concierge
2. Valets
3. General Manager
4. Doormen.

No wonder the other hotel staff were jealous of valets, and sometimes a real feud could develop. If we offered just to carry someone's bag from one room to another, for example, this could lead to a war with the luggage porters, as it meant that they had lost out on a tip. Such was the divide between the North and South blocks that it felt as if the Berlin Wall was between us, rather than Lutyens elegant colonnade. Between 1974 and 1978 I received an average income of £35,000 a year. Every week as I stood in a queue with thirty to forty other members of staff, waiting to sign for the little brown envelope that contained our wages, I would hear the same old joke: 'You're such a highly paid valet now. When are you going to retire, Kirby?'

Although money was obviously a great incentive to valets, the service we gave was really second to none. It was as if the apartments gave a five-star service, while the hotel was four-star in comparison. We offered a much more personal service than a hotel valet too – from running guests' baths to often selecting clothes from their dressing rooms for them to wear. Sometimes this meant undertaking a twelve- or fourteen-hour shift, but I preferred the apartment side as the service was more intimate, and whereas hotel guests might stay only a few nights and then never be seen again, the apartment clientele had by its very nature more continuity and stability.

Guests who had previously stayed in the hotel in the pre–Trusthouse Forte days now moved over to the apartment block, because they saw it as being old-fashioned and still offering a way of life that they had previously enjoyed in the hotel. The apartments were larger, of course, and even more luxurious than the hotel rooms. Some had as many as five bedrooms and all had huge sitting rooms, and the guests received the personal service as it *used* to be. The apartment block also had its own reception desk, separate from the hotel reception and so offered a greater degree of privacy and was close to the Grosvenor's Health Club, which many guests used. People like Jackie Stewart, Sean Connery and Roger Moore soon started to drift across from the hotel. Dame Margot Fonteyn, Lady Joseph and Margaret, Duchess of Argyll, were amongst those who had a permanent home there. The Grosvenor House apartments became *the* place to be.

My work brought me into daily contact with so many fascinating people, each with their individual quirks and foibles. David Cecil, Marquess of Exeter, the former Olympic hurdles champion, for example, had the personalised number plate AAA 1 (Amateur Athletics Association) on his Rolls-Royce. He once had a hip replacement operation and replaced the flying lady 'Spirit of Ecstasy' on the bonnet of his car with a silver-plated piece of his own hip bone.

As a keen footballer myself, I was thrilled when the legendary Billy Wright became a regular visitor to Grosvenor House, where his sister-in-law Babs had an apartment. He was the first footballer in the world to earn 100 caps and was really the David Beckham of his day, and even now remains the fifth most-capped footballer ever to play for England. His wife, Joy, was one of The Beverley Sisters and I would occasionally hear the three of them rehearsing in the apartment. Sisters Babs, Joy and Teddie were always together and stuck to each other like glue. They were always polite and kind to me, but I noticed that Billy was very careful with his money.

Lauren Bacall used to stay in film producer Sam Spiegel's apartment. She could be absolutely terrifying. Once, when she was about to depart, she over-packed her suitcase with far too many clothes. My fellow valet, Michael, struggled to close it for her. 'Bloody well get out of the way!' she shouted aggressively at him. Then she pointed at me. 'You! You look like a *man*. You do it!' Admittedly I was stronger than Michael and I managed to get the case closed. 'That's it,' she growled. 'Now get out, the pair of you!' She was one of the toughest women I have ever met in my life.

Glamorous, but really tough. We got out of that apartment like two scalded cats.

If Miss Bacall ever needed garments laundered or dry-cleaned, she would call down and ask for them to be collected. When we knocked on her door to pick them up, as requested, she would shout, 'I've left them there, now hurry up and bring them back, and *don't* be long!' She appeared to have no patience whatsoever. Miserable cow!

Margaret, Duchess of Argyll, the British socialite, had a house at 48 Upper Grosvenor Street just around the corner from us, but lived in apartment 148-149 at Grosvenor House on the eighth floor. Two apartments were knocked into one so that she could have more space. She had lived an extravagant lifestyle and her money had dwindled, so she opened her house up for public tours and retired to the hotel. Lord Forte was happy for her to be there, as it was good for the Grosvenor House's image to have a Duchess in residence. She had the biggest assortment of wigs that I have ever seen in my life. One whole room in her apartment was devoted to them. There was also a massive collection of shoes in her dressing-room, with racks almost touching the ceiling. She was a very elegant lady and looked tremendous when she was entertaining her guests, although very different if I ever saw her without her wig.

The Duchess had a permanent maid living with her and the two fought like cat and dog, always arguing over something. The maid undertook personal duties and dealt with the Duchess's laundry, so there was less for us to do and we did little more than clean her shoes – which was a free service that Grosvenor House offered. She was obviously on a tight budget and I never once received a tip from her. We did receive a Christmas gift, but I always suspected that the maid gave it to us out of her own pocket because she felt embarrassed for the Duchess.

Some of the apartment residents were more reclusive than others. I thought Shirley MacLaine was going to die of embarrassment when I one day caught her with curlers in her hair. After that, the Academy Award–winning actress and singer kept out of our way, and somehow seemed to get in and out of her apartment without being seen. We could never understand how, but discovered later that she was using the fire escape to make her entrances and exits.

Others were happy to lead a more public life at Grosvenor House and there would be an almost permanent contingency of media people visiting, especially if one of the resident celebrities had a film, book or stage play to promote. Their apartment would provide the location for television interviews, and occasionally we had to bring up extra flowers to make the background look even more extravagant. Often I would watch a major star being interviewed on a television programme and I would recognise the curtains and table lamp behind them.

Large companies such as Unilever, Shell, GKN, 3M, Procter & Gamble all had permanent apartments, which their chairmen and directors used to stay in at various times. They were more generous than the Duchess of Argyll and gratuities came monthly in an envelope, around £25–£30 a month for each member of staff that had looked after them. Because the personal items in the apartments were very valuable, they liked to have continuity of staff whom they knew could be trusted, hence the higher tips. Occasionally their families, friends and guests would also come and stay in the apartment with them and needed looking after; sometimes their business clients would be given accommodation too, so there was often a lot of extra work involved. I noticed that company occupants seldom seemed to plan ahead and rarely had their shoes ready to be polished, and clothes for dry-cleaning would be given to us at the very last minute. They might arrive at 6.30 p.m. for a function in the Great Room that evening and suddenly we would have to iron a shirt for them to wear or press a suit. This was annoying, as we could have thirty or forty boxes of laundry and many rails of dry-cleaning to return to other apartments during the early part of the evening, and it wasted our valuable time. It would not be long before the bleeper would go as other residents began screaming for their clothes. We were constantly on the run to keep everyone happy.

When we returned freshly laundered clothes to the apartments, we used to start at the top floor and then work our way down to the lower ones using the staff service lift. We were not allowed to use the guest lifts. It was crazy having only one lift for all the staff. Housekeepers, waiters, chambermaids and the like were constantly needing the staff lift to transport items up and down, and sometimes I could be standing by the lift door for ten minutes or more waiting to gain access. It really irritated me to the extreme, especially as there were three lifts in the apartment block for the guests use and they usually stood idle. Being young and impatient, I would sometimes sneak into one of the guests' lifts to go up to the top floor.

Robert Wiles was the Apartment Manager and occasionally he would catch me in the wrong lift.

'I do apologise, Mr Wiles, but I can't get into the staff lift. I waited a long time, but it's constantly in use, and I must get these clothes back to the guests,' I used to say humbly. 'They can't go out this evening until they get their laundry back, Mr Wiles, and the customer *must* come first.'

This was not true – at least it wasn't my motivation; I just wanted to get finished quickly so that I could put my feet up with a glass of whisky or brandy.

'Don't do it again,' he would smile.

'All right, Sir. Goodbye, Sir.'

The lift doors closed and he was gone. The next time I thought he wasn't around, I would be back in the guest lift again.

Customers really treated their apartment as if it were their own home, using it as their London base, with their main residence abroad or in the country. The company chairmen, for example, would arrive on Mondays, stay during the week and then return to their country estates on Fridays. We were treated as if we were their private staff.

Standards of cleanliness became of paramount importance. If the apartment was not kept spotless, or the housekeeping was not up to the mark, then the management would soon hear about it. Linen had to be changed every day, the bed cover was turned down at night, so they were really receiving hotel-style service in what was essentially a private apartment. In those days the apartment block had bathroom cleaners, who did nothing but clean bathrooms; chambermaids who cleaned the rooms and changed the beds, and a carpet-hooverer whose sole job was to vacuum the carpets and clean the corridors. Sometimes we would be called in to clean tall mirrors, chandeliers, or other hard-to-reach areas. A housekeeper would then go around with a white glove, running a finger over surfaces and across the top of picture and door frames to ensure that no dust had been missed.

Occasionally an apartment became vacant and the opportunity was then taken to give it a thorough clean and redecoration. The walls were generally plain-coloured, in cream or pastel shades, and so decorators came in and gave everywhere a coat of paint, including the ceilings. The carpet would be replaced, bathrooms would be regrouted and any worn fittings renewed. Furniture was french-polished, and really the whole apartment received a total makeover so that the standard was high enough for the next resident.

Many resident guests even chose their own furniture for the apartment, as if they owned it. Lord Forte's sister, Mrs Sanna, had one apartment and she installed an enormous marble fireplace in her sitting room there. No cost was spared where she was concerned. Every two years the carpets had to be changed in all the apartments, as invariably pale beige carpets were laid and inevitably the edges became dirty quickly with dust from the floor-boards below. Even on the hotel side, fittings really only had a maximum lifespan of five years. The wear and tear in any hotel is enormous.

For living in such surroundings and receiving five-star service, the rents on the apartments were not cheap. In the mid-1970s it was £25,000–£30,000 a year, but by the mid-1990s the Unilever flat alone was £135,000 a year plus VAT, just for the rent. That did not include incidentals such as telephone, food and, of course, staff tips. Even the smallest apartment at that time was £50,000 a year, with rents calculated on the basis of £50 per square foot of floor space. These were usually taken on a maximum five-year lease, although many only rented them for a year or two. The income from the apartment block was around £8,000,000 per annum.

A typical apartment had a highly lacquered mahogany outer door, so polished over the years that they reminded me of the mirror finish to the door of 10 Downing Street. Each door had brass fittings including a letter box, the apartment number and a doorbell. So it was very much like the front door to a private house. Once inside, the grandeur was equal to that of a stately home – richly carved cornices, deep-piled carpets, and sparkling crystal chandeliers in the hallway. Ahead would be double doors into the dining room; to the left a door to the bedrooms, another to the sitting room. The sitting rooms themselves were breathtaking in their splendour, often with pale-yellow walls, elaborate marble fireplaces, delicate antique furniture and clocks, and invariably white sofas. Throughout would be magnificent silver from the owner's private collection, glass decanters, superb-quality paintings in gilded frames on the walls, books strategically placed for show rather than to be read, and flower arrangements everywhere. Grosvenor House had its own florist, Caroline Dickinson, who used to provide floral decorations for all the function rooms, restaurants and public areas, and the guests ordered flowers for their apartments from her.

The florist actually had a shop within the reception, next to the hotel's resident hairdresser, Vidal Sassoon, who had a ground-floor shop with a metal staircase going up to his salon on the floor above. His business took up one whole apartment and many famous clients visited him daily. Another apartment was used as a doctor's surgery for guests. In many ways Grosvenor House was like a small town, as residents had so many facilities available without ever having to leave the building. And what we did not supply, they brought in. Some guests would employ their own private masseur; others had make-up artists and beauticians; acupuncturists and chiropractors would visit; even private dental treatment would be carried out, so there was constant movement around the apartments.

Each apartment had its own dining room and residents entertained on a lavish scale with dinners and cocktail parties. A few days before a dinner party, the Head Waiter would be called to discuss arrangements. This was strategic planning to establish whether they needed to borrow candelabra from the function rooms, what table linen was required, and so on. The Food and Beverage Manager would go in to discuss the menu and would liaise with the chefs. The apartments had their own kitchen and chefs, completely separate from the hotel kitchen. On the actual evening we would bring the food up to the apartment, where it would be served by tail-coated waiters wearing white gloves. Nothing extra was charged for this service but it meant extra tips, as the staff pulled out all the stops to impress the residents' dinner-party guests, and it really was above and beyond the call of duty.

Apartments had a very small kitchenette, not large enough to swing a cat in. A kitchen was not a priority for residents, and it was simply somewhere to house a fridge, a tiny oven, and store basic crockery and cutlery. They were badly designed because the smoke alarm system had a detector in the kitchenette which would go off with the smallest amount of steam or smoke. Although there was 24-hour room service, occasionally residents would decide to make themselves some toast and inevitably the fire alarm would sound. The fire brigade would turn up at all hours of the day and night, roaring down Park Lane, only to discover that the alarm had been set off by a slice of burning toast. Even if we knew the cause, the fire brigade insisted on seeing the scene of the incident, and for each false alarm they charged £50. The chairman of Procter & Gamble was a culprit that I particularly remember, and he stubbornly refused to let the fire brigade in at first but they were implacable. After an inspection of his kitchen they eventually agreed that all was well and returned to the station. Twenty minutes later he did exactly the same thing again! A second piece of toast set off the alarm and the fire brigade returned to Grosvenor House. They were furious and gave him a stiff talking to. It seemed rather strange to me, seeing one of the richest men in the world getting a dressing-down over a slice of toast. He was very embarrassed over the whole episode. What a twat!

On a sadder occasion, a resident fell asleep with a cigarette in her hand and burned to death as her bed went up in flames. That was why the fire brigade could never take any chances and were frequent visitors to the hotel. Fortunately for us they were invariably false alarms. Cigarettes, cigars and toasters were the most common triggers. I will never forget the terrible smell of her blackened and charred body; unlike anything I had ever smelt before.

Four valets looked after the 160 apartments in the block. Michael and I were responsible for the lower four floors containing eighty apartments; Charlie and Norman looked after the floors above. Trusthouse Forte housed the valets in a small one-bedroom apartment on the first floor, where we had three ironing boards, kettles and all the equipment needed for pressing and steaming clothes. Suits, trousers and dresses that had not gone out to the contract cleaners would be hung up on rails around us and we had to work our way through them, before personally returning each item safely to the relevant apartment. We were not meant to have a television in that apartment, but we had one hidden in a wardrobe just to help break the monotony of ironing.

Sometimes guests moved apartments for various reasons, or if the hotel happened to be full and an apartment was vacant then rich hotel guests would use them temporarily as a suite. Big companies such as Shell or BP might rent two or three apartments at any one time, and maybe a director would move from one of their smaller apartments into a larger one. Any move of this kind was our responsibility and involved transporting all the personal possessions on trolleys. We had to empty drawers, wardrobes and cupboards, and put everything in the new apartment *exactly* as it had been in the old one. This had to be done in pairs for security reasons, so that no guest could complain that a gold watch had been stolen or something was missing from a pocket.

On one occasion we had to move some guests to another apartment and they later claimed that they had lost jewellery to the value of £10,000.

The management had requested the move, they trusted us and knew that we would not steal jewellery, but the hotel still had to cough up £10,000 on their insurance. After that, all moves were undertaken with witnesses.

I also had to move an Australian family whose apartment had been double-booked. They had gone out for the day and so their possessions had to be moved without their knowledge. Unfortunately they returned to find that they were in a smaller apartment and kicked up merry hell. This is always a problem when people end up in a worse room than they had before; transfer someone to a bigger room and you never hear a word of complaint about having to move, and you often end up with a tip.

Generally we had a set routine, and the first two hours of the day were very vigorous as many residents wanted tasks done at a certain time and insisted that suits were back from the dry-cleaners and ready to wear when *they* wanted them. Shoes also had to be cleaned as early in the day as possible. We used to put chalk marks on the soles so that we knew which apartment they came from, but with a pile of shoes under our arms we invariably ended up with white chalk all over our smart black uniforms. We had to have all laundry collected by 9.30 a.m., so that we could get it back the same day. It was done off-site at Stevenson's Laundry. It was really our busiest period of the day and we ran from apartment to apartment collecting items and keeping everybody happy. Some of them wanted everything done yesterday. They would have wardrobes full of suits and fabulous clothes, yet they always wanted to wear the one garment that needed cleaning.

Most residents were busy people, and by 9 a.m. their chauffeurs would be waiting to take them to the office or a business meeting. Wives later had the chauffeur return to take them off for shopping sprees, maybe to meet friends for lunch at Claridge's, Harry's Bar, the Connaught or whatever eating place happened to be fashionable at the time. Although they could easily have eaten at Grosvenor House, these rich ladies just wanted a change of scene. And to be seen in the *right* place, of course.

Every resident had different habits and requirements. I arrived for work at about 6.45 a.m. and the first thing I had to do after changing into my uniform was to check the answerphone. There might be a message from Lord Grade in apartment 71 asking me to pick up a suit for him, or instructions to collect shoes from Lady Joseph for cleaning. She was the mother of Keith Joseph MP and would never leave her shoes in the corridor outside her door, as she was worried that they might be stolen, so left them just inside her apartment hallway. This meant that I had to knock on her door to collect them, but she would not allow me inside until I had removed my own shoes because she had very pale carpets. So I had to take *my* shoes off to collect *her* shoes! Many staff were unhappy about having to remove their shoes in case they had holes in their socks.

After I had dealt with these initial early-morning requests, six days a week I had to run down to apartment 31 at 8.30 a.m. to Sir Geoffrey Duveen, who had a four-bedroom apartment. I had to choose a suit for him to wear, a shirt and tie, and would lay them out in his dressing room, with shoes to match. Simultaneously I would go to his personal bathroom and start to run his bath. Sir Geoffrey was in his early nineties and unsteady on his feet, but would eventually come in wearing just a dressing gown. I would then sit beside him on a wooden laundry basket, making sure that the bath never overflowed, while he shaved. I was always amazed that he never cut himself, as his hands used to shake so much, and as he was deaf we had limited conversations and I am sure that he never actually heard a word I said.

When he had finished shaving, I helped him off with his dressing gown and into the bath. Afterwards I dried him with the towel and helped him put on his underpants and vest. It was not a pretty sight, but at the end of every week Sir Geoffrey gave me a £2 tip. He was a very rich man and once showed me his first million-pound business cheque, which he kept in his wallet as a souvenir. I could not foresee then that the day would come when I would have a million-pound cheque myself.

Sir Geoffrey was a great collector of ivory, and there were valuable items everywhere in the apartment, which was very grand and overlooked Park Lane and Hyde Park. Lady Duveen reminded me of the character Cruella de Vil from the film *101 Dalmatians*. Although they were a very wealthy couple, they could be very penny-pinching and the chambermaid had to steal croissants or rolls from the kitchen for them at breakfast time, as they were too mean to pay for them. When I collected their clothes for pressing, I would notice appalling stains on her dresses. Lady Duveen would not allow me to have them dry-cleaned because of the cost. Eventually the stains became too bad and I could not get them out with dry-cleaning fluid, and in the end I included her dresses with the staff dry-cleaning to keep the cost down and save her money. Sir Geoffrey died before his wife, and I could not help noticing in *The Times* that when Lady Duveen died she left between two and three million pounds in her will. Yet she was so tight and I never received a single tip from her after Sir Geoffrey's death.

After attending to Sir Geoffrey, I had to rush off each day to apartment 23, which was occupied by the prima ballerina Dame Margot Fonteyn. The headboard of her bed was hand-painted and depicted a scene from *Swan Lake*. She was always charming and would ask me to clean her ballet shoes and press her dresses, which would result in a ten-shilling tip each day. On the odd occasion when her husband, Dr Roberto de Arias, came to stay, he would bring his bodyguard with him who always appeared to have a gun under his jacket. A Panamanian diplomat and playboy, Arias had been shot by a rival Panamanian politician and was left a quadriplegic for the rest of his life. He would lie with a blackboard and easel at the foot of his bed, and the bodyguard would chalk up stocks and share prices while Arias was on the telephone to his broker. Dame Margot continued dancing until she was sixty, even though she suffered with an arthritic foot, just so that she could afford to pay for her husband's medical care.

One day Dame Margot Fonteyn called me to her apartment and handed me a carrier bag. 'These are my old ballet shoes,' she said. 'Throw them away. I don't need them anymore.' I looked in the bag and saw what I thought to be very dainty pink shoes, but not knowing much about ballet at the time, I threw the bag into the incinerator. How I wish that I had kept the shoes of the beautiful dancer, who was honoured with the title *prima ballerina assoluta* by the Royal Ballet when she retired. They would have been worth a fortune now. Hey ho.

Rudolf Nureyev came to stay in an apartment for four months while dancing in a ballet, and I noticed a bit of tension between him and Dame Margot. They would get together for coffee downstairs in the lounge and insisted that they got on well, but I was certainly aware of a feud of some kind.

'Mr Nureyev's staying upstairs, Madam,' I informed her one day.

'Oh, yes?' I could tell by her body language and manner that there was no love lost between them. 'Can you clean my shoes, and this dress needs pressing.' It was just as if I hadn't mentioned his name.

Once Dame Margot's requirements had been dealt with, I ran to the apartment of Lord Vestey, whose family owned the Vestey meat empire and the Blue Star Shipping Line. He was an elderly gentleman by this time and always seemed to be reading *The Times*. I would greet him with, 'Morning, M'lord', and he would just nod in return. I would go to his wardrobe and take the suit that needed pressing and shoes to be cleaned. That was also worth a two-pound tip each week, although once again he was not known for being free with his money. There was a joke doing the rounds that when Lord Vestey had been in the process of being made a baron he had been suffering problems with industrial relations. He was on one knee in front of the Queen, who dubbed him with a sword and said, 'Arise, Lord Vestey.' He did not rise. The Queen repeated her words, 'Arise, Lord Vestey.' Lord Vestey remained on one knee, whereupon Prince Philip said, 'Arise? He doesn't know what a rise is!'

I would then race along to Lord and Lady Grade's apartment to collect items of laundry and dry-cleaning. Lew Grade (christened Louis, he became 'Lew' after his name was misspelled on a theatre bill) was always polite, courteous and joyful. Although portly, he had once been a dancer, known as 'the man with the musical feet', and was crowned World Solo Charleston Champion at the Royal Albert Hall in 1926 by Fred Astaire. He was another two-pound tip.

Lord Grade was a larger-than-life figure, a very influential show-business impresario and television executive, and walked the corridors, smoking his specially made twelve-inch-long Havana cigars. He was seldom seen without these big fat cigars, and when he came round a corner you saw the cigar appear before he did. If you were in a lift with him, there was a real danger that you could have your eye poked out, the cigars were so long. The aroma of the cigars was so powerful too, that you could smell them from the floor below, and his wife made him sit beside a window in their apartment, puffing his smoke out into Park Lane rather than in their room. The cigars were his trademark, yet if he were alive today the smoking ban would prevent him lighting up.

Then it would be on to apartment 61, which was occupied by a Mrs Carmichael from South Africa who made two long visits to London each year for about six weeks at a time. She owned a large company that exported paper and card. She was a very tough woman – nothing was ever right for her and she was what might be called a professional complainer. She had a large four-bedroom apartment overlooking Hyde Park and did not get up until after 10.30 a.m. each day, when she would then get ready to go out for lunch. Her chauffeur would drive her in a Rolls-Royce to the Connaught, which was literally only two minutes' walk away, and then bring her back at 3 p.m. when she would promptly return to bed.

I particularly remember one day when the television in her apartment went wrong. One of the maintenance men came up to check it. He was black and she became exceptionally rude to him because of his colour and asked me to throw him out of the apartment. This was the time of apartheid in South Africa, and I was extremely embarrassed and felt like giving her a piece of my mind, but did not want to lose my job. He was very upset and complained to the management, but no action was taken because Mrs Carmichael was paying a lot of rent and they did not want to lose her custom. I think some staff spat in her coffee after that episode.

I decided to pay her back another way. Every day I had to press one of her dresses, and as she was an extremely large woman and probably weighed around 23 stone, I started charging her for two. The dresses really were like shapeless tents, each about three feet wide. Naturally I received my fifty per cent commission for everything I pressed. She also gave me a two-pound tip each week. I felt that I earned my money, as her dresses were always covered with stains. I could always tell what she had eaten for lunch.

After Mrs Carmichael, I would go along the corridor to where Columbia Pictures had two apartments, which always had a Hollywood film star in at least one of them. At any time an apartment might be a temporary home to the likes of Tony Curtis, Rosalind Russell, Rita Hayworth or William Holden. These apartments were so valuable to me as far as tips were concerned, because the whole bill was paid by Columbia Pictures and the tip would be five-pounds a week for the two apartments. Kirk Douglas, one of my favourite actors ever since I saw him in the 1960 film *Spartacus*, stayed there with his wife and I was delighted to discover that he was a kind and gentle man. His son Michael occasionally came to stay and was equally charming, though he could be slightly more demanding than his father. He was young then and could be a little arrogant, forever reminding us who his father was. Often the Hollywood stars would tip us very well, as they were staying there rent-free anyway and so had very few expenses. As the money kept rolling in, I began to think that I would soon be able to take an apartment myself.

Once, when Robert Wagner and Natalie Wood were staying in the apartment, I was summoned unexpectedly to the security office one morning and was questioned thoroughly for around half an hour. A £6,000 diamond ring had gone missing from the apartment. I had earlier returned shoes and clothing as usual, and had used my electronic master key to gain access.

This gave security a read-out and showed that I had been the very last person to go in there. I was in real danger of losing my job. The next day the ring was found down the back of a sofa in the apartment. Robert Wagner was extremely embarrassed, very apologetic, and gave me a ten-pound tip. The tight bastard! He had nearly lost me my job.

Another international film star, Laurence Harvey, lived in apartment 36–36a, which was leased by Romulus Films. He was one of my favourites and I saw many of his fifty films, including the iconic *Room at the Top*. At well over six feet tall he was a very elegant and well-dressed man. Most of his suits were handmade in velvet, and blue, burgundy or green were his preferred colours. These all had to be steamed, because if you ironed velvet it destroyed the pile. He also had slip-on velvet shoes with the letters *LH* embroidered on them in gold, which had to be brushed very carefully to keep them clean. His initials were also on the cuffs of his shirts, and his name was printed on the bottle labels of his own private stock of wine.

Whenever I went to his apartment, it always seemed to be in darkness with the curtains closed. I had to feel my way around, and soon I would hear his voice call out. 'Who's that?' 'It's Neil, Sir.' Then all was well. I think he often had somebody in bed with him, and had them hidden under the covers. At the end of each week he would give me a tip, but if one of the other valets attended to him when I was away they did not receive anything.

Often I would tell him that I had seen a film of his on television, and he would go straight into reciting lines from the script for at least five minutes. He always lived life to the full and never failed to make me laugh. He was also a very generous man and gave me five-pound tips. At the time he was married to the second of his three wives, Joan Perry Cohn, the very rich widow of Columbia Pictures movie mogul Harry Cohn, but she rarely came to England. He was having an affair with an actress called Pauline Stone, whom he had met on the set of the film *A Dandy in Aspic* in 1968, and she had given birth to his only child, a girl named Domino Harvey (who would later win fame as a bounty hunter). They visited the apartment regularly, but it was very hush-hush. On the occasions when his wife came over from America, he would say to me, 'Check the whole apartment for anything of Pauline's, take it away and keep it safe for me.'

I then used to search everywhere, even under the bed, and take any items downstairs and hide them in my locker. If anyone had searched it, they would have found her bra and panties and thought that I was a closet transvestite. Eventually Harvey divorced his wife and married Pauline Stone in 1972, but sadly died just a year later from stomach cancer aged forty-five. Laurence Harvey was bisexual and also had a long-term love affair with his manager, Jimmy Woolf, who had discovered him in the 1950s, but Woolf had predeceased him, committing suicide in 1966.

When I was a valet there was a room called the Closet Room in which all the celebrities' clothes could be stored on rails when they were not using their apartments. On one occasion Sean Connery's luggage was accidentally sent to America from this room by mistake. We managed to get it returned without him knowing and the next time he stayed at the hotel he had no idea that his belongings had made an unscheduled trip across the Atlantic and back.

During my time as a valet we had many Middle Eastern guests from Qatar, which had become a very rich state since the discovery of oil. An offshore field had been discovered in 1960 and within five years was producing 233,000 barrels of oil a day. In 1971 natural gas was discovered, too. It was as if they had tapped into liquid gold, so money appeared to be no object to the Arabs that stayed in the private apartments at Grosvenor House. Now tips could be in the form of a twenty-pound note, which we had not seen before. For some of us the weekly wage was then twenty pounds, so to receive the equivalent of a week's salary as a tip was beyond belief.

Surprisingly, with the Arabs came many high-class call girls. These were not ordinary prostitutes off the streets, but British girls studying to be a doctor, lawyer, or scientist, who had joined an agency to earn extra money to help fund their education. The girls obviously enjoyed it, as they would be taken to top restaurants, casinos and nightclubs by the rich sheikhs, before returning to Grosvenor House at around 2 a.m. to 'entertain' and earn themselves several hundred pounds. Then the girls just disappeared into the night.

The bodyguards and chauffeurs would organise parties for their bosses in the sitting room of the apartments. All the chairs would be pushed to the edge of the room so that Arabic dancers could perform in the centre. Many of the Arabs had mansions in Mayfair and Belgravia, so did not actually sleep at Grosvenor House and would return to their family homes once the evening's entertainment with the call girls had ended. We had to turn a blind eye to the parties, as they were not noisy so did not disturb other guests, and the Arabs were good customers and brought in a lot of money, paying a great deal for their suites. They would take luxury apartments on a two-year lease, yet maybe only used them a couple of times a year.

My eyes were certainly opened, especially as I had always been led to believe that the Arabs did not drink alcohol. At Grosvenor House I saw that whisky was their favourite tipple and bottles of Black Label were much in demand. Often we had to go in beforehand to help the waiters set up a bar. It was always spirits; I never saw any of them drink beer. When we went into the apartments afterwards we would see a large space in the centre of the room where the furniture had been cleared, and there would be little tables with peanuts and crisps all around, just as if an ordinary social party had been held. There were never any drugs of any kind involved, and it appeared to be simply men in their sixties or seventies having a good time with their friends, enjoying a drink and a pretty girl. Often the men would have two girls in a bed at a time, or they would sit around and watch a couple of the girls making love. We received a large tip the next day so that we would keep our mouths shut. I liked having the money, but their lifestyle with the call girls made me sick.

I have seen some unbelievable sights during my time in the hotel business. A very rich Arab once had two very pretty girls living in his apartment. One evening I entered the room, only to find the girls chasing each other around the room, one with a dildo strapped around her waist. I am not sure who was the most embarrassed, them or me. Finding naked men and women running around became commonplace. Whenever I returned dry-cleaning to apartments, the procedure was to knock three times on the door with the master key, and enter if nobody answered. On many occasions I found couples making love. Sometimes I deposited the laundry and left without them even noticing.

Although I was based in the apartments, I occasionally assisted with hotel guests when needed. I was once called to a room to help the occupier with his packing, which usually involved folding clothes and wrapping everything in tissue paper to stop them creasing. Instead the man took off his artificial legs in front of me and asked me to pack them in his case. 'I'm not allowed through airport security wearing these,' he explained, 'so they have to be checked in with my luggage.' They were not the realistic flesh-coloured prosthetics of today, but were made of stainless steel. He asked me to undo the bolts and take them apart so that they would fit into the case, but he had bought so many new clothes during his stay that I found it difficult to get everything in and I ended up with a foot sticking out of the side of the case. It was a bit macabre, but even he had to laugh.

Despite the generous tips and large income that being a valet provided, after twelve years I wanted to move onwards. I saw some of my colleagues who had worked at Grosvenor House all their life in the same job, and I did not want to end up like them, still pressing suits and polishing shoes into my old age. Also I had tired of the corruption that was going on daily: the pressing of two suits and charging for four, just to make a few pounds; often we would wash and iron long Arab robes by hand ourselves but charge a higher price as if they had been sent out to a professional laundry. As we also received ten per cent commission on garments sent to the outside laundry, we made even more money. But now that I had a wife, children, and my first house, I knew that I did not want to continue with that lifestyle. I had a goal to be General Manager of the hotel, and I wanted to be an honest one.

In 1983 the General Manager of Grosvenor House was Matt Buccianti, with Tony Murkett as his Deputy and Linda Woodhouse, the Personnel Manager. They had originally been at the Cumberland, another Trusthouse Forte hotel, and were referred to as 'BMW' because of their initials. I got on really well with them, and Tony Murkett saw something in me that he thought was management potential. As well as valeting in the apartments, for twelve months I had also taken on the role of Head Valet on the hotel side. I was able to get the staff motivated and raised the company's profits by taking a little bit of the apartment style across to the hotel, which improved the quality of service there. Having proved my capabilities perhaps, Tony Murkett offered me promotion to Back of House Manager, which meant taking charge of the Maintenance Department, the cleaners, store-men, washers-up, goods-bay staff, and so on. I would have a team of some sixty people working directly under me to ensure the smooth running of the hotel behind the scenes.

It meant a reduction in salary, as there was no commission or tips in management, but money had ceased to be important. I discarded my 'bumblebee' valet uniform for ever and put on my first navy-blue suit. It was the springboard to my dream.

5

Beds for All Who Come

*Will there be beds for me
and all who seek?
Yes, beds for all who come.*
Christina Rosetti, 'Up-Hill'

'You'd soon notice if there was a twenty-pound note on the floor, Kirby, but you don't bloody well see if a light bulb needs changing!'

Tony Murkett's voice rang out across the Great Room as we set up for a function. With some 350 light bulbs needing to be replaced *every* single day, out of many thousands at Grosvenor House, I knew then that I had got to be on my toes if I was ever to be successful as a manager. For so long I had been told what to do by heads of department, but now it was up to me to decide what should be done. The boot was firmly on the other foot. Three men were employed simply to keep the lighting in full working order, and I was on to them straight away. Each chandelier in the Great Room had 150 light bulbs, and there were eight chandeliers.

As Back of House Manager I was really in charge of the engine that kept Grosvenor House running efficiently, and at the time that I was appointed there were a few spokes in the wheels and cogs that required oiling. Staff morale was low at this point and I felt that part of the reason was that the working conditions below stairs, which guests never saw, were below standard.

Downstairs obviously covered the same area as the hotel upstairs, but the contrast between the two could not have been greater. We used to call it the aircraft carrier of hotels, because of its gigantic size covering approximately three acres. There were two-and-half miles of staff corridors beneath the hotel and they had become dirty and dingy over the years. In fact, it reminded me of a prison, with unplastered walls, the lower half of the brick-work painted in cream and the top half dark brown. For the staff it was depressing and it lowered self-esteem just to walk along these corridors daily. Higher management seldom ventured into the bowels of the hotel and simply ignored what they did not want to see.

I set myself the task of brightening up this area and had it painted over a twelve-month period. Initially we received a quote from an outside firm for £50,000 to undertake the work of decorating the walls and renewing the lighting. In the end we did it all ourselves at a cost of around £10,000. The corridors looked fantastic when completed, with clear lighting and newly panelled walls to protect them from the wear and tear caused by the constant procession of trolleys.

As I had been on both sides of the fence, I tried wherever possible to upgrade conditions for the staff. The locker rooms were refurbished, as they were constantly being broken in to. We upgraded the showers; renewed the staff toilets, which had previously been disgusting, and retiled the walls so that they looked fresh and clean.

I made sure that staff had safety shoes wherever needed, particularly chefs and maintenance men. Until then the boys were just wearing their own trainers and many were getting injured unnecessarily. Health and safety was becoming a big issue in hotels and catering establishments at this time, rightly so, and Westminster health inspectors were very tough about clean-liness in all areas. They used to take swabs to check that surfaces were uncontaminated, and it was my job to make sure that the kitchens and still-rooms were kept spotless. When I took over, there were two-inch-long cockroaches running everywhere. I quickly had them eradicated by a pest control company. There were no rats, but the occasional mouse put in an appearance.

I was conscious that staff had not been particularly valued before, es-pecially the black guys, and so I did all I could to improve morale. Ninety per cent of the staff below stairs were people that I had worked with in earlier years – they had not progressed – so they all knew me and still accepted me as one of the boys. It helped avoid the 'us and them' situation that management can often encounter and I used to have my coffee with them, and tried to make it feel as if we were all one team. I asked staff for suggestions as to how their situation and the running of the hotel could be improved. That not only helped me, but it also improved their outlook and they took ownership of problems. Even today, in my own hotel, I ask staff to give me one suggestion a week for improving how we work.

I was also in charge of the staff canteen, with eight chefs just to cater for the employees. I closed the four separate canteens and opened up a single large one, with all new equipment, where every member of staff could eat together, regardless of rank or race. That proved to be very successful from a motivational point of view. Previously management, middle management, uniformed staff and non-uniformed staff all ate in different canteens; even male and female staff would sit in separate areas. Regularly diners from the uniformed canteen had stolen items from the non-uniformed canteen because it served better-quality food, but now everyone was together and all had the exactly the same choice of menu. Management at one table ate identical dishes to the washers-up at the next. The food was excellent too, so I was really proud of that small but highly significant change below stairs. It became known as the staff 'restaurant' rather than just the canteen.

I was given a couple of hundred thousand pound budget for the new staff restaurant, and it was a new experience for me having so much money to play around with, but it was also essential that I came within that budget too. The only time I ever received a bollocking from Rocco Forte was when I once went over budget. Fortunately he is a kind man, bore no grudges, and that very evening we went running together and my overspend was never mentioned again.

As Back of House Manager I was given a small office in the basement, off the Laundry Room. Its position was probably not a coincidence, as laundry became a major part of my daily work. Purchasing everything from tablecloths and napkins to towels and bedspreads, I soon became an expert on the thread-count of Egyptian cotton. Although there was a specific Purchasing Department, I had to oversee their work just to make sure that they did not buy 5,000 new pillowcases when only 1,000 were required.

I did, however, increase stocks initially because the hotel had been working on a three-par basis – which meant that each hotel room would have three complete sets of linen: one set in use, one being laundered, and one resting in stock. A single set consisted of 4 pillowcases, 2 sheets, 2 bath towels, 2 hand towels, and 2 face cloths. I enlarged this to five-par, which made five sets available for every room. This was for two reasons. Firstly efficiency, as it meant that there was always plenty in stock so that the girls did not have to wait for the clean laundry to return before they could make up a bed; or if a guest accidentally spilt a cup of coffee or glass of wine on the bed, it could be changed immediately. Secondly, wear and tear on the linen was far less. If you keep using the same stock over and over again, it is going to wear out quickly and will need replacing sooner. If you rotate five sets, they obviously have a much longer life. The preliminary cost was enormous, with an increase to maybe 25,000 sheets and 40,000 pillowcases, but it saved a lot of money in the long term. Even so, around £250,000 a year was still spent on replacing linen. When I started buying linen, I used to get three quotes. Previously the same company had supplied Grosvenor House for years, and the hotel just paid whatever they had charged. By shopping around, I was able to save money, which went down very well with Lord Forte!

Increasing stocks also improved the quality of service for the guests, which I felt was important. Sheets that had been ripped were continually being reused and so I made sure that they were taken out of circulation and used for rags. This meant that guests always had a high standard of linen in their rooms.

I used to arrive for work at 7 a.m. each day just to oversee the laundry, as thousands of sheets, pillowcases, towels, tablecloths and napkins would pass through the Laundry Room daily, either on its way to be cleaned or back to the cupboards on each floor so that staff could function in both the hotel and the apartments. Huge trolleys transported linen up and down in the staff lifts to various floors, with room service, the restaurants, the chambermaids, all needing linen of various kinds to be able to lay up trays, dining tables, or change beds. The chefs needed clean whites, washers-up wanted clean tea towels, and it was a massive operation from around 8.30 a.m. until 5 p.m., always fighting against the clock to get linen. As an apartment valet my working life had been dominated by cleaning and pressing clothes; now, although in management, laundry was still a predominant feature of my day. Even receiving a set of tablecloths from a function room was not a simple process, as any cloth might have a champagne cork in it, confetti, or maybe candle wax that had to be removed before it could be laundered. I was relieved when non-drip candles became available, as around two thousand a day were used at functions and invariably wax would end up on the tablecloths. Every single item of linen had to be counted and documented too, so that I could keep track of what was going in and out of the hotel.

I introduced a linen chute, which enabled dirty laundry to be sent down quickly from each of the eight floors above, but I was shocked by some of the things that came down with the soiled sheets: knickers, vibrators, pornography, sex toys . . . After a while I made up my mind that the whole laundry system needed to be revamped, as linen was not always arriving back on time, and some of it was going missing. The housekeepers were forever screaming at me for fresh linen, and as it was travelling back to us from out of town there always seemed to be delays. I also felt that the outside laundry was charging us far too much money for its services. I decided that it would be cheaper in the long run to bring in new equipment, washing machines and tumble dryers, for laundering towels ourselves. These had been costing the hotel 45p per towel and £1 for a bathrobe, which was all going into the pocket of an outside contractor. By doing everything in-house, we were able to save a lot of money and it actually cut our laundry costs by sixty per cent. Another reason for Lord Forte to smile.

I tried to improve efficiency and economy wherever I could. Some changes might sound silly, such as my introduction of rags. In the past, staff had just grabbed a linen napkin to mop up a spillage, which was all unnecessary wear and tear. And if a napkin had been used to mop up coffee, for example, the stain was almost impossible to remove and so it either needed several extra washes or wasted an expensive linen napkin altogether. I had old towels and worn linen cut up into squares and made available as rags or cleaning cloths. Items that would otherwise have been thrown away were therefore reused, and ultimately this saved costs too.

China, glassware and silver were another area that I looked into. Far too many plates, cups and glasses were being accidentally smashed on a daily basis. I put signs on walls, saying exactly how much each plate or cutlery item cost to replace, so staff realised that, if they broke a saucer or carelessly threw away a spoon, it was an additional unnecessary expense for the hotel. When you consider that there would be between 1,500 and 2,000 diners in the Great Room daily, another 500 in the ballroom, plus three restaurants, the lounge, the bars, and 24-hour room service, serving breakfasts, lunches, teas, dinners, and catering for cocktail parties and the like, a tremendous amount of crockery, cutlery and glassware was in use at any one time. In one evening twenty thousand plates could need washing. We had four silver polishers whose job was just to keep the teapots, cutlery and candelabras gleaming

I introduced trays so that crockery and glassware could be stacked safely during storage and throughout the dishwashing process. I had to make sure that the china, glassware and silver had been cleaned properly too, as it was all beginning to look rather jaded. A foreman was given a little wage increase to keep an eye on this situation, which improved matters enormously. Glasses and silver gleamed, breakages and damage were greatly reduced. I found the staff to be loyal and hard working, and a little financial incentive now and again worked wonders and made them feel valued. I introduced an Employee of the Month scheme, which gave a small bonus in someone's wages, all to encourage the people that really matter within a hotel and to say 'thank you' to them. There can be far too much snobbery in five-star hotels and I liked to reward the industrious staff, rather than see some of the dinosaurs in middle management get an undeserved pat on the back.

Because wages were not high, many members of staff joined the Transport and General Workers' Union (TGWU) as it made them feel safer. But when I got into management I tried to introduce the ethos that we were all working as a team and the hotel was there to help them. I made sure that they were treated like human beings and received recognition for their work, and many subsequently left the union. I had once been a lowly worker in the basement, so could put myself in their position.

Not all staff members were honest, unfortunately, and I had to stamp out theft. There was a lot of pilfering going on, particularly within the loading bay, which was just above my office. The sheer quantity and variety of goods coming in was astounding, with around two hundred lorries a day arriving with supplies. Alcohol, meat, fish, produce of all kinds would be delivered to the hotel by one of the five loading-bay staff on a special electric cart that could drive through the staff corridors, but the delivery notes would not always be signed. This meant that I could not tell what had actually been received, and items could be stolen without it showing up on any paperwork. This was a grey area that I had to sort out. I also discovered that one of the employees driving the cart was a heavy drinker and usually drunk on duty. He was regularly knocking back left-over wines and spirits from functions, drinking the dregs that remained in the bottom of bottles and glasses. He was an alcoholic and so I had to fire him. I couldn't have a drunk in charge of a vehicle in my newly decorated corridors!

Staff absences were a constant headache for me, as thirty to forty people a day would ring in saying that they were sick. It might be a cleaner, it could be a chef, but the gap had to be filled to ensure that the service to the customer carried on as normal. In a five-star hotel, we could not get away with saying, 'Sorry, your room can't be cleaned today as the chambermaid is ill.'

Heating, lighting, plumbing, and air-conditioning all came under my jurisdiction, with around forty-four maintenance men to keep everything in working order. There was always a report of a loose door handle or a failed heater, and probably around a hundred problems a day for the maintenance men to resolve. I had to have eyes like a hawk to ensure that nothing was missed. As a runner, I was able to walk the 2½ miles of corridor very quickly and regularly to ensure that all was as it should be. Whether the swimming pool had been cleaned, if there was enough food available in the staff restaurant, and that nobody was skiving in the toilets or locker room. Nothing could escape my eye. If there was a hair on the floor in the Health Club, I would get a complaint from a customer, so every detail had to be checked.

Cleaning and decoration was unremitting, almost worse than painting the Forth Bridge. There was always furniture to be repaired or reupholstered, and carpets needed constant attention through the thoughtlessness of guests. Timing was crucial because if we closed a whole floor for refurbishment it meant loss of income, so redecoration of rooms had to be done generally one at a time, and as quickly as possible to ensure that they were not out of commission for too long. While painters set to work on the walls and ceiling, french-polishers would be restoring the finish to the furniture in their workshop, upholsterers could recover a chair in around two days in fabric to match the room decor, and within a week the room would be back in use. During quiet periods, such as early January, then there was the potential to close an entire floor and redecorate each room in one go or give them a thorough spring-clean. But even then I had to make sure that everything was completed without delay. If I had taken a floor off for maintenance and then reception had to turn down a sudden booking for twenty rooms because of it, I would have been in trouble. Often painters worked through the night.

There were seventy-eight rooms per floor, and each floor had a standard design with the same curtain material, bedcover pattern, and carpet in each room. Suites would be slightly different, but nothing in the hotel had the individuality of the apartment block – because the rooms there were people's homes, whereas in the hotel guests were staying only for a few nights. In the apartments the customer had some input; in the hotel guests naturally had what they were given with regard to decor.

Carpets in hotels are a major problem because of the constant wear and tear. Cigarette burns in carpets were once the curse of any hotel. Until the change of law in 2007 banning the smoking of cigarettes in indoor public places, carpets frequently received cigarette burns. Nylon carpets or similar were out of the question, and we had to use good-quality Axminster carpets which allowed a small repair to be undertaken. The lush pile enabled a small section of carpet around the damaged area to be cut out and a new piece of carpet inserted into the hole without the repair being obvious. We had to keep a supply of the various carpets in store, just in case a patch was needed.

Once, when a party of rich Arabs came to the Grosvenor House, they cooked a whole lamb on a fire in the middle of their room and burned a huge hole in the carpet! In that instance the entire carpet had to be replaced, and we presented them with a bill for many thousands of pounds to restore the room to its original condition, as hot dishes had also been placed on french-polished tables destroying the surfaces. This type of behaviour was not uncommon and sometimes it cost around £20,000 to put right the damage, but they always paid up without question. No chairs appeared to be used, as they sat in a big circle on the floor around the food that was being prepared in the very centre of the carpet. If smoke from their meal set the fire alarms off, we would be told that it was the room of a Saudi Prince and we were not allowed in.

Entrance halls, receptions and staircases in particular receive the greatest amount of traffic and we had to change the carpets frequently in those areas. In later years marble and granite floors became popular in hotel lobbies and corridors, but then guests kept slipping over on the shiny surfaces. So an anti-slip surface had to be applied to prevent hotels being sued. With a hard surface, damage is caused by ladies' high-heel shoes and men's steel toe and heel caps, so wear and tear to hotel floors is an ongoing problem whether carpeted or not.

Cigarettes were the bane of the hotel industry before the smoking ban came into force. Guests smoked everywhere: in the public rooms, the lifts, the toilets, the restaurants and bars, the afternoon tea lounge, you name it. Probably seventy per cent of our guests smoked and the smell was horrendous. Chambermaids spent their lives trying to rid rooms of the odour, as smoke permeated into curtains, upholstery and carpets, and guests would complain if there was a lingering reek of tobacco. Windows could be left open to ventilate the room, but this meant that pigeons often ventured in, creating another problem. Dry-cleaning curtains and bedspreads cost the hotel a lot of money. Whoever invented sweet-scented air fresheners deserves a medal, as they were a godsend for combating cigarette smells and improving the atmosphere in a room.

At Grosvenor House there were buckets of sand available to throw on small fires in an emergency. The surface of the sand was kept smooth and was stamped with the hotel logo. Smokers used these fire buckets continually as if they were large ashtrays, and I regularly had to remove all the cigarette butts, re-smooth the sand and stamp it again with the logo. The next time I walked past, the bucket would be full of cigarette ends again.

Today most hotels are completely non-smoking zones, although the law does allow for some bedrooms to be set aside for smokers. Guests still try and get away with it in a non-smoking hotel, having a crafty cigarette in their en-suite bathroom, the hotel toilet, or by puffing smoke out of their bedroom window, but there is simply no getting away with it as cigarette smoke can *always* be detected. Housekeepers and chambermaids were thrilled to see the end of smoking, and it must save UK hotels millions of pounds a year with the subsequent reduction in cleaning and repairs. I have stayed in American hotels where guests are fined $200 if they light a cigarette, with charges for cleaning the curtains, carpet and bedspread.

Candles are still a major fire risk. Many a time men catch their ties alight in the restaurant, or menus fall against candles and go up in flames, and people burn themselves when napkins or tablecloths accidentally catch fire. On a table of ten in the Great Room people used to lean over to speak to someone across the table and either burned their hand on a candle or set light to their hair. We used to get a lot of complaints, and some unscrupulous guests would even try and claim the cost of a new suit or evening dress out of the hotel. Rarely did we pay up in those instances, as we had put candelabras on tables at the organiser's request and it was not our fault if a guest burned a hole in a sleeve through their own carelessness. As it was, we received an average of three claims a day from guests saying that food had been spilled on them by waiters. It was silver service in those days and inevitably someone did very occasionally get splashed with gravy or have a potato land in their lap, but definitely not as many times as the number of demands that landed on my desk to settle dry-cleaning bills or pay for a completely new outfit. Seven times out ten guests were simply trying to make themselves some money out of the hotel.

Fire drills also became my responsibility and they could be horrendous, as I had to evacuate all the staff from the building. Some took it all too lightly, so the Head of Security and the Chief Fire Officer came up with the idea of blocking off some of the exits as if they were the scene of a real fire. The staff thought that they could just casually stroll through an exit to the meeting point in Park Street, where they were supposed to line up with others from their own department, and had a shock when they couldn't get out of the building. We could not help smiling at the panic this induced, but it certainly made them think about what would happen in the event of a real fire.

Within a few months of becoming Back of House Manager, once I had settled into the job, I was also appointed Duty Executive Manager to take control of the whole hotel whenever the General Manager or his deputy were off duty. I had worked at Grosvenor House for many years by this time, knew the building inside out and so was considered to be an ideal candidate for the job. I also have a suspicion that nobody else wanted the responsibility.

On my very first shift as Duty Manager, I was standing in the lobby of Grosvenor House at 8.19 p.m. thinking that for the first time I was actually in charge of the whole hotel. How proud I was, so very proud. I looked around me and suddenly smoke started pouring out of the air-conditioning vents. The alarm sounded in the entire hotel and simultaneously my pager bleeped. I replied on my walkie-talkie to central base, which informed me that there was a fire on the top floor. At the time we had 1,600 guests in the Great Room, 500 in the ballroom; the apartments, bedrooms and restaurant were all full, and there were between 300 and 400 staff on duty. And I was now responsible for what happened to them all.

Fortunately there had been a recent fire drill and so I was au fait with the procedure, but now it had to be put into practice. I ran to the back-door security office and picked up a yellow tabard, loudhailer and checklist, and ran to the Reeves Mews entrance at the rear of the hotel where everyone was supposed to assemble in this kind of situation.

I managed to commandeer at least six heads of department, got them to put their tabards on and to calmly assemble staff and guests. Three members of staff went around the perimeters of the hotel in Park Lane, Upper Grosvenor Street, Mount Street and Park Street, gathering guests from the thirty fire exits and soon three thousand people were assembled in Reeves Mews. We tried to group the staff in departments and make sure that guests were safely on the pavements, but at times there was pandemonium. The road was coned off as we awaited the fire brigade, and I nervously took the megaphone to address this vast crowd.

'Ladies and gentleman, can I have your attention please!'

Nobody took any notice whatsoever. Three times I tried with the same result. One head of department tapped me on the shoulder.

'You want to switch it on, boss.'

When I shouted down it again, the crowd finally reacted. What a relief that was. The fire had first been seen coming from the roof and now I could see twenty-foot flames lighting up the sky on this cold winter's night. The fire brigade took just twelve minutes to arrive, but to me it felt like thirty; time just seemed to slow down. It took forty-five minutes to bring the fire under control and, with such a famous hotel, the incident made the national news. Some of the guests' relatives watched it on television and immediately tried to telephone the hotel. Getting no answer they naturally became very worried, but we were all outside. Today everyone would have a mobile phone.

As we stood and waited for the fire to be extinguished, there was suddenly a huge bang, followed by a sickening crunching noise. One fireman had accidentally dropped a fire extinguisher, which fell eight floors on to the forecourt below where all the guests' expensive cars were lined up. Did it land on the tarmac of the forecourt? No. Where else, but on the bonnet of what had a moment before been a beautiful Rolls-Royce.

The reason for the fire was that a few of the best rooms were being refurbished, and some asbestos had to be removed safely. A wooden shed had been built on the roof containing a shower, so that workmen could undress and wash off any particles of asbestos for health and safety reasons. They had left a heater on which had overheated and set light to the shed. Being positioned next to the air-conditioning units, smoke had been sucked into the vents and was pumped out throughout the hotel, giving the appearance that the whole of Grosvenor House was ablaze. I was relieved that the destruction was not as bad as it might have been, and some rooms on the top floor had only suffered water damage.

The all-clear was eventually given over the tannoy and everyone was asked to go back into the hotel calmly. Then came a further message: 'Chef will do his best.' The chefs ran back to their ovens, but the Italian banqueting chef began panicking. 'I dunno what da food is like. I left de ovens on with da food inside.' Needless to say, the meal was ruined, and I had to announce to the function rooms that drinks were on the house until more food could be prepared. I was unable to get home until I had finished filling out various forms and dealing with loss adjusters, insurance investigators, plus health and safety officers. It was a nightmare, and I shall never forget my first night as Duty Manager. Fortunately no one was hurt and the situation could have been a great deal worse.

Those dreaded fire alarms have haunted me all my life in hotel management. When they go off, you do not know what to expect or what panic they might cause.

Another time the alarm sounded, we rushed up to the roof of the top floor where contractors were working. One of them had set the alarm bells off when he hit a live cable. We discovered the young man's body, burnt black. It made me feel very ill, as it was a terrible tragedy. Unfortunately dealing with bad accidents is part of a Duty Manager's job. My pager went one day and I was called to the outside of the hotel in Upper Grosvenor Street. One of the window cleaners had not used a safety harness and had fallen out of a first-floor window on to railings below. Fortunately he had not pierced his body, just his legs, and was back at work six months later. He was extremely lucky.

The bleeper on my pager sounded another time, and there was a message for me to rush up to one of the apartments as a lady was screaming. I knocked on the door and a very beautiful woman, half-naked, opened it. An elderly gentleman was lying naked at the bottom of the bed and was quite clearly dead. A post- mortem later revealed that he had suffered a heart attack while making love to this beautiful lady. What a way to go.

'Are you his wife?' I asked the lady, as she covered herself up with a dressing gown.

'No. He hired me,' she replied. 'He died while I was on top of him.'

The police arrived and statements were completed one-and-a-half hours later, then the lady vanished into the night. The biggest concern was that the man was chairman of a very large South African company and they were keen to hide the manner of his death.

'Was anyone with him?' a member of his family later enquired.

'He was alone,' I said.

Bleep, bleep.

'Mr Kirby, can you please go to the Great Room. There is a bit of a disturbance.'

It was half-past midnight. I was tired after a long day and people were going home. At the Great Room I found a couple making love by the fire exit, underwear around their ankles. I stood and watched for at least thirty seconds, not knowing what to do. They were in a 'doggy' position and completely oblivious to me. I coughed extremely loudly, whereupon they both jumped up and quickly began pulling their clothes back on. In my sternest schoolmaster voice, I said, '*What* is going on here?'

At that moment, the man's wife walked round the corner, slapped the woman around the face, slapped her husband even harder, and stormed off in tears. I stood there with my mouth agape. They were not even staying at the hotel.

Bleep, bleep.

'Mr Kirby, I think we've seen two prostitutes roaming the corridors of the sixth floor. Could you please investigate?'

I made my way up to the floor and found two girls wearing cheap fur coats, with boots up to their thighs.

'Ladies, I am the Duty Manager. Are you residents?'

'No. A man invited us to room 643, but we can't find it.'

'Sorry, but as you aren't residents, you will have to go down in the lift and leave the building.'

'Please, Sir, please let us go. It's our livelihood. We need the money.'

They offered me a bribe. If I had still been a valet, I might have been tempted to take it, but I was now a manager and wanted to be General Manager one day. As we got closer to the lift, their language became worse and then they offered me oral sex. I declined and immediately called for back-up. With the help of another manager, we escorted them off the premises. Their language throughout was not pretty. As I left the hotel at 1.30 a.m. and was making my way home, thinking that I could do without this kind thing, I turned from Park Street into Mount Street and saw the same two prostitutes. They chased after me, wielding handbags, and I had to jump into a taxi to escape.

Prostitutes are rife in big hotels, and I soon discovered that there was a mass exodus of them between the hours of 3 and 5 a.m. In the end all one could do was turn a blind eye. I even came to recognise some of the girls, as they became regulars over the years. Their faces were haunting, as they were obviously selling their bodies because they needed the money, and yet there was a sense of revulsion in their eyes at what they were doing. Some prostitutes went on to 'greater' things, becoming part of Arab entourages, working for the same men for months at a time. The Arabs were very generous and a girl could make her fortune. One can only hope that they used the money wisely.

I quickly realised that being a Duty Manager was a tough job. You have to be very diplomatic with customers complaining about everything from the food and drink to the quality of service. It taught me to be quick thinking, to be able to deal with any situation, and that the customer is always right. However well you try to do something, there will always be one customer who will complain. As the old adage goes, 'You can please some of the people some of the time, but you can't please all of the people all of the time.' Some guests are simply beyond help. I was called to room 324 one day, but the lady was gone when I arrived. She had jumped from the window and lay dead on a ledge below.

Another day dawned and my pager sounded with the message: *Armed robbery. Wages office.*

I ran there as quickly as I could and discovered that men wearing balaclavas had broken into the wages office, threatened the staff with sawn-off shotguns and forced them to open the safe. The gang had taken £25,000 in cash and made their escape through the loading bay to a get-away car, never to be seen again. At that time all staff members were paid weekly in cash, so the hotel carried a lot of money. People in the wages office were unable to speak due to shock, but fortunately no one was hurt. We were all worried that we might not get paid that week!

The pager could send messages at any time and I had to respond immediately.

Bleep, bleep. Two staff are arguing over tips. I have to look into it.

'Who are they and where are they?' I ask switchboard.

'Luggage porters and they're in the Baggage Room, Mr Kirby.'

'OK. Tell security to meet me there.'

When I arrive they are nearly at fisticuffs. Both are shouting in Portuguese. I tell them to calm down and stop shouting. I get between them and when security arrives, we separate the two and take them to the Section Office to listen to their side of the story. Very simple really. One luggage porter took two suitcases to a room. The guest wasn't there at the time but came down later and gave the other luggage porter a £5 tip. The second guy sees it and says, 'That's my tip, you didn't take the cases up!' And the fight began.

While I'm trying to sort this out: *bleep, bleep.*

'Couple of drunks in the Red Bar refusing to pay their bill. Not happy with the service, Mr Kirby.'

'I'll be there in two minutes.'

The luggage porters are still hot under the collar.

'That's enough! You are both suspended on full pay until tomorrow. Come back and see me with the Personnel Manager at 10 a.m. Now go and cool down. Both your jobs are on the line. Fighting is gross misconduct, a dismissal offence. Good night.'

They both look contrite as I tell security to see them off the premises.

I am needed in the Red Bar.

'Yes, Sir, I'm the Duty Manager, what's the problem?'

'Your barman is trying to rip us off.'

These two have been to a function in the Great Room and I can see that they are both as pissed as farts.

'How do you mean?'

'There's no way a whisky costs £5 a single. Where's your price list?'

'We have one on the wall, Sir, and also one on every table.'

'Oh . . . yes, I see them now.'

'What whisky did you have, Sir?'

'Red Label.'

'And as the price list says, that's £5 per single measure.'

'Well, that's f***ing disgraceful!'

The pitch of his voice goes up two decibels.

'You are entitled to your own comments, Sir, but that is our price. You're both drunk and I'd like you to leave the bar now, please.'

That request does not go down well. I have to keep my cool as both become belligerent now.

'Are you residents?'

'Yes, we are, and we want another f***ing drink!'

'I tell you what, Sir, I'm just going to pop down to the Great Room to see your boss. I'm sure that the organiser of the function will have a word about your state of affairs. Abusive and drunk. It doesn't look too good, does it?'

I've never seen two people sober up so quickly.

'I'm really sorry, please don't do that. We're straight to bed.'

It always works, that one.

Sometimes natural elements rather than people could cause problems, too – notably the great hurricane of 1987. On the night of 15/16 October that year I was at my family home in Sanderstead in Surrey. I awoke to find devastation all around me, trees down everywhere, with roads and railway lines blocked. The only way I was going to be able to get to work was to run the fifteen miles to Central London. I put on my running shoes and ran all the way to Grosvenor House, which took me two hours. When I arrived, I found that many staff members were stranded at home, there were 800 guests staying at the hotel and very few people to attend to them. There was no laundry, food supplies could not get through, and that night there was to be a banquet for 1,200 guests. Fortunately there was great camaraderie amongst the staff, and with a fantastic team spirit we somehow managed to acquire food and kept as near normal service as we could manage. And, yes, the banquet went ahead as planned.

Even management had to help out with menial tasks that day and found themselves receiving tips from the guests, as they delivered room-service trays and helped out in the restaurants. They realised then just how much the staff were making on gratuities. Many of us worked for forty-eight hours at a stretch until the full complement of staff were gradually able to return to work.

If there were no specific problems to resolve, there was always something to be done and my mind was continually active.

Must put together a speech. Two members of staff are leaving after thirty-five years' service. One in the Linen Room, the other a waiter from floor room service. Can't let them go without some kind of recognition. Maybe we'll give them both a cheque from the hotel, plus a gift from the staff. I'd better organise some flowers for their wives too. A cocktail party with canapés has been arranged. Their families have also been invited, so there'll be over a hundred people to cater for . . .

I hate writing speeches. Personnel have given me the dates when they first came here and some information about them. Which departments have they worked in? Oh, they seem to have stayed in exactly the same departments that they started in. Obviously they felt comfortable, I suppose. Also they will have earned very good tips from the regular guests that keep coming back . . .

Oh no, that reminds me . . . the Inland Revenue has been in touch with us again over tips. They want to interview the doormen, as they're not declaring any tips at all. The Personnel Department has told them before – they must declare something . . .

The whole tipping business was becoming a bit of a nightmare. On his visits, the tax inspector always interviewed the Head Doorman first and went through all his bank accounts with him. And the questions! How much is your monthly mortgage repayment? Do you smoke? Do you drink? What holiday did you have this year? How much do you spend on food per week? On average how much petrol do you use? In the end they work out that these guys are spending well over their salary. 'So where is the money coming from, because you're not in debt, are you?' 'No.' It was really the third degree.

Eventually they would come to an agreement and the doormen would declare so much per month, just to keep the tax inspector happy.

This episode sent shivers throughout the rest of the hotel, including me. We had to start thinking differently where tips were concerned, so that all staff paid the tax inspector his dues. We introduced departmental till boxes for staff to put their tips in, with the idea that the money would be shared equally between them. All this did was make matters worse. In reality, if someone received a £5 tip, they put only £1 in the till and kept the other £4 for themselves. The scheme resulted in a lot more bad feeling around the hotel – there were many more arguments and departmental personnel frequently had to get involved when near fights broke out.

Working Back of House ultimately gave me much greater respect for employees in the basement and made me feel that staff below stairs had a harder life than some of their counterparts above ground. The concierges and doormen upstairs, for example, had a relatively easy time of it and were lining their own pockets with tips, whereas downstairs the staff received no gratuities whatsoever. The 'class divide' amongst staff always rankled with me, and the fact that even in those days the colour of your skin could prevent career progression really needled me. Even though I was in a smart suit like the other managers, I never forgot where I came from and preferred to eat my meals with the non-uniformed staff rather than with some of the toffee-nosed management who thought they were superior. I am delighted to say that the most snobbish amongst them never became hotel managers.

I like to think that I was very much a 'hands-on' manager and I was genuinely prepared to work hard. My immediate bosses, Matt Buccianti, Tony Murkett and Linda Woodhouse, were always very supportive and encouraged me to move forward. When the Trusthouse Forte board of directors moved out of the apartment block to new offices at High Holborn in 1986 and left the whole of the first floor empty, Matt Buccianti and Tony Murkett decided to convert the space into meeting rooms for conferences, seminars, business presentations or corporate entertaining.

In between each meeting room was a bedroom, but for some reason this layout did not attract business clients as they had hoped. I made the simple suggestion that they should forget about including bedrooms and concentrate on providing more meeting rooms instead. It seemed logical to me that if businessmen wanted a bedroom they would just take one in the hotel; they did not necessarily want to be staying right next to a meeting room. Designs were drawn up by architects and I was sent to see Dennis Hearn, Forte's Deputy Chief Executive, to present a feasibility study. He seemed enthusiastic about the project.

Before I knew it, I was sitting with Dennis Hearn in the boardroom at High Holborn facing Rocco Forte, his sister, the designer Olga Polizzi, and the Grosvenor House General Manager, Matt Buccianti, explaining the scheme to them in detail. They loved it. Rocco gave the go-ahead for it to proceed and I was given a £3.5 million budget to oversee the work. By a very lucky chance I now had another job and a new title: Projects Manager.

6

My Wife, My Mistress, My Mother . . .

Sleep, riches, and health, to be truly enjoyed, must be interrupted.
Jean Paul Richter, *Flower, Fruit, and Thorn Pieces*

My life had now become a mixed-up world of extraordinary contrasts. By day, I worked amongst the splendour of a five-star hotel with its trappings of glamour and untold riches. Royalty from around the globe, Hollywood film stars, heads of multi-national corporations, all provided my income. Yet at night I returned to a council house in South London, where the Kirby family were not exactly known for their wealth.

We were one of the first tenants to be given a new house on the Roundshaw council estate, Wallington, as soon as building work was completed in August 1967. The terraced house that I lived in with my family is still there today, although so much has changed around it. It was once an area to be proud of, surrounded by greenery and fields, and we were thrilled to live there. Today I would be frank and call it a dump. Some parts have been regenerated, but others are so run-down that it is frequently used as a location for the television police drama series *The Bill*, whenever they need a particularly grotty estate.

When I first started working at Grosvenor House, the whole family of eight was living at home in what was a four-bedroom house. There were six children: my two elder brothers, Philip and Michael, my sister, Sandra, and younger brothers, Andrew and Stephen, with whom I shared a bedroom. There was no space for a wardrobe in that room, so our clothes ended up in a heap on the floor. No valet service for us. I couldn't help wondering how Shirley Bassey would have coped.

Housework was not a great priority for my mother, Kathleen, who really only cared about bingo and cigarettes, and would rather gamble her money than buy a tin of furniture polish. My father, George, was working seven days a week to maintain a roof over our heads. He had a regular job at the Advance Laundry in Camberwell, plus two days a week at Hackney Youth Club, for which he also received a salary. The hours were long and he seldom got home until eleven o'clock at night. And was there a hot meal waiting for him? Not on your life! My mother just couldn't be bothered to cook. My father never complained and just made himself some toast. Their relationship had deteriorated and they now slept in separate rooms. No child likes to think about their parents' sex lives, but I was streetwise and well aware that if she wanted money for bingo, my father only gave it to her if she agreed to have sex with him first. Sad but true.

We always knew when she'd had a win, but my mother never let on how much money she lost. Eventually this led to divorce, because she spent all her money on cigarettes and going to the large bingo hall in nearby Croydon, and had no cash left to pay the household bills. My father would leave for work at 7 a.m. and so was unaware that people were knocking on the door requesting payment. Any final demands that came through the post, she simply tore up. After about a year of this, bailiffs arrived to take away our furniture. This was the final nail in the coffin and their marriage ended. My father left home and took a small flat, and gradually started to pay back the debts that my mother had accrued, which came to around £1,000 – a lot of money to us in those days. The older children that were working, like me, had to contribute towards paying off the debt too.

Just once during the marriage my father had an affair. He had been working nights at a petrol station and returned home from work one Sunday morning, wearing a blazer with a pink handkerchief in his top pocket. It was not something he usually had, so my mother pulled it out and it was not a handkerchief at all. It was pair of ladies' knickers! She immediately slapped him around the face. He must have got dressed quickly with his lady friend and hastily put her knickers in his pocket. He had really only played away to pay my mother back, because he had discovered that she had herself been having an affair with a bingo caller, just so that she could play for free. I always joke that my two younger brothers are really the bingo caller's. *Six and nine, sixty-nine!*

In spite of this, they were good parents. They were certainly not arguing all the time – it was just not their style – and they simply drifted apart because of financial problems. Despite her troubles, my mother was a natural comedian and frequently had us all in stitches as if we hadn't a care in the whole world. And she treated all six of us exactly the same – there were never any favourites amongst her children. 'Am I your favourite, Mum?' I would ask sometimes when I was feeling insecure. 'You're *all* my favourites.' Her response was always the same.

On my eighteenth birthday in 1970, I had a joint party with my sister. Sandra is one year older than me, with my birthday on the 15th November and hers on the 20th. My father came to the party, and was not in the best of moods as he had just had an operation on his foot. The subject of money came to the fore, and before I knew it he and my mother were having a major row in the middle of the party. I had never seen them going at it hammer and tongs like this before. Talk about embarrassing! I ended up having to get my mother out of the house and driving her through the night to Bournemouth to stay with my grandmother. I had only met my grandmother once. She and my mother had fallen out when I was still an infant and had scarcely spoken since, but my mother really had nowhere else to go. Suddenly we were turning up on the doorstep of a grandmother whom I did not know, with my two younger brothers in tow.

Leaving my mother and brothers in Bournemouth, I was desperate to get back to London where I was due to play in a football match. I had all my kit in the boot of the car and set off on the return journey. But I was so tired that I almost lost control of the car and could have killed myself as I fell asleep at the wheel. In the end I arrived late for the match and was suspended from yet another match as a punishment. Eighteenth birthdays are usually memorable occasions and mine was no exception, but for all the wrong reasons.

My father stayed on at the Roundshaw house to look after the four of us who were left, and we continued to help him pay off the debts, which we eventually did. After ten months my two younger brothers were home-sick, and my father agreed that my mother could return to London and he moved out once again. I think at the root of it there was friction with my grandmother, who was well into her eighties, and my mother was relieved to get away from Bournemouth.

There was tension at times between me and my father. I was not earning a great deal at Grosvenor House at that time, and yet I had to help bail out my mother, which was not my fault, and it rankled. I was young and foolish and did not spend my money wisely either. I paid my share of the housekeeping, but went out at the weekend with my mates and by Monday had no money left, and so I borrowed money back from my mother out of the housekeeping. There was no thought of saving for the future either. Early on I spent my money on a car, a blue Ford Cortina, even though I hadn't passed my driving test.

I had £300 in my Abbey National Building Society account and was just about to buy the car, when my mother said that she had an urgent electricity bill to pay and asked if she could borrow £100 from me. Of course I lent it to her, but a few weeks later when I asked for it back, she denied that she had ever had it. My father was there at the time, and he backed my mother. He said that I must have spent the money myself and forgotten about it. There was nothing I could say to convince them. So I lost £100 and had to save more money before I was able to buy that first car. I found it hard to forgive my mother for that.

I used to drive that Cortina everywhere, and inevitably crashed it one day through driving far too fast after a few drinks. Panicking, I abandoned the car in a ditch and ran away. But as I began to sober up, I gave myself in to the police and a blood test showed that I was over the limit. I was fined £30 and banned from driving for a year. I decided then that perhaps I ought to take a driving test, so I booked a few professional lessons. I used to drive up in my car, have a lesson with the instructor in his vehicle, and at the end of it get back into my own car and drive away. I had bought a second-hand V8 3.5-litre Rover by this time, which was actually a much better car than the driving instructor had. I finally passed my test on the third attempt.

One day things came to a head at home and I had an almighty row with my father and he threw me out of the house. I rented a room with my mate, Paul, who lived on the same estate, but he eventually threw me out as well. I was not taking life seriously, drank too much, was always messing around, and Paul also feared that he might get into trouble with the council for sub-letting a room. So I rented my first bachelor flat in Sutton at £14 a week, when my gross weekly wage was £20.

Instead of settling down sensibly, I bought myself a golden retriever puppy. I named him Waggy, because his tail was always wagging. Having a dog when I was working full-time was absolute madness. I had to set off early to get the train to Victoria station, and I would leave the poor dog in the garden. At least a dozen times he jumped over the fence and went in search of me. The dog would be found wandering the streets and each time I was called to the police station to collect him. After that, I left him in the flat all day where he chewed up the kitchen lino!

The tips that I was receiving as a valet helped pay for my rent and food, but I had to continually feed the electricity meter with half-crowns for heating and light. That wretched meter would only take half-crowns and was the bane of my life. I smartened the flat up before inviting anybody round. I was not going to live like my parents and wanted an impressive bachelor pad, whether I could afford it or not. I bought black sheets for the bed, a leopard-skin bedspread, a black-leather sofa and armchair, and filled a bookcase with leather-bound volumes of Dickens and Shakespeare which I ordered from a Littlewoods catalogue. I never read the books, but they looked good and that was all that mattered to me. As a final touch, I bought a cut-glass decanter with matching glasses. Something of Grosvenor House was rubbing off on me, and I felt that my flat looked like a palace, but I bought everything on the 'never-never'. Nothing was actually paid for. It is exactly what my mother would have done. I held many great parties there, and enjoyed it when my father came round and mixed with my younger friends. Deep down, I suppose I wanted him to see that I was making something of my life.

After my parents' divorce, my brother Stephen bought their house as an investment once he had started work. My father took a small flat in Croydon, found himself a much younger girlfriend, and decided to take life a little easier and became a gardener. He always had an eye for the ladies and even at the age of ninety-seven in 2009 he had a girlfriend twelve years his junior. He never let medical problems get him down either and sailed through four hip replacement operations, cataracts, bunions, prostate, appendix, and had a double-hernia repaired. He was as tough as a horse and I just hope that this has been passed down to me in the genes. Ultimately what I really learned from my parents is the importance of health, money and sex . . . in that order. You need money to be able to survive, but you cannot enjoy life without good health. Sex is the icing on the cake.

During one of my shifts in 1972, my eye was taken by the new secretary to Robert Wiles, the Apartments Manager. She had red hair, which I loved, was petite, slim, and wore the shortest of miniskirts, which showed off her legs to perfection. I was immediately attracted. I used to watch her whenever she was in the staff canteen, and started to say 'Hello' if we passed in the corridor. But I had to be careful because Mr Wiles was my immediate boss. I soon found that I could make her laugh. She giggled at my jokes when I spoke to her on the telephone at work and eventually I plucked up the courage to ask her out.

Her name was Wendy Golding. There was only seven months' difference in our ages, and like me she lived in a council house, came from a large family and had four brothers. I just knew from the outset that she was the one for me. At first we kept our relationship secret, as we did not want anyone at the hotel to know that we were going out. If ever we were working late together, we would sneak a quick kiss and a cuddle in one of the guest bedrooms. Once we became more serious, then I wanted the world to know about us.

Like many men when they fall in love, I showed off with cash. The repayments on my Rover car alone were costing me £44 a month. I began falling into debt with having to pay the rent, hire-purchase costs and other outgoings, and trying to impress Wendy. I spent a fortune buying her gin and tonics whenever we went on a date. It was lucky that I had no credit card in those days, as I would have gone even more into the red. Sometimes my landlord, Mr Ferminger, would come knocking on the door because I owed him several weeks' rent, and I had to hold the dog's nose to keep him quiet so that it would look as if I was out. I was becoming like my mother and squandered money away. After I crashed my car, the insurance company sent me a cheque for £2,000 to pay for the repairs, but I quickly spent it on new clothes and entertaining. When the time came to settle the garage bill, I had very little of the money left and Wendy had to lend me some of her savings.

After going out together for eight months, I popped the question and we became officially engaged in 1973. First I had to meet Wendy's parents. Her father, Donald Golding, was a former Royal Navy man and was working at Barclays Bank as a nightwatchman, and her mother worked in a plastics factory making ice buckets. Their house was filled with plastic ice buckets. There were potted plants everywhere and each plant pot was an ice bucket. Even the tea and coffee containers in the kitchen were red and green ice buckets. They were used for absolutely everything and we still have some in our attic even now.

Mr and Mrs Golding were very old-fashioned, so I had to sneak Wendy back home late at night as she was not allowed to stay over with me at my flat. After an evening together I always had to drive from Sutton to her home in Merstham, then all the way back again. Getting very little sleep, as I had such early starts at the hotel, I often nodded off at the wheel. This went on for months, but I lived to tell the tale.

Once we were engaged, I confessed to Wendy about my debts. She took control of the finances and, by the time we were married, all my debts had been cleared. Even to this day, she controls our finances. If only my mother had been like Wendy. We were married at St Katherine's Church, Merstham, on 14 September 1974, with a white wedding and over a hundred guests. Although it had rained all week, that day the skies cleared and it was perfect weather. It was a memorable occasion for me, not least because it brought my parents together again, though sadly for that one day only. It seemed like a large wedding to us, with a buffet reception at Reigate Manor, followed by a two-week honeymoon in the Cornish seaside town of Looe, but it was absolutely nothing when compared to the multi-million pound weddings that I was later to organise at Grosvenor House.

Wendy adored dogs and had been brought up with golden retrievers and spaniels, so Waggy was not a problem for her and he loved her to bits. She had a retriever called Jane, and the two dogs used to romp happily together. On the eve of the wedding, I took the dog and his basket round to my mother's in Wallington so that she could look after him while we were on honeymoon. My youngest brother, Stephen, was playing with Waggy on the floor, when the dog suddenly went for him and bit him on the head. Stephen had to be rushed to hospital where he had eight stitches. My father was also bitten as he tried to intervene and needed four stitches.

I had no opportunity to tell Wendy what had happened, as it is considered unlucky to see your bride before the wedding, so I waited for her to process down the aisle at the ceremony. She looked wonderful in a dress that her mother had made, but as we knelt side by side at the altar with the priest's hands on our heads, I said to her surreptitiously out of the corner of my mouth, 'We've got to take the dog on honeymoon with us.'

'Why's that then?' she whispered back from under her lace veil.

'He's bitten Stephen.'

'Oh no!'

I messed up my words by saying 'awful wedded wife', but we later set off for our honeymoon in Wendy's white Mini with Waggy in the back seat. As we were about to depart, Mr Golding slipped £200 in my hand towards our expenses. He was a very generous man.

Working at Grosvenor House had its benefits too, as the printers did our wedding invitations for free, and the chef made us a three-tier cake. We kept the top tier for when the first baby was born, which is traditional, but when the time came and we opened up the tin, the cake had gone mouldy. It could have killed us.

Although we were young when we married, it has been a wonderful partnership. We decided right from the start that we had to be friends as well as lovers. Wendy has been a great inspiration and has supported me in everything that I have done, and I have never regretted the day that I first fell in love with Miss Golding in her short skirt. We bought our first house in New Addington after Wendy's mother and father gave us the £700 deposit, and eventually had three children – Nicola, Neil junior, and David. Money was still tight and so we did all our own decorating and even built an extension ourselves. Later we purchased a family home at Sanderstead in Surrey, very posh and a world away from the Roundshaw council estate.

I have to confess that I also had a mistress. She was beautiful, elegant, and very demanding. And time-consuming too, as she kept me away from my family for long periods. Her name was the Grosvenor House Hotel. Once we were married and had the children, Wendy gave up working to become a full-time mother. She later took on a typing job that could be done at home and sometimes sat until the early hours of the morning to meet a deadline. I had to be up at 6 a.m. to catch the train for work and often did not return home until 10 p.m. or even later. The children would be in bed by this time, so I rarely saw them. I only had one day off a week too. I feel sad that I missed out on so much at home and did not really see my children growing up.

The hotel business takes over your life. Even if you are a receptionist on a shift that finishes at 3 p.m., you never get away on time. Something always happens that keeps you there for another half an hour or more. In a hotel you are part of a team and working hours have to be flexible. You might be about to leave the building when there is a telephone call to be answered or a guest requires attention and, particularly in five-star hospitality, the hotel has to come first. If staff charged for the extra time that they put in, most hotels would go bankrupt. This inevitably puts a strain on personal relationships.

Most of the general managers that I worked under at Grosvenor House had failed marriages, simply because of the pressure of work and the long hours. Heads of department, housekeepers, receptionists, doormen, so many people found it difficult to sustain personal relationships for the same reason. If they worked a fifteen-hour day, there was no extra wages; it was simply expected of them as part of the job. And if you did not like it, well there were plenty of people that would be only too happy to come to Park Lane and fill your shoes. Nobody is indispensible.

Inevitably a lot of staff members had relationships with each other too, as the opportunity was always there. Especially for any men in a managerial position, as women that were attracted to power just threw themselves at them and were there for the taking. Not just management either. Staff from all levels often had girlfriends or boyfriends, even if they had a partner at home. Who was shagging who became a constant source of gossip in the staff bar – it was like the pubs in *Coronation Street* or *EastEnders* at times. Some got caught in a compromising position and either resigned or were quietly moved to another job.

At the hotel a garage project became my next task. Grosvenor House owned the freehold of a garage in Park Street; above it was accommodation for some housekeepers and a few middle managers, with eighty-eight car parking spaces below. Twenty-five years earlier it had been leased out to another company, and this lease was now coming to an end. I did a feasibility study and felt that if we took control of the garage again, rather than renewing the lease at £25,000, there was £100,000 a year profit to be made.

So the garage reverted to Grosvenor House, which now charged guests to park their cars, as well as offering some corporate parking for company bosses. I was way out in my estimation, however, as in the first year we made £300,000 profit! It became an unexpected money-spinner. Trusthouse Forte were thrilled and considered me to be their blue-eyed boy with the Midas touch.

As a result, I was given the whole of the reception area to refurbish – which was a two-year project. Lord Forte's daughter Olga Polizzi was in charge of the design, and as Projects Manager I organised the work and saw that it was all finished correctly and on schedule. I particularly had to see that disruption to paying guests was kept to a minimum, although noise

89

and dust were unavoidable. A temporary reception desk was set up until the new one had been installed.

I learned a great deal about design from Olga Polizzi. The quality of materials that she chose was second to none, and she advised me, 'Always have the best that you can afford, Neil.' And it is a principle that I have tried to follow ever since, as high-quality craftsmanship is inevitably longer-lasting and better value overall. I was particularly impressed with Olga's attention to detail, and it was often just those little finishing touches to carpets, curtaining or lighting that made all the difference. Olga knew exactly what she wanted and would spend hours going through fabric samples. Occasionally she would have curtains made for a room, but once they were in place she would have them taken down again because they did not look exactly right. I get a slight thrill when people say to me in my own hotel today that I must have a marvellous designer, and I can reveal that I have designed it all myself. But really I have Olga Polizzi to thank, because she taught me so much.

The eldest of Lord Forte's five daughters, Olga Polizzi was a delightful person to work with – very honest, chatty and bubbly. She was slim, dark-haired, a very elegant lady too, and expensively dressed. When she walked into a room, you knew immediately that she exuded wealth and class, and could easily have been mistaken for one of the film stars that stayed in her father's hotels. If she came on-site to inspect building work there were no dirty old clothes, but a chic blanket-like shawl or serape to protect her. She was extremely loyal to her father and the company, and the staff loved her. I never heard a bad word said about Olga. Although she was the designer, she allowed me to have some input and asked my opinion.

An entourage of architects or designers always seemed to accompany Olga Polizzi, such as staff from the top firm of Richard Daniels Design of Wandsworth. She was a busy lady and not only undertook design work at Grosvenor House, but at many of the eight hundred Forte hotels. With many different hotel refurbishments on the go at the same time, she was constantly flying between Paris, New York and London. There could be family feuds, however, as Lord Forte's sister, Mrs Sanna, was also a designer and she and Olga had different ideas and methods of working. Mrs Sanna frequently overspent on projects, which could cause problems. It was not just the Kirby family that had upsets over finances!

Olga and I worked on the first floor of the Grosvenor House apartment block, once it had been vacated by the Forte board. It was renamed 86 Park Lane and became nineteen separate function rooms. She had many of the internal walls knocked down to create spacious, airy rooms, although she kept her father's old office suite as it had been. The new function rooms were intended to be multi-purpose with up-to-date equipment, so what appeared to be solid wood panelling could actually be raised at the touch of a button and there was a back-projection screen behind it. It was all very James Bond. I gave each room a suitable name, so we had, for example, the Waterloo Suite, named in honour of the Duke of Wellington who had lived at nearby Apsley House (also known as Number One, London). On this particular project I did not allow enough money in the feasibility study for the kitchen to be refurbished and so the overall budget was too low. I overspent by £50,000 to £60,000 and had to submit another capital expenditure form, which needed to be signed by the bosses. Rocco Forte was not pleased. 'I remember Kirby sitting here gloating that it would be done within the budget,' he said at a meeting grimly. I thought I was going to be in real trouble, but he signed it off without another word; otherwise the project would not have been completed.

'I only did it for you,' he said that night when we went running together in training for a marathon, 'but you deserve a good bollocking.'

'I'm sorry about that, Sir. I forgot to allow for the kitchen.'

'Well, don't let it happen again. That's your bollocking over. Now, let's go. How far are we running tonight?'

He never mentioned it again.

Many other schemes came my way, such as the total redevelopment of the hotel kitchens, which was a major project as so many of the tiles were broken and the equipment was outdated. I also refurbished the Health Club and Sir Jimmy Savile came to advise me. We first met while doing the London Marathon together one year and he came and had lunch at the hotel. Downstairs in the Health Club, he tried out some of the machines, still smoking one of his trademark cigars which were almost as large as Sir Lew Grade's, and helped me test out the equipment that had been brought in as samples for us to look at. I tried to get the guests involved too, to see what they actually wanted. Rather than having management saying what would be available, I thought it best to see what the guests would actually prefer. The customer must come first, after all.

I was still Duty Manager even while working as Projects Manager, as the mortgage had to be paid and I had a family to support. Even though I was in striped trousers now, I continued to work as private valet to Rocco and Lord Forte. I am really a workaholic. All my life in hotels I have averaged ninety to a hundred hours a week, certainly never less, which does nothing for family life.

My mother had mellowed over the years, and in 1992 we moved her into a flat to be near the family. My children loved to go and see their grandma. She was very generous with them, even though she still frittered her income away. If she gave them a gift, it was usually with *my* money! My sister and I supported her financially and I paid her utility bills, bought her new carpets, and arranged for redecoration to be done. My father refused to take a penny from me, and cut his own path, but my mother was happy to have a son with a bit of money.

She was her own worst enemy at times, particularly where her health was concerned. She ate all the wrong foods, was four stone overweight, and still smoked sixty cigarettes a day. It was always butter, never a low-fat spread. If we had pork, she would want the fat and the crackling. Eventually she became ill with gallstones and had an operation. I'll never forget those stones, which she kept in a jar. They were exactly like pebbles from a beach. Although she appeared to recover from this, she later developed kidney stones. The pain was so great that a catheter was inserted to relieve the pressure when urinating, but after a year these tubes irritated her and she felt uncomfortable.

One Sunday she came to our home at Sanderstead for a picnic in the garden. Our children were playing on the swings, we had friends round and it was a glorious afternoon, but my mother was clearly in pain. The next day she went into Sutton Hospital to have the catheter removed, at her own insistence, as the irritation had become unbearable. Wendy and I were due to take our children to Florida that Wednesday for our first trip to Disneyland, so I went into the hospital on Tuesday to see how she was recovering from the operation. Instead of the simple procedure to remove the catheter, I discovered that my mother had unexpectedly undergone a hysterectomy – far more serious surgery than I had anticipated.

She had a drip in her arm, but was in good spirits and her usual self.

'I hate that bloody ward sister,' she complained. 'She's a miserable old cow.'

We were laughing and joking, but as I sat on the end of her bed I suddenly felt a shiver come over me. My mother clearly noticed.

'Are you cold?' she asked. There was a small window behind me and she thought that I was in a draught.

'No, I'm fine, Mum,' I said.

'Oh, I'll be glad when I'm out of here so I can have a fag.'

We were told that the operation had been a complete success, and returned home to pack for our trip to Florida the next day. Later I received a telephone call to say that her lungs had collapsed. The years of cigarettes had finally caught up with her. She was in intensive care when I arrived at the hospital, but the nurses gave no cause for alarm. The lung collapse was not unexpected in a heavy smoker and they insisted that she would recover with medication. Very reluctantly, Wendy and I flew to Florida with the children, but I rang my sister Sandra daily to check the situation. Sandra was absolutely marvellous and has always been a great source of strength to me.

I returned to England after two weeks to find that my mother was in a coma. Arriving at the hospital, Sandra and I were taken to one side by the doctors to be told that the treatment had failed.

'Why did you operate in the first place?' I asked angrily. 'You knew what condition her lungs were in.'

'She insisted that we operate.'

'I'm not interested in what she insisted. You're the doctors, you should have done what was best for her.'

'We're sorry, Mr Kirby, but there's nothing that can be done for her now.'

I was completely shocked. Only a machine was now keeping my mother alive.

'We'll call you when it's time,' they said.

It was Wendy who received the call at home which we so dreaded and we rushed to the hospital as fast as we could. We went into a side room to find three of my brothers, with my sister and her husband, at the bedside. We watched the screen that showed my mother's heartbeat. Up and down. Up and down. Up and down. The rhythm was mesmerising. I sat on one side of the bed and took her hand. We told her how much we loved her. It all seemed so surreal, as if we were watching a movie and it wasn't really happening to us. And such a feeling of helplessness! There was absolutely nothing that we could do. After about an hour, a single tear rolled down my mother's cheek and the machine went flat. She was gone.

My father had not visited the hospital at all, even when he knew that my mother was dying. He just could not face it, but he joined us six children for the funeral. It was the very last time that we were all together as a family. Although my own children have flown the nest, we have remained a very close-knit unit as I have been so determined that history will not repeat itself. I have learned from my parents' mistakes.

Tearfully, I drove away from my mother's funeral and back to my other world at the hotel.

7

Who's in the Next Room?

Who's in the next room? – Who?
I seemed to see
Somebody in the dawning passing through,
Unknown to me.
Thomas Hardy. 'Who's in the Next Room?'

I now rubbed shoulders with celebrities on a daily basis, so thought nothing of it when film stars James Mason or Howard Keel came to stay in the apartments or I saw Michael Caine walk through the lobby on his way to the restaurant, smoking a large cigar. I was unfazed when I spotted Bette Midler with bright-red lipstick and a chest that reminded me of Dolly Parton's; if Telly Savalas asked for his short crocodile boots to be cleaned, or some giggling chambermaids revealed Barbara Windsor's bra size to me – it was all in a day's work.

The General Manager, Matt Buccianti, and his deputy, Tony Murkett, had decided that the Apartments Manager was not up to the job. His figures were down, there was not enough profit being made and they were under a lot of pressure from the boardroom to increase takings. Fortunately their faith in me as Back of House and Projects Manager had not been unfounded. They considered that the changes I had implemented were a success, and so they offered me the position of Apartments Executive Manager to see if I could turn that around too. I had gone from washing up in the hotel to valeting in the apartments, then back to the hotel in managerial positions, and now I returned once again to the apartment block with a brief to look after all 160 apartments. When I was last there I might be pressing a lady's dress as a valet; now I found myself negotiating the rent on her apartment.

Having gone up in the world, an apartment actually became my office;

I had a plush desk, a boardroom style table, and my own secretaries, Susan and Marianne. When my wife took a photograph of me sitting behind my desk, I was filled with a sense that I had really made it. I was soon to be brought back down to earth when Rocco Forte, congratulating me on the promotion, added knowingly, 'You've got a very tough job there!'

My job was really to rent out as many apartments as possible, because some had been lying empty for months, which meant a loss in revenue. Some people that rented apartments were only in them a couple of times a year, so there was very little income from servicing those particular apartments. My brief was to obtain a minimum of £50 per square foot for an apartment. They were all measured and the floor space of the smallest turned out to be 850 square feet, the largest was 3,200 square feet, so annual rents were going to range from at least £42,500 to £160,000. There was room for negotiation and I was often able to obtain a higher rent from a very wealthy client or company. The maximum lease was three years, which was then renegotiable, but it gave Trusthouse Forte the option of altering an apartment and giving it another use if they wanted, and they were never landed with a resident for years on end who could not be removed.

I also had to oversee all maintenance, redecoration, servicing and cleaning. There was hiring and firing of staff, with sometimes disciplinary action to be taken. Security was a major issue too, as there was such great wealth there. Diamonds were everywhere – if you happened to go into an apartment during the evening, it would look like a Bond Street jewellers – and I did not want anything stolen while I was in charge.

With VIPs arriving continually, I made sure that there were flowers and champagne in their rooms, together with their favourite magazines and newspapers – a hotel practice that I felt would add a welcoming touch to the apartment block. But the apartments had much higher standards overall: towels were a thicker weft of 750 grams, rather than the 450 grams at the hotel; sheets were linen with a greater thread-count; toiletries were more luxurious; everything we did was superior. I looked after the Health Club and facilities for the residents too, which was a constant headache. One day I came in to find that the Health Club ceiling had collapsed into the swimming pool. There were forever problems with contract cleaners, demanding guests, fire regulations, health and safety. I thought I knew it all from being Project Manager, but there was so much more to learn. I felt as if my brain was going to explode at times.

From an academic point of view, I was not good at reading or spelling due to dyslexia. It would often take me three times longer to do something on paper that the average person could do quite quickly. Once a month I had to present a report to the managers and heads of department with the latest figures, outlining profit and loss, budgets and cost control, and I found this very tough. So much preparation had to be put into giving presentations, and I used to wake up during the night in a hot sweat. At my first management meeting I could literally feel the sweat pouring down the back of my neck, I was so nervous. I apologised to the board. At least I felt that I was being honest with them. They were very understanding, but often they asked me questions that I simply did not know the answers to, which only made me feel worse. But I brought in new staff to work under me and we managed to make the apartments profitable again, with a turnover of around £5 million a year.

Although the hours were long and the work was demanding, managing the apartments brought me into contact with some of the most amazing people. Archbishop Makarios of Cyprus stayed with us, arriving in his chauffeur-driven black car complete with a flag on the front like royalty; Sidney Lipton and his band were still the regular orchestra at Grosvenor House, so it was a delight to be able to hear them with some of the top vocalists of the day; Hollywood stars that I had only ever seen on the silver screen were suddenly there in the flesh, such as Bette Davis. She came to England in the early 1970s with *Bette Davis in Person and on Film,* a stage presentation in which she spoke about her career and answered questions from the audience. She had a room in the hotel block and I was shocked at how tiny she was, although she was big in personality and didn't suffer fools gladly.

Her Highness Sultana Fawzia Binti Abdullah of Johore rented apartment 48 and had the most beautiful daughter, Princess Miriam, living with her. All the male members of staff fancied the Princess like mad, she was absolutely gorgeous. The Princess later married the British pop singer Barry Ryan. The Sultan of Johore was known as one of the richest men in the world during his reign.

Many members of the aristocracy rented apartments, such as Lord and Lady Astor in number 8, but it was the British socialite, Margaret, Duchess of Argyll, who really stood out. She is best remembered for her divorce case in 1963 which featured salacious stories of the Duchess and a notorious photograph of her having oral sex with an unknown man in her bathroom. This was shown as evidence of her adultery. She was wearing nothing except three-strands of pearls. A list of eighty-eight men was also produced in court, all said to have been her lovers, which included two government ministers and three members of the Royal Family. The magistrate stated that the Duchess had a voracious sexual appetite 'which could only be satisfied by a number of men'. Her extravagant lifestyle forced her to leave her home at 48 Upper Grosvenor Street in 1978, and move into the hotel suite with her maid. Famed for her elegantly coiffed hair, as I said earlier, she had a huge number of black wigs in her room, and clearly had a penchant for shoes.

The Duchess was never without a black poodle, once famously saying, 'Always a poodle, only a poodle. That and three-strands of pearls. Together they are the *only* essential things in life.'

Once I was called to the hotel's Italian restaurant where I found an extremely angry Restaurant Manager. He was completely white in the face. When I asked what the matter was, he simply said through gritted teeth, 'The Duchess of Argyll is here.' He pointed to a large puddle on the restaurant floor.

'Don't panic,' I told him, 'If anyone asks, just say it was the dog.'

By the time she became a resident at Grosvenor House, she had frittered away most of her money and there were always problems getting rent from the Duchess of Argyll. One day my bleeper went and I was summoned to the apartment of the General Manager, Mr Buccianti. He had just been to see her about the rent which was due. As he spoke to the Duchess in her sitting-room, her poodle suffered from an attack of diarrhoea and made a large mess on the carpet.

'I am *so* sorry,' said the Duchess, 'My doggie has a dodgy tummy. I'll get something to clear it up.'

As she left the room to find a cloth, the dog ran straight through the mess and jumped up all over the manager. The dog's dirty paws were everywhere. Over his suit, his shirt and tie, even his face. Mr Buccianti ran straight out of the flat and called me.

'What do you want me to do?' I asked.

'Get me a brandy!' came the reply.

The Duchess was eventually evicted from her apartment and left the hotel owing £27,000. She died in a nursing home in 1993, a sad ending for a once glamorous woman, who will always be remembered (from her first marriage to the American golfer Charles Sweeney) as the 'Mrs Sweeney' in Cole Porter's song *You're the Top*.

In 1990 former *James Bond* actor Roger Moore was staying at Grosvenor House. He was due to make his musical theatre debut, playing Uncle George in the Andrew Lloyd Webber show *Aspects of Love*. I had the dubious privilege of hearing him rehearse and I can only say that his singing was absolutely awful. Just one week later he withdrew from the show before his escape clause expired in the contract. From what I heard, I think it was the right decision. If Sean Connery happened to be staying with us at the same time as Roger Moore, we had to keep them apart. Having both played the coveted role of James Bond on screen, there was a certain amount of professional jealousy between them and they refused to speak to each other in private.

Roger Moore had stayed with us earlier, at the same time as Tony Curtis who was starring with him in the popular television series *The Persuaders*. They got on really well together and ate in the hotel restaurants. Many stars did not want to be seen in the public areas because there was too much pressure from press and fans, but Roger Moore and Tony Curtis did not seem to mind. Guests who stayed in the apartments were given a discount if they ate in the restaurants, just to encourage them to eat there.

Tony Curtis liked his privacy and, when I was still a valet, I frequently passed him running up and down the concrete staff staircase. He would never use the guests' lift.

'Morning, Neil!' he would shout as he flew by at speed.

'Morning, Sir. I've finished cleaning your shoes . . .'

'Thanks, just leave them in my apartment . . .' And he would be gone.

His wife, Leslie Allen, was a beautiful dark-haired model and pregnant when they were staying with us, but like so many of the star guests at Grosvenor House the relationship did not last and he married five times altogether. I found Tony Curtis to be a very kind and generous man, and I confess that I was so impressed by his sartorial *je ne sais quoi*, that I started to copy his style of dress.

American actor George Peppard, popular for his role in *The A-Team*, almost got me into serious trouble. He congratulated me one day on the girls working at the hotel reception, who were all very smart and attractive. He was appearing for seven weeks at the Wyndham's Theatre with Elaine Stritch in a play called *Love Letters*, and said that he had another show coming up and there might be an opportunity for one of our girls to be in it. He offered to audition them and requested that they wear bikinis. I agreed to this, as I did not want any of them to lose out on the chance of appearing in the West End. The girls duly went to room 145 and paraded in front of him in their swimwear. I later got my knuckles wrapped. There was no show at all . . . George Peppard turned out to be a dirty old man. I fell for it hook, line and sinker. He obviously had an eye for the ladies and was another star who married five times.

Sean Connery's wife was another guest who caused a problem for me. Micheline Roquebrune was a French painter and always very smartly dressed. One of her blazers was ruined by Watford Steam Laundry, which the hotel was using at the time. The colour of the garment faded during the dry-cleaning process, so I received an angry telephone call and was summoned to her room. 'This is *not* acceptable!' she shouted. 'This blazer cost me a lot of money.' The laundry had to pay her £300 for a new jacket, as they admitted that it was their fault, but I was the one that received the flak. Admittedly she had cause for complaint, but I was not happy with the way she went about it. It was as if I had ruined her blazer myself. Although most guests allowed us to launder clothes, many would not allow their expensive garments to be sent for dry-cleaning, just in case they came back damaged. After my experience with Mrs Connery, I was quite glad.

When Shirley Bassey stayed in one of the apartments we used to press her clothes too, but I drew the line one day when she gave me a heavily sequinned evening dress to be ironed. If we had ironed or even steamed it, the sequins could have been damaged and we were frightened as to what her reaction would be if we ruined one of her expensive stage costumes. I just sent it back to her room un-ironed and hoped that she wouldn't notice. She had a very powerful voice and you could almost see the chandeliers shake if she was rehearsing. She was a very demanding guest and liked being the star. I could not help noticing that, whenever she arrived or departed from the hotel, it was not discreet. She wanted to make an entrance or an exit and made certain that everybody saw. Some celebrities wanted to be inconspicuous, but not Shirley Bassey.

The flamboyant performer Liberace was actually a very unassuming guest and, apart from a regular supply of champagne, one of his few requests was to have a mini grand piano installed in his room – at his own expense – so that he could practise whenever he felt like it. I was amused to see that he brought his trademark candelabra with him to place on the lid, even though nobody would see it other than him. When he first came to stay in suite 657 he brought his own valet, but he took a liking to Tom Nutley, a Grosvenor House employee, who eventually became his butler. The personal valet was dispensed with.

Larger-than-life opera singer Luciano Pavarotti was a frequent guest at Grosvenor House whenever he was in London. His actual weight was a closely guarded secret, although was said to be in the region of 330 pounds. The bed had to be made bigger and stronger for him, and initially I thought this was because of his huge girth. Later I discovered that it was because he wanted it to be large enough to accommodate four people! He also had the most enormous appetite for food. While at Grosvenor House he was served six plates of chicken at a time. Despite his bulk, the ladies seemed to find him attractive and there were various scandals about his love life. At the age of sixty he divorced his wife, Adua, after thirty-five years of marriage when he became romantically involved with his personal assistant, Nicoletta Mantovani, who was twenty-six at the time. Italian newspapers featured the couple frolicking in the sea, and Pavarotti told *Chi* magazine that Nicoletta was 'the favourite of my harem'. The world-famous tenor also had a much-publicised fling with model Lucia Debrilli. To occupy his time at Grosvenor House, prostitutes used to be brought to his room, usually three at a time – hence the larger-than-average bed.

The first that we knew of his arrival would be a telephone call from Pavarotti's personal office, saying that he would like to stay in the apartments. We usually gave him number 85, which was a large apartment on the fourth floor with two double bedrooms and a single. It had recently been refurbished with a very large walk-in shower, which was one of his requirements. Another was the very large bed, which we had to have custom-made for him, and extra strong too, as he had broken a bed during an earlier stay. The other prerequisite was a huge fridge so that he could fill it with his own food, especially whole pre-cooked chickens. He booked on a room-only basis, paying extra for any food that he wanted, and the rate I gave him was £950 per night, including VAT, for his ten-day stay.

'He will be arriving on Saturday at around 3.30 p.m.,' his assistant would say. 'He will have a few friends staying over. I think you understand, Mr Kirby.' I understood perfectly. Just a few lady friends was what she really meant. We all knew what was to happen, but had to keep it quiet from the press and from our bosses. The Fortes being Italian would not have been amused by his actions at the hotel. Pavarotti's sexual appetite was clearly as large as his love of food, and the girls were all very beautiful. I just used to pray that he didn't die on the job. I would have had to call the fire brigade to lift him off. 'I can't imagine him in that position! It would kill all three of the girls at once!' We all used to joke about it over a cup of tea in the staff restaurant.

Most celebrities that stayed with us did not bring a lover with them, possibly for fear of a scandal. Footballer George Best, however, obviously didn't care what the newspapers wrote about him, as he had a fling at the hotel with Swedish beauty queen Mary Stavin, who was then Miss World. He stayed in apartment 8, which was rented by a rich South African, and is said to have thrown £15,000 up in the air and made love to her on the bed surrounded by notes. He then called room service for a bottle of champagne. When the waiter arrived and saw George Best with a naked Miss World on the bed, and money strewn around everywhere, he is reported to have grinned and said, 'Where did it all go wrong, George?' Known as 'the fifth Beatle', Best later said of those days, 'I used to go missing a lot: Miss Canada, Miss UK, Miss World . . .'

The Miss World Beauty Contest was organised in those days by Eric Morley and his wife, Julia, who also had an apartment. Boy, did they argue! Huge rows used to go on between them. One year we hosted the Miss United Kingdom contest in the Great Room at Grosvenor House, with a huge amount of staging, as the set was made to look like a railway station, and they fought like cat and dog. The show attracted 2.5 billion viewers across 155 countries, and Eric Morley afterwards acted as agent for the winning girls, so made himself a lot of money, yet he always wanted something for nothing. That really irritated me, and I used to dread it when he came to stay. He left £2.6 million when he died.

The film producer Sam Spiegel lived in apartment 108 on the sixth floor. He was responsible for many classic films, such as *Lawrence of Arabia* and *Bridge over the River Kwai*, and was extremely rich. The apartment at Grosvenor House was just one of his many homes and he had a chauffeured Rolls-Royce. Many of his film-star friends would come and stay in his apartment while he was away filming. Although I looked after the first four floors of South Block during my years as a valet, I would sometimes attend to apartments on other floors when the two valets, Charlie and

Norman, were on holiday. So I occasionally had to look after Sam Spiegel's guests.

One visitor was Yul Bryner, who starred in such great films as *The King and I* and *The Magnificent Seven*. I am a great movie fan, particularly westerns, and was thrilled one evening when Yul Bryner rang to have his shoes polished. I went up to the apartment and rang the bell, expecting to see a six-feet-plus man open the door. I am five-feet nine-inches, and I waited at the door looking slightly upwards. When it opened, I looked down and saw the top of a bald head! Even though he was not wearing any shoes, I was amazed to see that this great man on the cinema screen was so much shorter than me. He was a very gentle man with a kind face, and he gave me half-a-crown before I had even done anything for him. I took his boots down to valet service to clean them and saw that they had been specially made with built-up heels and a built-up lining to give him at least an extra three inches in height.

A great number of people stayed at Sam Spiegel's apartment over the years. One of the funniest and at the same time worst things I saw was when a very famous film producer had an actress in his room. He always had a succession of young actresses visiting him, but on one occasion I walked in to find him completely naked, with an actress in the bath and he was urinating over her. I am told that this is called a 'golden shower'.

Lord Grade often used to have guests staying in his ITV apartment if he was away, such as Julie Andrews and her husband, Blake Edwards, who produced such films as *The Pink Panther*. A fellow valet, Mike, and I once came out of the apartment and began larking about, dancing along the corridor singing 'A Spoonful of Sugar' from *Mary Poppins*, which Julie Andrews had made famous. Unbeknown to us, Julie Andrews came out of the apartment behind us and watched us dancing and singing her song. Suddenly her voice rang out down the corridor: 'Very good, boys, very good. You two can appear in one of my shows any time!' She took it in good part, but we were so embarrassed. She stayed with us for three weeks and gave me a ten-shilling tip. Many a time I would hear her singing in the apartment, soaring up to the high notes, but I never attempted to sing in front of Julie Andrews again. We enjoyed dealing with Lord Grade's apartment, because we never knew which celebrity we would find staying there next.

Entertainer Sammy Davis, Jr stayed on the Crown Club Floor. His wife and three children came and stayed in the George V Suite with him. He had a circular bed brought in to his bedroom for himself and his girl-friend, while his wife and children were in the next room. She obviously knew what was going on. He always used to have a little walking cane with him, maybe because he was a song-and-dance man. Drugs were part of his life, too, and he regularly used cocaine. So it was a cane *and* cocaine with him.

Some occasions were tinged with sadness. A lesser-known producer of West End shows and lessee of the Haymarket Theatre, Louis Michaels, used to have an apartment where he entertained some of the top actors of the day, and Richard Todd was a regular visitor. Louis Michaels was a very well-dressed man, in his early sixties, and very generously gave me free theatre tickets to his shows. He was a very heavy smoker and succumbed to lung cancer as a result. I used to go to the apartment daily to collect his suit and shoes for cleaning and will never forget the day in 1981 when he said to me, 'I won't be needing my suits any more.' He had lost so much weight through this terrible disease and died in the apartment.

In 1972 the film star Gregory Peck contemplated staying at Grosvenor House and arrived at the hotel with his second wife, Veronique Passani. My wife, Wendy, showed them around and happened to be wearing a very short skirt that day, which was fashionable at the time. Mrs Peck eyed Wendy up and down, looked at her husband and said, 'I don't think we'll take this apartment.' And the couple swept out. We did later get one of Gregory Peck's sons staying with us, however, who certainly had his father's charm.

Having so many famous guests at Grosvenor House meant that we were plagued by paparazzi trying to get photographs. They tried every ploy to get into the hotel and we would often find them floating around the corridors. You could not miss them, as they always had a huge camera around their necks. We'd ask them who they were looking for, and they would say Shirley Maclaine, Liza Minnelli, Rita Hayworth or whoever they knew was staying with us at the time. We would then give them detailed directions, which took them as far away from their intended target as possible. The route we had given them always took them to a fire exit, as we did not like them hounding the stars. Although security was tight, photographers had the audacity to worm their way in and would blatantly make their way to the corridors whatever we did. Sometimes they would be well dressed, looking like a guest or one of the many non-residents attending a function, and would sneak in through the Health Club that was between the hotel block and the apartment block.

Grosvenor House had an almost permanent press contingency outside, always on the lookout for who was arriving or departing, and it could reach ridiculous proportions if a major celebrity was staying with us. I remember that, when David Cassidy was at his peak and stayed in the Columbia Pictures apartment, the press went absolutely mad every time he appeared. He was a charming, unassuming young man and stayed in the apartment alone. The hotel kitchen had to make hamburgers for him in the American style, which was something new for them in those days. David Cassidy gave me his guitar plectrum as a souvenir of his visit.

Autograph hunters were another problem, especially if we had a pop star or Hollywood actor staying. Unlike many London hotels, such as the Dorchester or the Savoy, which have one main entrance, Grosvenor House had entrances at the front, the back, at the ballroom, at the apartment block, and so it was a difficult building to try and field off fans. If a major celebrity was staying, fans would stand shouting up at windows sometimes, even if they didn't know which room the star was staying in.

The Monkees – Davy Jones, Micky Dolenz, Peter Tork and Michael Nesmith – came when they were at the peak of their pop career and also had a hugely successful television series. Although they initially stayed in the hotel, we had to move two of them over to the apartment block as they became tired of the girl fans screaming outside and trying to climb up the fire exits to get to their rooms. The Monkees used to travel together in a big black Princess car, which could seat six people, so everyone knew when they were leaving the building.

Sean Connery was always being hassled by the switchboard, receiving a lot of telephone calls from fans purporting to be friends. The calls had to be vetted, and in the end we had a blackboard put up in the switchboard room saying: *Mr Connery is not accepting ANY telephone calls*. This happened to many big stars, and messages were taken by the telephone operators, but absolutely nobody was put through. We could never put his name on the laundry dockets, only the room number, otherwise his underpants would have been kept by souvenir hunters. It was the same with all the major stars.

* * *

Not all of our patrons had celebrity status as such, but most made up for it in wealth. A Mr and Mrs Laurence Graff asked to see me one day in 1973. They wanted to take an apartment, so I showed them three possible choices. They particularly liked apartment number 42, which had a double and a single bedroom (which we referred to as a 1½ apartment). They took it and agreed on a rent of £30,000 per annum, but said that they would bring their own housekeeper with them. We had a few clients who had their own housekeeper and butler, even though these services were provided by the hotel and included in the price that they were paying. I discovered later that his firm was Graff Diamonds of Bond Street, so money was no object to them. In 2008 Laurence Graff ranked thirty-first in the *Sunday Times* Rich List. Mrs and Mrs Graff hit the headlines in March 2009 with reports that their 47-year marriage had ended and there would be a possible £1-billion divorce settlement. But in an official statement the couple later insisted that they had no intention of splitting up. I think it would have been one of the biggest divorce settlements in history if the couple had legally separated.

Dr Rupert, the South African chairman of Rothmans Cigarettes rented apartment 122. He was extremely rich, and when his apartment was refurbished I had to liaise with him continually through telephone calls to South Africa. He shipped many valuable paintings over to the UK; however, whilst they waited in a warehouse at Heathrow to be transported to London, the entire collection was destroyed by fire.

Many other wealthy people had apartments, such as the Barlow family from South Africa, the famous Oppenheimers, Colletts the milliners, and a Mrs Chivers of the well-known jam-producing family. Every Christmas Mrs Chivers used to give all the staff a pot of jam; we were not impressed and would have preferred cash. Ghanshyam Das Birla was another. Known as 'G.D.', he was a very influential Indian entrepreneur and a close associate of Mahatma Gandhi. He always stayed in the George V Suite and used to give us boxes of tea instead of tips. What were we supposed to do with loose tea? He left instructions that wherever he died, that is where he wanted to be buried. He died in Catford, a somewhat monotonous and down-at-hill suburb of South London.

The controversial Labour MP for Coventry Geoffrey Robinson was another who lived at Grosvenor House and was mocked for being a 'champagne socialist' as a result. He was in apartment 34 and our valet service apartment was number 23, just along the corridor, only about ten yards away. I thought he was a super guy, great fun, and I always had a laugh and a joke with him, but he could be a dirty old bugger. He was chairman of Jaguar cars at the time and used to stay at Grosvenor House two or three nights a week. The press were always hounding him over his wealth, but when he became involved with a Belgian multi-millionairess, Joska Bourgeois, who had apartment 70 above him on the fourth floor, they had a field day. When I was Apartments Manager and negotiating leases, he specifically asked me if I would give her a special rate, which I did.

Much older than him, Joska Bourgeois became a close friend until her death at the age of eighty in 1994. There was a public scandal when it became common knowledge that Madame Bourgeois had set up a £12 million trust fund for him, called Orion (and I had been letting her have an apartment at a reduced rate!). And a further scandal erupted when it was later revealed that Geoffrey Robinson, by then Paymaster-General, was at the centre of one of Peter Mandelson's political downfalls. Robinson had lent him £373,000 to purchase a house but Mandelson, as a Member of Parliament, had not declared it. So Geoffrey Robinson was clearly not short of a bob or two either.

Politicians staying at Grosvenor House were often colourful characters. The Conservative MP Sir Gerald Nabarro, famed for his much-lampooned handlebar moustache, was definitely larger than life with his booming baritone voice and plummy accent. He certainly liked his drink and almost drank us dry during his stay. His motto was *Audax et fidelis*, ('Spirited and faithful'), and the former was certainly appropriate. Other well-known politicians, who are still alive and cannot be mentioned by name, brought their lovers rather than their wives to the hotel.

To my surprise, some of the high-profile guests who stayed frequently became personal friends. Formula One World Champion Sir Jackie Stewart was a regular guest and a great help to me when I became Apartments Manager. He pointed out where improvements could be made with regard to the decor and, like Olga Polizzi, he had a good eye for detail. Service was another area where he pointed out any failings. 'I arrived today and did not receive a welcome,' he might say. 'Just thought you ought to know.' He did it in a very gentle way, not complaining as some guests would have done, but I made sure that there was always someone to greet him whenever he arrived in future.

Like Sean Connery, Sir Jackie Stewart always left his clothes in store at Grosvenor House while he was away in some other part of the world. His main home was in Geneva and he could be resident in the UK only for ninety days a year for tax reasons. He was very fussy about his clothes and shoes, and had a special wooden box made for storing them. You lifted the lid and there were all his shirts, tidily arranged; if you pulled out a drawer, his handmade shoes were laid out neatly in a row. It was another instance of his love for detail and precision. I first met him while I was still a valet and he sometimes used to visit the service apartment personally, rather than wait for us to collect his clothes. Maybe he was checking up that we were pressing his tartan trousers correctly! He was very tight with his money where tips were concerned, but the staff were all very fond of him.

I really got to know Sir Jackie Stewart when he learned that I worked privately for Rocco Forte. He invited me to his apartment and asked if I could persuade Rocco to sponsor him. I was able to get Rocco to agree to this and he eventually sponsored Sir Jackie's son, Paul Stewart, for his British Formula Three Championship to the tune of £50,000. The Forte Gold Cards that guests and staff had were also printed with an advert for Paul Stewart Racing on the back. Sir Jackie frequently went shooting with Rocco and brought many celebrities to the hotel, so it was a mutually beneficial relationship in the end.

Sir Jackie invited Wendy and me to a couple of races, where we once found ourselves chatting with George Harrison of The Beatles – who had just arrived with his wife and son in a private helicopter. We were in Sir Jackie Stewart's private box at Silverstone and beside me were the King and Queen of Jordan; nearby were Princess Anne and her then husband, Captain Mark Phillips, and there was me from a council estate in South London. It was unbelievable really. About eighty of us then had lunch in Sir Jackie Stewart's VIP tent.

On another occasion I was flown up to the Gleneagles Hotel in Scotland for dinner. Sir Jackie's chauffeur picked me up from the airport in his private car with the number plate 1JYS (the initials of Jackie Young Stewart). At the hotel Sir Jackie had established a very successful clay pigeon shooting school; before he became a racing driver he was considered to be one of the finest shots in the country and could have been part of the skeet shooting team at the 1960 Olympic Games, but decided to go into motor racing instead. The next day I was given an opportunity to try my hand at clay pigeon shooting. I was terrible and could not get to grips with it at all.

'Neil, you're leaning all wrong, you need to do it like this,' Sir Jackie said. He shot successfully at the clay pigeon, and then in a split second shot the same clay pigeon again. 'You stick to running hotels,' he added with a grin.

After breakfast next day, where I was seated next to Gordon and Ena Baxter of the Baxter Food Group, famed throughout the world for their soups and preserves, Sir Jackie asked me which flight I was on back to London. He was booked on the same flight and so offered to take me to the airport. I had my bags packed and stood waiting for him, but he seemed to be taking a long time to get ready and I was certain that we would miss the plane. When we finally got outside and approached his car, he suddenly told the chauffeur that he would drive the car himself. I got into the back seat, with the chauffeur in the front passenger seat, and Sir Jackie then drove us at 120 miles per hour to the airport. My knuckles were white as I clung on for dear life. The car lights were all flashing, the Ford Cosworth engine roared, and yet Sir Jackie chatted away as if it was nothing and we caught the plane on time. It was a journey that I will never forget. I knew then that I was not cut out to be a Formula One racer.

I once went with Sir Jackie to the factory where his racing cars were actually made, and saw the huge lorries that transported the vehicles to the Grand Prix races around the world. The interiors of the lorries were absolutely immaculate, with everything neatly arranged. There were drawers for all the spare parts needed, and it was reminiscent of his clothing box back at the hotel. Even the floor of the factory was spotless, and he prided himself in the fact that you could eat your food off it. That was Sir Jackie Stewart – everything had to be perfect. He taught me a lot about high standards and I learned a great deal from him.

Some celebrities that stayed at Grosvenor House shocked me by their behaviour. Not because they were outrageous, but because they were so different from the personae I had seen on the cinema or television screen. I expected Groucho Marx to have his trademark moustache, eyebrows, glasses and cigar that I had seen so often in films, and yet he was almost unrecognisable. Where was that famous walk? And the familiar voice? I only caught a glimpse of them once at Grosvenor House. He had been staying at the hotel and was queuing to check out one morning. Normally bills were sent up to a celebrity's room so that they could settle up in private without being hassled by other guests, but Groucho Marx came down to reception himself and was in the queue with everyone else. Suddenly he did *that* walk, and I heard *that* voice. 'Excuse me, honey, do you mind if I push in front of you?' he said to a female guest, 'I've gotta plane to catch.' He cracked a joke, did the walk, pretended he had a cigar, and everyone in reception laughed. They let him go right to the front of the queue.

'Thanks very much, Dr Hackenabush!'

Many stars, like Groucho, were the exact opposite to their public image. I had only seen actor David Jason as the cockney wheeler-and-dealer 'Del Boy' in the television sit-com *Only Fools and Horses*, so was amazed at how well spoken he was in real life. No wonder he is now Sir David Jason. Yul Bryner did not have his *King and I* accent either. The American slapstick comedian Jerry Lewis, however, was an entertainer both on and off stage, and he did go into a few routines for guests and had the crazy voice that we all expected. Everybody loved him, especially the staff, as he was a very good tipper.

That great actor, Sir John Mills, used to come and visit Louis Michaels and Lord Grade, and was a real gentleman, always immaculately dressed, but I was shocked by his height. He was so small and reminded me of Arthur Askey, especially when he wore a striped suit. He occasionally stayed in the apartments too, and was visited by his daughter Hayley Mills and her sister, Juliet. The Mills were a great theatrical dynasty, as Sir John's wife, Mary Hayley Bell, was a dramatist, and his sister Annette Mills found fame with *Muffin the Mule*.

Members of other theatrical families stayed with us too, such as Jane Fonda. She was at the hotel while making an appearance on the popular chat show *Parkinson*. In preparation for the show, she put some curlers in her hair and the style went wrong. It was only hours before the programme was due to be recorded and I found her in a huge panic, wearing dark glasses and her hair a mass of curls. I suggested that she visit the hairdressers at Grosvenor House, which was then called Edward's Salon, where they would be able to put it right. But she refused to go down as she did not want to be seen in public and I had to fetch Mrs Edwards, who came up to the apartment and restyled her hair in time for the recording. I never once saw Jane Fonda smile, but maybe she had worries, and she did not come out of her room unless she had to. She had an aide, like a member of the Royal Family, who arranged everything for her.

One of the saddest sights was when the legendary Marlene Dietrich came to Grosvenor House to perform in the Great Room in September 1974. It was her first cabaret appearance in the West End for two decades, so there was a great deal of interest. She was over seventy and had broken a leg in her Paris apartment just a month earlier, so had to be pushed in a wheelchair in private. So that no guest would see her, we took her down to the basement in the staff lift, through the kitchens, and on to the lower floor of the Great Room behind the curtains. She got out of the chair and made her entrance on to the stage, and none of the audience knew that she had a problem. At the end, with the applause still ringing out, she got into the wheelchair for the journey back through the kitchen and into the staff lift. Then it was into a luggage lift to get her to the guest floor where she was staying. Because of her poor health, she rarely went out and had room service most of the time. If she had to leave the hotel for any reason and go out in public, the wheelchair was dispensed with and I just held her arm to help her along the corridor and into the guest lift, then down to her waiting car. Appearance was everything to her, and she used to wear the most amazing gowns on stage, which, she said, distracted people away from her awful singing voice.

Although the show went on, Marlene Dietrich cancelled a star-studded party in her honour. Princess Margaret had organised a pre-show reception, with a guest list that included actor Christopher Lee and director Franco Zeffirelli, but Dietrich rang down beforehand to say that she would not be attending. Not because of her injured leg, but because she had nothing suitable to wear to compete with Princess Margaret. The party was abandoned, but the Princess joined the audience in the Great Room to watch a memorable performance.

Working in the apartments, as both a valet and a manager, brought me into contact with some amazing characters and I never knew who or what each day would bring. Although I enjoyed the challenges, I seemed destined never to remain in the same position for long and I was keen to progress. Recently an employee at Grosvenor House received a long-service award, having worked in the same department for forty-five years, but that is very unusual these days and it is not a distinction that was ever going to be bestowed on me. My tenure as Apartments Manager came to an end in 1990, when the General Manager, Matt Buccianti, moved on to a hotel in

Dubai and Tony Murkett took his place at the helm. I returned from a holiday to discover that in my absence I had been promoted to Deputy General Manager.

Rocco Forte immediately rang me and offered his congratulations. Yet I was now placed in a very difficult position with him: he was my boss, we had a friendly relationship as running partners, and I was also his private valet. But with the huge responsibility that this promotion placed on my shoulders, my time became much more limited. It seemed ridiculous that I sometimes had to break off from a task that I was doing as Deputy Manager to go off and press Rocco's suits. In the end I paid another valet, Johnny Salmon, to undertake these private valeting duties for me. Actually I subcontracted the job, as Rocco still paid me, then I paid Johnny and kept a percentage for myself. I had spent far too many years receiving tips and making an extra pound or two where I could, that it was difficult to give up the habit.

I packed up my plush office in the apartment block and moved across to a new one at the hotel. It was only a short walk from one block to another, but the journey I had taken from washing up in the basement of Grosvenor House to becoming Deputy General Manager of the entire building seemed like a million miles.

8

The Guests Are Met

The guests are met,
The feast is set.
May'st hear the merry din.
    Samuel Taylor Coleridge, *The Rime of the Ancient Mariner*

Even though I was now Deputy General Manager, I was actually given the former General Manager's office on the first floor of the hotel block, which was huge. The new General Manager, Tony Murkett, decided that he did not want the upheaval of transferring and so he remained in the Deputy's office, which was opposite mine and much smaller. There were some significant differences, however, between the General Manager and his deputy. I used to arrive at 7 a.m. each day; Tony would arrive at 7.45 a.m. He travelled in his BMW; I travelled by train. But I was at least permitted to get taxis to and from the station, which the hotel reimbursed.

Tony and I had many similarities. We were both born on council estates and were also almost identical in age, with just a month or so between us; he started in the business as a waiter, I began by doing the washing up. As managers we both used to have our double-breasted suits made by Boehler in Germany and I had over thirty, each of them numbered so that I could wear them in rotation. The number was on a small white label inside and it became a talking point with some of the regular customers.

'Which suit are you wearing today, Mr Kirby?'

'Hang on a second . . .' I would flip open my jacket to look at the label. 'It's number 16.'

'He's got thirty-eight suits, you know.' The Americans loved it. 'There's the label – look, number 16!'

The navy-blue suits would be pressed for me each day by a valet. In a strange turnaround, whereas once I was pressing suits, now a valet was pressing mine. And I gave him a tip too! Tony and I used to buy our shirts and ties from Thomas Pink in Jermyn Street, although occasionally Hermès ties came as gifts from guests. I would have preferred the cash instead, as they cost around £70 and the choice of design was not always to my taste. As I looked in the mirror each morning, my mind often went back to the clothes my mother used to buy for us children from a jumble sale. For years I wore second-hand clothes that had cost her sixpence in pre-decimal currency, or hand-me-downs from my brothers. Sometimes I went to school with holes in my shoes, patched from the inside with a piece of cornflake packet. Now I was putting on shoes that were £350 a pair, and buying clothes from the Royal Family's tailors. It used to be bread and dripping when money was tight, now I was regularly lunching at Michelin three-star restaurants with exotic food. Whatever happened to me, I could never forget my roots.

The first thing I would do on arrival was walk the floors, and speak to reception and the night manager just so that I was kept abreast of anything that had happened since the previous evening. I kept my two secretaries, Susan and Marianne, which was a great advantage to me. Being dyslexic, I could dictate everything to them rather than having to write it down. Despite my promotion, I still continued to manage the apartments and negotiate the leases. I knew the job inside out and it saved Trusthouse Forte money by not employing a replacement Apartments Manager. Times had changed in the apartments and a lot of long-term residents, the lords and ladies, were beginning to dwindle away because the rents had risen dramatically. They found that it was cheaper to buy a property or rent an apartment elsewhere in London. For the first time, we began renting out apartments on a nightly basis without contracts, so it was becoming very much like the hotel.

I had a large boardroom table in my office where we held a meeting every morning at 9.30 a.m. This was known as 'Prayers'. I would be briefed beforehand by Tony as to what needed to be done. At the meeting there would be around ten people, which included the Banqueting Manager, the head housekeepers of the North and South blocks, the Reception Manager, the Personnel Manager, the Food and Beverage Manager, the Head Concierge, the Head of Finance, the Head of Security, and myself. We would begin by going through the arrivals and departures for that particular day, and looked at which VIPs were expected. Usually there were around fifty VIP arrivals a day and each had different requirements. In fact, there were three categories of VIP:

A List
Champagne, flowers, chocolates, and their favourite magazines were placed in their rooms.

B List
Champagne and chocolates.

C List
Chocolates only.

Some of this was based on their room rate, rather than their celebrity status. If someone was paying £2,000 a night for a suite, then, as an 'A Lister', the Guest Relations Manager would be bleeped the moment they arrived and he would personally escort them to their rooms. They would bypass reception altogether and register within the privacy of their own room. In 1972 the executive rooms on the eighth floor became known as the Crown Club. Guests paid extra to be a Crown Club member, but received the same perks as a VIP in that they were able to check in to the hotel in their room; they were given a butler and a valet; a free bar in case they wanted a glass of wine or a drink, and received complimentary gifts such as umbrellas, bags and coat hangers, all with the Grosvenor House logo. The Crown Club meant that anybody could receive celebrity treatment, just as long as they had the money to pay for it.

Returning VIPs received a signed card from Tony Murkett or myself, welcoming them back to the hotel. The top payers were given the very best treatment. We got to know VIP guests' birthdays, anniversaries, their favourite food, alcoholic drinks, so sometimes we could alternate with different gifts. For example, a whisky drinker would be given a complimentary bottle of whisky in his room rather than champagne. If we knew that someone enjoyed gardening, then a selection of gardening magazines would be placed in their rooms. We felt that this added a personal touch. Detailed record cards were kept for each of our regular guests and, as staff discovered something about them, it would be added to the card. Lists of likes, dislikes and individual preferences were eventually transferred to computer, so that we had a personal history of our visitors and corporate clients.

Staff taking guests to their room or suite were briefed to fish for information.

'Are you here for a special occasion, Sir?' The question would be asked very casually.

'Actually it's our wedding anniversary.'

'Congratulations, Sir.'

Another detail to add to our records.

'Can I get you a bottle of champagne, Sir?

'I'd rather have a brandy.'

A note would be made of brandy for the future.

'You're looking very elegant today, Madam.

'Oh, thank you, it's my birthday . . .'

At the end of each month staff were awarded a bonus in their wages, depending upon how much information they had discovered. This gave the staff an incentive and put us ahead of our rivals. Five-star hotels have to continually come up with new ideas to make the guests' stay special. The days of chocolates on pillows is now old hat, and to my mind was a ridiculous practice anyway. I never forgot when one man staying overnight after a function was so drunk that he went to bed with the chocolate on his pillow, and woke up next morning with it melted all over his hair. Rather than being upset, he found it very funny and still tells me that story every time I see him.

After discussing arrivals and departures at the prayers, which could take fifteen minutes to go through, I would ask if there had been any complaints. There were *always* letters of complaint to be dealt with, probably seven a day, which were kept in a file as thick as a door. The guest didn't like the room – the size, the decor, the lack of a view – or they had found some dust in the bedroom; the food was cold, the other guests were noisy, they didn't receive their wake-up call, a member of staff was impolite or had body odour, the air-conditioning either wasn't working or the metal grill rattled when it was . . . These were the most common complaints. We had good boilers though, so never received any grumbles about lack of hot water as some hotels do; although on the apartment side there could be complaints early in the morning from the top floors when everybody was trying to have a bath or shower at once and the pipes couldn't cope.

Another regular complaint was slow service at breakfast, and this is one that I have heard more than any other throughout my working life in hotels. Often this would be accompanied by the irritating phrase, 'You haven't got enough staff.' Unlike lunch or dinner, breakfasts are not booked in advance and too many guests tend to congregate in the morning at the same time. It is impossible for staff to anticipate exactly when people are going to come down, and one might open the dining-room doors at 7 a.m. and serve just two guests during the next hour; then 120 people will suddenly arrive all at once and demand breakfast. Within half an hour there could be 220 and a queue of angry guests outside the door. Some would go off and not have any breakfast at all, while others opted to have room service instead. We used to have around a hundred breakfast trays to make up every morning, served by waiters, with a hot box to keep the food warm, which meant that guests could have breakfast without hassle.

An occasional criticism was that Grosvenor House was too expensive, either the cost of the room or the price of food and drinks, but maybe the complainers shouldn't have been staying in a five-star hotel on Park Lane in the first place, if they couldn't afford it. And there was one gripe that always made me smile: 'I never see the General Manager.'

In the days before email, letters of complaint were a daily chore. The higher the calibre of hotel, the more complaints you seem to get. Guests are paying a lot of money and so nitpick about the least little thing. Their expectations are so much higher. Sometimes they would write directly to Head Office, and occasionally even to Lord Forte or Rocco personally. Then the Area Director would immediately be on to us for a full report to obtain all the facts. Fortes rarely gave money in recompense, but usually offered a room upgrade on the guest's next visit instead; otherwise the profits would be eaten in to.

Bad attitude from staff was another area for complaint. As Deputy General Manager I was responsible for the hiring and firing, so when interviewing anyone for a new position I began to ask them if they had a chip on their shoulder about anything. It is a question I still ask to this day. How they answer it is crucial. A normal person tends to smile, maybe shrug, and say that they don't think they have. If someone becomes defensive or aggressive, and vehemently insists that they haven't got a chip on their shoulder, then I will not employ them. Experience has taught me that they're the type that always *have* got a chip and will be difficult employees to work with.

After complaints, we would go through the list of maintenance problems. A door handle loose here, a leaking toilet there, a faulty light fixture above, a lift out of order below . . . the list was endless. Plumbing was always a major issue: blocked sinks, dripping taps, a flooded bathroom. Scratched walls in corridors were another cause for complaint, as the service trolleys for chambermaids and linen porters inevitably scraped against them as they passed through. Whoever designed the metal trolleys which maids use to transport soaps, toiletries and cleaning products from room to room needs to be shot. With seventy-eight rooms per floor, without a trolley maids would be forever running backwards and forwards along corridors, so it was an essential piece of equipment. Yet they were so heavy that the girls could hardly push them and, like a supermarket trolley, they seemed to have a mind of their own and were forever whacking the walls. In the end I had new lighter trolleys designed with padding on the corners, which were easier to push and protected the walls from damage. A simple but very effective solution.

If there was a major issue, I would later accompany the maintenance men to see the situation for myself. Air-conditioning was always a problem, as condensation used to gather in the units and would eventually leak through a ceiling. Temperature control was a concern too, as guests would complain that rooms were either too cold or too hot. Whilst discussing maintenance, we would list which rooms were next scheduled for redecoration and decide whether any additional work was required. Maybe a new door could be fitted while the room was out of action, or the bathroom could be retiled.

Next, revenue had to be discussed. The Finance Manager would give a breakdown as to what had been taken in the hotel, the apartments, the bars, the restaurant, and the function rooms, so that we knew from a budget point of view the occupancy and what had been taken in revenue as a result. Food, beverage, room hire, and telephone sales were the key figures. We forget now that in the days before mobile phones all calls had to go through the switchboard, which resulted in annual revenue of over £1 million for Grosvenor House. Today hotels make nothing, as everyone uses their own mobile phone.

I found sorting out budgets quite stressful. We were always being hassled by the management to make more money for the company, so we used to temporarily hide income if we had made a good profit for one accounting period. Then we had an amount to carry over whenever there was a less successful period. The Finance Director, Roy Tutty, was a canny man. He used to come round and say, 'Right, Mr Kirby, how much are you hiding this month?'

'Twenty-five thousand, Mr Tutty,' I would say, even though we had probably put a hundred thousand aside. We never gave it to him all at once.

'OK, put it back in the pot. We've had a bad time with two hotels down the road. The Cumberland and the Strand Palace have been useless this month. I need every penny we can get.'

When figures for the London hotels were collated, the Grosvenor House would always come out as the biggest profit earner for Trusthouse Forte.

Finally, we reviewed staff issues: how many new staff were starting work that day, how many of the regular staff had not turned up for work or had rung in sick, who was booked in for training, and maybe who was likely to be employee of the month. Worse still, we inevitably had to discuss who was due to be fired. I enjoyed meeting all the new staff and liked to think I could encourage them by revealing my own career progression within the hotel, but I did not relish firing people. Usually the Personnel Department dealt with this, but occasionally I had to arbitrate and make the final decision. We used to call it 'going for a walk around the car park', because if someone was due for the chop I would take them outside for a walk.

'I'm not sure it's really working out for you here.'

'Perhaps not, Mr Kirby.'

'You're always calling in sick.'

'I know.'

'And we've received quite a lot of complaints about your attitude. You've seen the letters?'

'Yes, Mr Kirby. Maybe I ought to resign.'

If handled correctly, employees invariably jumped before they were pushed.

Another method of firing people was to highlight their faults in front of everybody at the meeting, which was guaranteed to cause them maximum embarrassment.

'Now, John, will you tell us what the problem was yesterday? Mr Smith didn't get the service he had ordered, did he?'

They would shift uneasily and try to explain the situation.

'So, why did that happen?' I would continue calmly

'Because I forgot.'

'You forgot. So will you just tell everyone again exactly what happened.'
The staff member would reluctantly outline his mistake in more detail.
'This is the second time, isn't it, John?'
'Yes, Mr Kirby.'
I would then maintain a period of silence, which made the offender squirm even more, before moving on to the next item on the agenda. The next time it happened, I would repeat the procedure in front of everybody at a meeting.
'This is the third time you've forgotten to organise this, isn't it, John?'
'Yes, Mr Kirby.'
'Three times you've made the same mistake. That's unbelievable . . .'
Within two days they would hand their notice in. It worked every time and I didn't have to sack them.

The morning prayer meetings were held seven days a week – even on Sundays – and took around forty minutes to get through. But they were crucial for keeping heads of department informed and ensured the smooth running of the hotel. They became a fundamental feature of my life.

'Good morning, everybody. What a day we have today! There's a St George's Day lunch in the Great Room. One thousand five hundred guests are expected and they will be big drinkers, so be prepared. There will be 450 in the Ballroom for a charity lunch, which Princess Diana is attending. She should be arriving at 12.45 p.m. for a 1 p.m. lunch. Security is obviously at its highest today. Sniffer dogs are currently doing their last check, police are sealing and taping air ducts, and will seal the Ballroom until one hour before she arrives. Remember that no one except management can enter. The kitchen has been checked, and the staff and waiters have been vetted to ensure that we have nobody new working in the kitchen or Ballroom for this function.

We have full occupancy in the hotel today, with all 452 rooms booked, and the apartments are full as well. So bear in mind that we are going to have around four thousand people passing through the doors over the next twelve hours.

Ninety-eight per cent of today's arrivals are VIPs. Sammy Davis, Jr and entourage have booked four suites and two doubles. They're paying the full rate. James Mason and his wife will be in the Columbia apartment. Sir Jackie Stewart and wife are in the Park View Suite. Have you put champagne and fruit in those rooms? Don't forget the golf magazines he reads. Sir Jackie also has a meeting with Sir Rocco Forte in the lounge at 6.30 p.m. this evening, so we need to make sure that it is spotless and the service impeccable. Otherwise I'll hear about it.

Sean Connery and wife are on the Crown Club Floor. Champagne and fruit in there, too, please. His suits and bags are here in store, so can they be transferred to his room. Have the valets been instructed? The same for Sir Jackie Stewart's clothes. Reception Manager, please check that these have gone in and have been unpacked. We have the Italian Prime Minister in a suite and two double rooms for his security men. Could our security please liaise with the Embassy as to his time of arrival?'

'Already done, Mr Kirby.'

'Thank you. Alan, and can you make sure that you're on hand personally when he gets here?'

'No problem.'

Head of Security, Alan, is a former policeman and I know that he can be trusted to do a good job.

'Moving on, we had seven no-shows last night. No reason given. I have checked the correspondence. All of them were corporate clients so, Reception, can you make sure that we charge them all? And tonight I see we are over-booked by eight rooms.'

'We are holding eight rooms at the Dorchester, just in case, Mr Kirby.'

'I hope they're at the same rate as our bookings?'

'The Dorchester say they are nearly full, Mr Kirby. I'm afraid they want the full rate and they have no double rooms left, only suites.'

'Pull the other one! I bet if we called saying we were a client looking for a double room, they would jolly soon find a double room. Give me the phone, let's try. Quiet, everyone!'

I call the Dorchester Hotel.

'Reservations, please. Oh, hello, I'm in London for a conference and am looking for a double room just for tonight. Do you have anything available? You do! And the room rate? £350 per night, room only. Now, I have a few clients with me, do you have other double rooms available? I'll probably need about eight altogether. That's great. I'll call you back in a few minutes, many thanks.'

Everybody laughs as I replace the receiver.

'Bingo! OK, Reception Manager, can you please make the call and book

those rooms. And can you also check that we have no double bookings for tonight either. Are there any provisional bookings?'

'Yes, two, Mr Kirby.'

'Can you check with them as to whether they are now definite? We need to be one hundred per cent sure, especially as we had seven no-shows last night. We can charge them if they don't bother to show up.'

'Will do.'

'OK, Princess Diana and the charity lunch. Her office will call from the Palace to inform us when she has left and will give a definite time of arrival. I will wait by the Ballroom door with Alan, and no one else, please. We can't have any hangers-on . . . Now, any new staff today?'

'We have twenty men starting this morning, Mr Kirby.'

'OK, get them all together at 10.30 a.m. and I'll call by and say hello. Are there any maintenance issues?'

'We replaced 180 light bulbs yesterday. Air-conditioning in rooms 320, 160 and 408 will be fixed today ready for letting. The french-polisher is varnishing eight lounge chairs, so we need to put in some replacements just for today. The chairs should be back tomorrow.'

'Banqueting Manager, anything to report?'

'Last night's function was very busy. We took over £125,000. The Italian restaurant has a new lunch menu starting today, so a leaflet has been sent to all our corporate clients with a ten per cent discount. Bookings look good for tonight and the rest of week.'

'Housekeeping?'

'We're OK for laundry in the bedrooms, but the delivery back today was a bit short of napkins. I have spoken to the Laundry, and they have promised to send 2,000 more napkins by tonight. But we really need 5,000.'

'OK. Let me have an order for 3,000 napkins and I will sign that off today.'

The meeting finally comes to a close.

'Have a good day, everyone. Remember the guest is king.'

Only after the prayer meeting could the day's work properly begin. After going through the morning's mail with my secretaries, I would then spot-check a few rooms to make sure they had been cleaned correctly, that there were no maintenance problems, and that the strawberries and champagne were in place for the VIP arrivals. I would visit the restaurants and function rooms, look around the bars and lounges, showing my face to the staff, and acting as mediator and problem-solver wherever needed. I was a hands-on manager and loved every minute of it.

As Deputy General Manager there was a huge amount of responsibility on my shoulders. I had to oversee most of the huge functions that regularly took place in the Great Room, which involved as much planning and preparation as a military operation. Especially as most had a public figure in attendance – royalty, a politician or a household name of some kind. The Great Room at Grosvenor House is one of the largest function rooms in Europe, seating 2,000 for a lunch or dinner, or 1,100 theatre-style, so is a major venue for award ceremonies, charity balls, theatrical galas, and many prestigious events each year.

One of the most historic was Queen Charlotte's Ball. An annual event since King George III first held a ball in 1780 to raise funds for a maternity hospital named after his wife. Over the years it developed into a debutante ball as part of the London Season and eventually came to be held in the Great Room at Grosvenor House. The presentation of debutantes at Court ended in 1958, as Queen Elizabeth II considered it outdated. Princess Margaret famously said, 'We had to put a stop to it. Every tart in London was getting in.' But in an attempt to keep something of the debutante system alive, society ladies still came out at Queen Charlotte's Ball every September, curtseying to a large cake rather than Her Majesty in person. We used to get around eight hundred people attending, with maybe eighty girls being presented. There would be a procession of girls, all looking fabulous in their virginal white dresses. Some would be the daughters of well-known aristocrats, others were untitled and just wanted to climb the social ladder, but as they were all dressed in a similar way, they became unidentifiable. Occasionally a member of the Royal Family would be guest of honour, such as Princess Michael of Kent

A three-course dinner would be served, usually quite a simple meal as it was a charity event and therefore not a big money-spinner for Grosvenor House. Later all would dance to the music of The Dark Blues, under the direction of bandleader Nigel Tully. The Dark Blues have played for many private royal functions at Windsor Castle or Buckingham Palace, notably Prince Charles's fortieth birthday party. Years ago it was intended that girls might find a suitable marriage partner at the ball, usually an eligible brother of one of the other girls, who would be known as a 'Deb's Delight'. Queen

Charlotte's Ball eventually died out in the late 1990s, as it relied on young ladies 'coming out' and there were fewer and fewer each year. For around forty years, a famous 'fixer' called Peter Townend worked hard to keep the debutante system alive. If you wanted your daughter to come out in society, he was the man to fix it for you. Every year he wrote hundreds of letters in turquoise ink to mothers of suitable eighteen-year-old girls, suggesting that their daughter might like to come out. When he died, the flame of the debutante system finally faded. Queen Charlotte's Ball was, however, revived in September 2009 to raise money for neo-natal research at Queen Charlotte's Hospital – very much as King George III had intended at the first ball over two centuries ago.

Queen Charlotte's Ball was always preceded by the Berkeley Dress Show, traditionally marking the start of the London Debutante Season, which still happens every year and is patronised by royalty and high-society ladies. Debutantes often used to attend the Sally Clayton Finishing School for a couple of weeks to polish up their appearance, posture and social skills, before showing themselves off at the Berkeley Dress Show.

The Water Rats' Ball was a particularly star-studded event for this theatrical organisation. Virtually every table seemed to have a famous face at it. The Duke of Edinburgh, the Prince of Wales and Prince Michael of Kent all attended at various times as Companion Water Rats – people recognised for their charitable endeavours but not actually in the theatrical profession. Sometimes the King Rat that year was somebody that I had never heard of, but I do remember when magician Paul Daniels had the honour. He was brilliant in all respects from our point of view, because he turned out to be a marvellous organiser as well as being a superb act when entertaining his fellow Rats. The Music Hall star Dan Leno was one of the earliest King Rats and his great-nephew Danny Leno used to attend each year and brought other functions to us as well. The hotel dealt mainly with the Scribe Rat, who did all the administration. It was a big job for the hotel, with around 1,400 guests, but the cabarets were wonderful. They were an utter shambles sometimes because we didn't actually know who was appearing, but still wonderful. We knew the menu, we knew that the organisers would arrive at 5.30 p.m., but a man might also turn up with an elephant because he was one of the acts. We just never knew what was going to happen. If we did have a list of performers, they were often unknown to us and we had no idea what their act was, but they would get up in between courses and entertain.

One memorable act was a man with a crossbow, which was mounted and attached to a timer. Members of the audience were invited up to help strap the man tightly into a chair. He was tied, padlocked, and blindfolded, so that he could apparently neither move nor see. A German woman then shouted out, 'I vill set zis timer to two minutes. And after two minutes it vill fire ze crossbow!' The timer was set, and each second could then be heard ticking away, with the crossbow aimed directly at the man strapped into the chair. He seemed totally unperturbed and made what looked like only a minimal amount of effort to release himself. And all the time the clock was ticking. Tick-tock. Tick- tock. The tension in the room mounted. With just one second left, he shifted himself very slightly in the chair, and boom!, the crossbow fired and missed him by just a fraction of an inch. It seemed such a close call and we felt that he had really taken a risk that night.

The act was so impressive that we booked him for more events at Grosvenor House, and each time it was equally dramatic. Only later did we discover that the crossbow was operated by a beam of light and not the timer. The man had just enough leeway to move slightly, and he knew that as soon as he moved out of the beam of light, the crossbow would fire where the light had been and he was safe. It was an incredible act and just the sound of the timer ticking had the audience on the very edge of their seats, hearts in their mouths.

The cabaret acts were always a joy to watch. Once a man built a ladder out of newspaper and a girl climbed up it. The Grand Order of Water Rats was blessed with many top comedians as members, and the year that Les Dawson was King Rat was a hoot. Little wonder that they always point out that the word Rats reversed spells 'star'.

Brian May from Queen attended the ball and was on the top table at around the time that Freddie Mercury died in 1991. Michael Simcock, our Head Waiter, had a flat opposite Freddie Mercury's house in Logan Place. It was a former council flat that he had bought very cheaply from Westminster Council, and it had suddenly become worth around £2 million. At the morning meeting Michael often used to report that there were, say, 250 bouquets of flowers outside Freddie Mercury's house and thousands of fans. So we came to know a lot about Queen.

Princess Margaret used to attend the Caledonian Ball every year, having been born at Glamis Castle in Scotland. There would be a dinner in the

Great Room, followed by a break while the dining tables were cleared away and were replaced with smaller tables around the outside of the room, and along the balcony. The carpet would be rolled up so that Scottish dancing could take place in the centre of the floor. Princess Margaret used to be taken up to a retiring room, where a bottle of Famous Grouse whisky would be waiting for her. By the time she returned to the Great Room to watch the dancing, she would have consumed almost the entire bottle. Over the years the ball changed, so that there would be just a small dinner for 300 in the Ballroom, and then 1,500 guests went straight into the Great Room for the ball itself. The Muckle Flugga Band played, sometimes until 3 a.m. Often we had no idea who would be arriving for the ball, and on one occasion Princess Anne turned up with a mystery man.

The Great Room was an ideal venue for award ceremonies because of its size, and we could easily accommodate television crews, and all their cameras and paraphernalia. We hosted the Society of West End Theatres (SWET) Awards for many years, which in 1984 changed its name to the Laurence Olivier Awards in honour of the great actor. The room would be filled with hundreds of people from the world of theatre, and it was easy to nod and say hello to someone you knew, only to realise afterwards that you didn't actually know them personally at all; they were just a very well-known face. You felt such an idiot afterwards.

We also hosted the British Academy of Film and Television Arts (BAFTA) Award Ceremonies, which would be preceded by a dinner. One year the organisers miscalculated on the numbers attending, and some people had to sit in the crush foyer – where guests usually made their entrance – and would have seen nothing of the ceremony at all. We had to put televisions out there so that they could watch the action on screen. They might just as well have been at home. Although the Great Room can seat 1,500 for a dinner, this number is reduced for an event that is being broadcast because all the technical equipment takes up so much space.

Annual general meetings were regular events too, such as that of Amstrad with Sir Alan Sugar in attendance. I particularly remember a Burton Group AGM, when chairman Sir Ralph Halpern was speaking. He had been dubbed 'five-times-a-night' by the media, following a high- profile sex scandal with a model. We had to bring him in through the loading bay and the kitchens because press photographers were chasing him. He came out on to the stage, chaired the AGM, and then we whisked him out the same way so that he could avoid the paparazzi.

Marks and Spencer held their AGM at Grosvenor House too. We used to provide the food, and each time the organisers would insist on coming to inspect the hotel kitchens beforehand to make sure that they were up to their standard. We felt a bit put out about this. Of course our kitchens were of a high standard! One year my Director of Banqueting, Andrew Coy, had a brainwave.

'We're missing a trick here,' he told them, 'why are we not serving your shareholders Marks and Spencer's food?'

They thought it was a marvellous idea, and he sent them a suggested menu list to see if they could supply the food. Then he said, 'But, of course, I'm going to have to come and inspect your kitchens.'

There was a silence.

'You always come and inspect our kitchens before we serve the food,' he added, 'so I want to inspect your kitchens if you're providing it.'

They agreed, and Andrew went to look at the Marks and Spencer kitchens in Baker Street, which he found to be immaculate.

We used to find at several AGMs that some shareholders would attend that only owned about five or ten shares. We called them 'bag ladies', because they would arrive with lots of carrier bags and then practically sweep the tables of food, putting as much as they could into their carrier bags. Even plates disappeared into them. They were like vultures.

John Jarvis of Jarvis Hotels was another client. He used to come in to arrange a dinner with our Banqueting Manager, and expect to receive a knock-down price on the £14-a-head menu.

'You must have forgotten how it works, Mr Jarvis,' Andrew Coy would grin and say, 'Do you still cost menus at Jarvis Hotels?'

'Of course I do.'

'I used to negotiate on your behalf, Mr Jarvis, when I worked for you.'

'Yes, I remember, damn you.'

'Then the menu is £14-a-head and not a penny less.'

We regularly used to host lunches and dinners for the Variety Club of Great Britain, a very worthy theatrical charity which often had cabaret-style performers to entertain them. The organiser for many years was Lottie Samuels and her husband. Mr Samuels would call and say that he was putting on a lunch, there would be 400 people, and he would state how much he intended to pay. And that was it. There was absolutely no room for negotiation. He just asked for a copy of the menu to be sent to him, and that was virtually the function organised.

Not all meals ran smoothly, as sometimes there were circumstances completely beyond our control. A horrifying situation was the day a sewerage pipe burst into one of the fridges! Large pipes travelled across the ceiling of Grosvenor House above two vast walk-in fridges. The principle in banqueting is 'prepare for tomorrow today'. So in Fridge 1 would be today's desserts, prepared yesterday, and in Fridge 2 would be tomorrow's desserts, prepared today. That way you always worked a day in advance.

In the middle of a banquet, a sewerage pipe leaked into the fridge containing the puddings for that day's meal. There was absolutely nothing for it, but to serve the guests 'tomorrow's pudding' instead. It was a completely different dish to the one printed on the menu, but not a single guest commented. They ate strawberry parfait instead of crème caramel, and nobody appeared to notice the change. Out of politeness, the Banqueting Director approached the organiser and apologised about the switch.

'It's was either strawberry parfait or a plate full of shit,' he said.

At a St George's Day luncheon, a bishop was the guest speaker and was halfway through his speech when a drunken man ran from the back of the room straight towards him. The Banqueting Manager and the waiters rugby-tackled him just as he reached the Bishop, and escorted him off the premises.

Organisers used to book the room early for that particular event, and so some guests drank a great deal during the day. A man was once so drunk at the lunch that he fell and hit his head on the floor. There was blood everywhere. Another guest who had drunk far too much plummeted head first off the balcony straight on to a table below; he just got up and had another drink.

For the annual Cottage Homes Ball, which was attended by around 1,200 people in the retail trade from big chains such as Next, Marks and Spencer, and Debenhams, the menu always had to be slightly off-the-wall. The organiser was Richard Haywood, and one year we sold him the idea of serving a chilled fruit soup. He was sceptical at first, but we served it to him at a trial run, with the chairman of the board. We used to prepare three different starters, main courses and puddings, so that a choice could be made. The chairman walked in for the tasting and immediately asked for a large scotch, which we gave him. He drank scotch throughout and really sampled very little of the food. At the end, he selected the menu for the ball and opted for the fruit soup as the starter.

As the soup was cold, we were able to have it made in advance and preset on the tables just before the guests arrived. Their timings were short anyway, and this speeded the whole meal up. I don't know what happened, but on the day of the ball the kitchen seemed to have a completely different selection of fruits to those at the trial, and the finished soup bore absolutely no resemblance to the one that had been sampled earlier. The Banqueting Director warned Richard Haywood, who went immediately to inform the chairman. 'Don't worry,' he replied, 'I can't remember what it was like anyway. I was far too pissed!'

Once we had the hotel power station blow up and had to evacuate guests out in to Park Lane in the middle of a meal. We also hosted a brewery AGM where they always gave out free beer. Many of the people got terribly drunk and used to sleep it off on the traffic island outside the hotel. And just before another function there were essential changes to the hotel fire exits due to an amendment in safety regulations. The Fire Officer insisted that the maximum number of guests to be served in the Great Room was reduced from 2,000 to 1,500. We already had a few bookings for more than 1,500, so I decided to take a gamble and allow the functions to proceed. Halfway through the first dinner, the fire alarms went off in the apartment block. It was only someone accidentally burning a slice of toast, but the Fire Officer said that while he was in the building he might as well have a look around the hotel as well. He asked me if there was a function in the Great Room, and I walked him along the balcony looking down on the diners below. At that precise moment, the speaker got up and welcomed the guests, saying, 'It's marvellous to see you all. We have 1,700 people here today. Isn't it wonderful!' The Fire Officer turned to me and said, 'You're nicked.' I was in all kinds of trouble for breaching fire regulations and was taken off to make a statement. After around ten years the regulations changed once more and now the Great Room is again allowed to cater for 2,000 people.

There was one event that I always dreaded: the annual Hunt Ball. Each time there were protesters, but one year we had a call from the police asking to set up an urgent meeting. With much talk about a possible ban on deer hunting in the UK, they expected the protests to be even worse than usual. I met up with two Special Branch officers, who informed me that three to four hundred protesters were expected. We usually only had about thirty. It looked as if it might be a tough night for our security men, although the police said that they would have a strong presence themselves; but our position was very clear: we would not be cancelling the function.

We were told to check the guest list carefully in case of infiltrators. There were always around 1,200 at the Hunt Ball, with about fifty per cent staying overnight, so there was a lot of checking to do. We printed copies of the arrival list to share with the organisers. Three or four suspicious names stood out, which I passed on to the police.

When the night arrived we had all our security men in place, plus backup from a private security company that we had hired to help us, just to be on the safe side. Grosvenor House has so many entrances that fourteen men plus Alan, the Head of Security, were needed to cover them. We closed the gates to our main entrance on Park Street, so that only *bone fide* guests could get in. There were around two hundred protesters outside, but about ninety minutes before the guests were due to arrive, I received a telephone call from the switchboard.

'Mr Kirby, we have a warning message saying that a bomb will go off tonight.'

My heart began to race.

'OK. What did they actually say?'

'That there is a bomb due to explode in twenty minutes.'

I called the Bomb Squad.

We had a good search, but found nothing suspicious. A decision was made not to evacuate the hotel.

'Mr Kirby, it's getting a bit rough out here,' Alan paged me.

When I looked outside it was like a scene from *Les Miserables*. Protesters had now increased to eight hundred, all shouting, screaming, throwing flour bombs and water bombs. What a mess all over the forecourt of the hotel, and over the cars too! Then they began throwing eggs. Noisy protesters stormed the gates every time a car or taxi had to be let in. Some even managed to run through, outmanoeuvred the police and got into the hotel. Soon we had reports that protesters were running around the corridors. There was a chance that things could be turning dangerous

I sent in two security men to chase them and get them out. Then, just as things seemed to be at their worst, an idiot got out of a taxi wearing a red hunting jacket with horns on his head. The crowds went absolutely mad. Water bombs, stink bombs, flour bombs, everything was aimed at us. I had flour all over my navy-blue suit and shoes. Despite the clamour and possible danger, my immediate thought was, 'That's OK, I've got a spare suit and shoes in my office'. We rushed the guest through as quickly as we could, but we were furious at him for wearing an outfit that was guaranteed to inflame anti-hunt protesters. I was delighted when a police officer had a go at him.

What a night! None of us on duty got a chance to eat anything until after 2 a.m. By this time the protesters had long since gone home, most of the Hunt Ball guests had left, and there were only around twenty late drinkers in the bar. I told them twice to keep the noise down, before having a word with our night chefs. They made us club sandwiches and chips, which we had with a well-deserved beer. Staff were not meant to drink on duty, but I could not have cared less by this time.

I finally got to bed at 2.45 a.m., and had to be up and back on duty again in barely four hours. I liked to have a run before work too, but I was completely exhausted. I realised that I had not even had time to telephone Wendy, but she was getting used to it. Before putting the light out, I wrote a report to our bosses at Head Office about the Hunt Ball, with recommendations for the following year. The organisers needed to know that we could not tolerate their guests stalking and mocking the protesters. Next time there really could be a bomb.

Other events were much more dignified. The world-famous Grosvenor House Antiques Fair began in September 1934 and continues to be a major annual event. Now held in June each year, it has been opened no less than thirty-eight times by members of the Royal Family, including Queen Mary, Princess Diana, Princess Margaret, the Queen Mother, Princess Grace of Monaco, and it is now patronised by Princess Alexandra. The first Antiques Fair in 1934 consisted of eighty-seven stands in the Great Room, where a Chelsea plate sold for one guinea and a Chippendale table for eight. Today there are antiques worth around £500 million on sale, with prices ranging from a few hundred pounds to several million for just one item.

The fair used to take up four weeks of our time, as an entire week was needed just to set everything up, and another week to take all the stands down again, so it was a major operation. The fair attracted dealers from around the world, each with magnificent antiques, paintings, furniture, jewellery and *objets d'art* on display. Some of the items were huge and had to be transported down to the Great Room in the 'jumbo' lift, which was used whenever large pieces of equipment had to be moved between floors. It was called 'jumbo' not because of its size, but from the time when a baby elephant put in an appearance at an event and got stuck in the lift. The poor animal naturally became frightened, could not control its bodily functions and the lift filled with elephant poo. From that day onwards it became known as the 'jumbo' lift.

Security for this particular event was inevitably a nightmare, with hundreds of thousands of priceless antiques stored at the hotel for weeks, plus royalty and high profile visitors in attendance. So many doors had to be locked, with security men posted at them twenty-four hours a day. Visitors used to queue down Park Lane to get in each day, and the knock-on effect for the hotel was that the lounges and bars overflowed with people wanting refreshments, and the restaurants would be packed, so it was an enormous money-spinner.

Once the doors had closed at the end of it, there was another logistical nightmare. Every single antique that had been sold then had to be sent off to the buyer, which could be anywhere in the globe. Maybe a £50,000 sideboard was destined for China, or a £200,000 grandfather clock had to be packed up for shipping to America. There would be lorries and vans everywhere, waiting to collect the treasures, and when the very last stand had been removed and the final antique had been taken, we were left to restore the Great Room. The carpet would be in need of repair, the walls would be damaged where antique dealers had knocked in nails (even though expressly asked not to), and a great deal of time and money was needed to restore the room to its former glory.

Function rooms always had to be adapted to suit the event. Sometimes organisers did not want the eight chandeliers that hung in the Great Room, they were either in the way for a television broadcast or they were going to bring in their own lighting. It was no easy task taking down huge chandeliers, so they were charged £150 per chandelier, £1,200 for all eight, to have them removed and put in storage during the function. The hotel had a special wooden platform that the chandeliers could be safely lowered on to, and then each had its own wooden box.

There were one hundred sets of pin spotlights on the ceiling so that every table could be lit as necessary. Function organisers were charged separately for the use of these lights, such a cost being known in the trade as an 'add-on'. In the early 1990s Grosvenor House had four technicians in the Maintenance Department. If Banqueting needed them to carry out work in the Great Room, such as erecting lights, then they had to be booked and so it became a cost, because it always involved them working overtime. Eventually accountants decided to make the technicians redundant to save on costs, but this meant that an outside production company would need to be hired to attend to lighting requirements, which was ridiculous. So in the end the technicians went on to the payroll of the Banqueting Department rather than Maintenance, at a cost of £40,000 a year.

Grosvenor House did not actually own any spotlights at that time and just rented them as necessary, hence the additional cost to the function organisers. We knew that we could save money if we had our own lights, but there was no capital available to purchase them. So we bought them 'on the drip', a few at a time. If we had a dinner for 800 people which required forty pin spots to light the tables, we sent the technicians out to buy the forty lights and charged it to the function. The next function might require sixty pin spots, so we bought twenty more. Gradually over a period of time we were able to build up sets of all the lights that we might ever need, with clients being charged for their use. Once we owned them, of course, the income generated from the lights became profit, because we no longer had to hire them. Even when offset against the cost of the technicians' wages, there was still a profit. The accountants saw the income but never seemed to notice the expenditure. Suddenly we had all this lighting kit hanging from the ceiling, and nobody once queried how it had all been paid for.

To set up for a dinner, the Banqueting Department had 2,000 sets of cutlery, 6,000 napkins, our own Grosvenor House tablecloths in either salmon pink or white with *GH* embroidered in the centre, 150 table number stands with the Grosvenor House crown logo on, between 5,000 and 7,000 wine glasses, and 2,000 Slim Jim drinking glasses. Or that was the theory anyway. Often not enough napkins came back from the laundry in time, and occasionally damp linen was laid on the table, and sometimes the last of the cutlery would be laid as the first of the guests arrived, because it had to be washed and reset from a previous function. For the Great Room alone there were 135 tables, each five feet in diameter, which could seat ten guests, and 80 tables, six feet in diameter, which could seat twelve. There were 2,000 chairs with arms, as Sir Rocco Forte had insisted that all dining chairs had arms. Everything in the Great Room really was great in size, even the carpet covered an area of one acre.

The hotel became a venue for many sporting events. Every year the Football Association Dinner and awards ceremony would be held there on a Sunday, with all the top footballers of the day present. In 1992 I received a call from the Sultan of Brunei's office to say that he and his entourage were on their way and he wanted the whole of the eighth floor. Of course, it coincided with the Football Association Dinner that year, and the eighth-floor suites were already full of prominent football personalities, including Terry Venables.

One of the Sultan's daughters was apparently ill, and he was flying the Princess over to England in his private jumbo jet for treatment. The Sultan insisted that every room on the eighth floor was emptied, so it was left to me to approach the footballers, and explain that we had an important person flying in with a daughter who had internal bleeding, and we desperately needed the top floor for security purposes. I told them that they could have suites on the floor below and that the client would settle their bills. As they were in £500-a-night suites, none of the footballers objected to moving and they stayed free at the Sultan of Brunei's expense, and each received a bottle of champagne. It took several hours to track each footballer down and then move all their clothes and possessions to a lower floor, but we managed it just before the Sultan's entourage arrived. If just one of the footballers had refused to move, I would have been in trouble, but fortunately I got away with it through a combination of bullshit and charm. Another crisis solved. The Sultan of Brunei took over the whole of the eighth floor for three weeks, and his daughter thankfully recovered.

For many years boxing was also a popular event and the famous promoter John Solomon used to organise an evening at Grosvenor House. A boxing ring would be set up in the centre of the Great Room, and three to four hundred people would have dinner at tables set up around the outside and watch a match. Eventually the event moved to the four-star Hilton Hotel in Park Lane, because the numbers were dropping to around 250 people. We had been turning away a function with a potential 2,000 guests to mount boxing for just a couple of hundred, so we decided to say goodbye to that particular event.

Cricketers used to visit with the Lord's Taverners Club. One year they auctioned a Vauxhall 4 x 4 car, then worth £19,000. The England Captain, Graham Gooch, put his hand up, and people thought that he had made a successful bid, but he hadn't and so the car wasn't sold. We had such problems getting the car into the Great Room too, and had to remove the wing mirrors to get it into the jumbo loading lift.

Many entertainers came to perform at functions in the Great Room too. Military bands were particularly popular with Americans, so members of the Irish, Welsh or Grenadier guards would march in after a dinner and play music. For the Casenove Quinquennial Staff Party in 1992 the American Motown group The Four Tops were booked to perform the cabaret. Their rider included the provision of eight oxygen bottles backstage to keep them pumped up, and eighteen brand-new Grosvenor House bath towels still in their wrappers.

Luciano Pavarotti 'appeared' in the Great Room during one of his stays. A special chair had to be commissioned to bear his weight, and an exclusive menu was created just for him because of his vast appetite for chicken. Guests paid between £150 and £200 to see the great tenor in the flesh. He arrived, wearing his trademark scarf, ate his meal and then left. Not a note was sung that night. When he performed at a concert in Hyde Park in October 1991, I stood with guests on the roof of the North Block to hear it. The singing was magnificent, but the rain absolutely bucketed down. Even Princess Diana in the audience got completely drenched that night.

Jimmy Tarbuck and Kenny Lynch were a favourite act. In those days they usually received £10,000 for an hour's comedy and a few songs. One of Kenny's singles was 'Half the Day's Gone and We Haven't Earned a Penny', which certainly wasn't true when they worked at Grosvenor House. The audiences remembered him for his big UK hit of 1962 'Up on the Roof', but I don't think he ever had the credit he deserved as a singer. It was a joy to have them, as they were always laughing and joking. They both liked a drink, Kenny particularly. Off the balcony encircling the Great Room there was a secret room for performers to use as a dressing room or have a meal. It was called the Green Room and was behind a hidden panel, so that it was not obvious to anyone walking by. While a show was going on we would often have our meal in the Green Room.

Events taking place each week were so varied, and could be regular dates, such as the Performing Rights Society Lunch for 1,200 writers and singers which was held every year, to one-off events like the new ownership launch of Channel 4 in 1994, when the franchise changed. Eight different cooking stations were set up in the Great Room and the food was cooked by chefs in front of the guests. It was organised by a man called Alan Zafer, who ran one of the most innovative production companies and was responsible for such events as the Sony Awards at Grosvenor House. I had always assumed that the Sony Awards were organised by Sony, but Alan Zafer was the creative director behind it.

For a Forex function a televised link was arranged so that the event could be broadcast directly from Grosvenor House to all the hotels on Park Lane where other similar parties were taking place. Forex used to put on a dinner dance for 1,400 people, organised by David Black. It was an incredible occasion as practically every single guest was fabulously rich, because they were all financial traders. They would book apartments and suites so that they could stay overnight, then they would enjoy a champagne reception, followed by the dinner and cabaret, before dancing to a band. The Miss United Kingdom beauty contest, mounted by Miss World supremo Eric Morley, was often held in the Great Room too. I remember the time when we had to make the room look like a railway station for the event. The Miss Great Britain contest has also been held at Grosvenor House.

Every New Year's Eve there would be a dinner for the Teenage Cancer Trust and we were not told the final number of guests expected until they actually arrived, because people used to book between Christmas and New Year. There was a booking station in the middle of the dance floor on the night, so if we had laid up tables for 800 people and heard the bookings suddenly go past 800, then we quickly laid up for 900. If they reached 900, then another 100 places would be laid. Until they sat down for dinner, we never really knew the final numbers.

One day a call came unexpectedly from the BBC producers of the popular television programme *Gardeners' World*.

'We want to do a programme of sound bites at a large function.'

'Fine,' said Andrew Coy, the Banqueting Director.

'Our plan is to walk in and record the whole event, including all that goes on behind the scenes, and it should make an entertaining programme.'

'Brilliant. If you come and see us on the Friday before the Antiques Fair, I'll show you around and you can record a dinner.'

The BBC were delighted with this and arrived to film as planned. On the previous evening, Thursday, there had been an Action on Addiction ball, which Andrew had designed with a circus theme. Where guests went to get a drink there were hoop-la stalls, coconut shies, and fairground games. At the dinner itself there was entertainment from trapeze artists, stilt-walkers, jugglers, clowns and so on. It was a very complicated occasion to coordinate, with so much going on at once, in addition to serving the food. Although it went smoothly, there was endless potential for it all to go wrong, with a lot of shouting and swearing behind the scenes to ensure that the timings were kept to. The function that the BBC filmed on the Friday, however, was the Association of Criminal Lawyers Dinner with a thousand diners. They all had pre-dinner drinks quietly before going down into the Great Room for the meal. This was followed by two speakers from the Queen's Counsel, and then they all went home again.

The film crew arrived and recorded the laying up of tables, the staff briefing, followed by the dinner moving swiftly over the next two hours. They filmed the toastmaster, the speakers, the whole proceedings in great detail, and at the end of it all the producer said, 'Wow! Everything just runs like clockwork. I can't believe how you can feed a thousand people so effortlessly.'

'There are degrees of difficulty,' replied Andrew, 'and this was an easy one.'

On the following Monday morning she telephoned him to say that the BBC had decided that they were not going to proceed any further with the Grosvenor House programme.

'Why?' asked Andrew, rather baffled after her earlier enthusiasm.

'We have every admiration for the way that you organised it all,' she told him, 'but there's no drama. It was all too slick.'

'You should have come the night before!' said Andrew. But it was too late. The clock could not be turned back.

Occasionally a function would have a very quick turnaround for staff. A St George's Day luncheon for 1,500 people, where the Baron of Roast Beef was paraded before the guests before being carved at the top table, was once followed by a Xerox Group dinner for two thousand. At a given time, tables had to be taken away and lunch guests were left standing, still drinking their wine, while the room was prepared for the dinner guests. Otherwise the room would just not have been ready in time.

A man from Xerox Group had come down to the Great Room at around 3 p.m. to see how the setting up of the evening dinner tables was going, and was stunned to see the St George's Day lunch party still merrily celebrating and listening to speeches. Obviously he had not worked in hospitality himself, and just knew that he had a dinner in three and a half hours and panicked that the room would not be set up in time. At 4 p.m. he returned, and the lunch was just finishing. At 5 p.m. he was back and, although staff were clearing up, a few St George's Day guests were still standing around with drinks. I thought he was going to have a heart attack. At 6 p.m. he stood watching ashen-faced as the dinner tables were laid up with the necessary cutlery, crockery and glasses, while the Banqueting Director bawled orders to the staff. At 6.29 p.m. the room was ready for the Xerox guests and they came in for their pre-dinner drinks as planned. This was Grosvenor House banqueting at its best, and the sheer logistics of turning a room round in this way from one function to another was a sight to behold.

The Xerox Group used to have very tight schedules too. They would give us dates for maybe eight separate dinners, back to back, and booked around 250 rooms as well. Sometimes their representatives would end their stay and be taken to Heathrow airport, just as the next lot of Xerox Group representatives were flying in, so there was a very quick turnaround to get all the rooms ready. In theory there was only an hour's transfer, but we used to give Housekeeping up to three hours, by waylaying the new arrivals with a drinks reception and entertainment in the ballroom. They were exhausted from their flights, but we needed to keep them from their rooms for as long as possible.

Once they booked an end of conference dinner at Grosvenor House about two years in advance. This date was pencilled in the diary, but there was no other paperwork about the dinner. Unbeknown to our Banqueting Director, a woman from Xerox rang in every few months to check that the booking was still valid. A receptionist simply confirmed that it was, made no record of the call, and left it at that. As the date approached and we had no further paperwork, it was assumed that the dinner was no longer going ahead, and the Banqueting Director rubbed it out of the diary.

The next time the Xerox lady rang to make her regular check, she was horrified that the booking no longer existed. The Banqueting Director was summoned to her office and faced an inquisition from ten people.

'And how many letters have you written to us?' he asked calmly.

'Well, just the initial one.'

'I see. And how many letters have we written to you?'

'Just the original acknowledgement.'

'Would you care to show it to me?'

Just as Grosvenor House had no paperwork, it turned out that Xerox hadn't got a file either.

'There are two ways of playing this,' said our Banqueting Director, keeping his cool. 'I can sit here all day and take your abuse. You're absolutely right, and I apologise for the mistake, but it does not get you a date for the dinner.' In the end we booked the dinner for them at another hotel and Grosvenor House paid half the bill.

During the 1992 General Election campaign, Granada Television built an amphitheatre in the Great Room and invited the three party leaders to attend in front of the same audience. John Major, the then Prime Minister, Neil Kinnock and Paddy Ashdown had to be shown in and out of the hotel through separate doors so that they did not meet each other. Each took his turn individually and was asked identical questions for forty minutes, so that the audience could judge which of the three they felt was best. They were then asked how they would vote in the General Election, based on what they had heard that afternoon. Just before the event, the Labour Party had created a political storm by raising the issue of a five-year-old girl who had waited over twelve months for a simple operation to correct glue ear. It became known as the 'War of Jennifer's Ear', and Labour leader Neil Kinnock declared, 'If you want to vote Conservative, don't fall ill.' It became highly contentious and resulted in around eight hundred pressmen outside the hotel all trying to get a story. The PM, John Major, went on to win that election, however, notoriously campaigning from his soapbox.

Political occasions could often be fraught. For fifty-five years the Conservative Party held their Winter Ball at Grosvenor House on the sixth Monday of the year. The ball raised funds that enabled marginal constituencies to fight at the next general election. One year it was organised by Sandra Howard, wife of the then Tory leader. She engaged the services of top chef Anton Mosimann to provide his trademark bread-and-butter pudding. Our chefs cooked the starter and main course for the 1,300 guests, and an Anton Mosimann employee delivered two very tiny trays of pudding.

'Hang on!' said our Banqueting Director, 'You haven't delivered enough.'

'That is the correct amount,' came the response. 'Mr Mosimann's portion size is like this,' and he indicated an amount that was barely the size of his index finger.

When it was time to serve the third course, there was great anticipation in the Great Room as the much-vaunted bread-and-butter pudding was brought in. Then guests looked at their plates in disbelief.

'Excuse me, have I got the right amount?'

'Yes, that's Mr Mosimann's portion size.'

Edward Heath, Margaret Thatcher and John Major all gave speeches at the Winter Balls during my time at the hotel, and the formidable committee of ministers' wives used to have an inventive theme each time. One year the Great Room was filled with stressed willow, imaginatively lit with uplighters. The chairwoman of the day would lean on her own tradesmen and suppliers that she used privately to provide fantastic prizes for the auction and raffle.

Because there were so many politicians present, security was extremely tight. An airport-style gate was set up in the crush foyer for every guest to pass through. Police sniffer dogs would search everywhere beforehand and, once they had completed their job, the handler would always throw something down for them at the end. It turned out to be a piece of Semtex plastic explosive, as a reward for the dogs so that they actually found something. Fortunately it had no detonator.

A regular guest at the Winter Ball was Bob Payton, founder of the Chicago Rib Shack, London's famous barbeque restaurant, and the man who also introduced the deep-dish pizza to Britain. He supported the London Broncos, an American football team in England, and was instrumental in bringing the Captain's Club to Grosvenor House, which was an organisation for managers and executives. Bob Payton was one of those guests that stood out to us at any function because he would always ask to be served a different menu to everyone else. At every meal he wanted a simple dish of chicken, a bowl of grapefruit segments, and a glass of Coca-Cola. He once organised a London Broncos dinner, for which the main course was roast ox, and insisted that the Banqueting Manager wore a Chicago Rib Shack baseball cap, with his black tail suit, throughout the proceedings.

'I'm not doing that!' was the inevitable reaction.

'I am the client,' Bob Payton insisted, 'and you will wear your tails and my baseball cap.'

And so he did. Sadly, Bob Payton was killed in a car crash in 1994, shortly after his fiftieth birthday.

Organisers of functions continually had to come up with new ideas. For the Chief Executives Officers (CEO) Club of America, we once had to turn the Great Room into a farm, with real live animals. There were pens of sheep, cows, pigs and chickens. The CEO chairman always wanted to outdo his predecessor by having an even more impressive theme. I was once flown to Cannes for three days to see for myself how a CEO event was organised, so that the following year in London we would be able to top it. Three or four hundred CEOs then came to Grosvenor House with their wives the next year, when we turned the Great Room into a circus venue, with clowns and men on stilts, coconut shies, jugglers and so on. At the end of it all the CEOs always marked their events by filling out a satisfaction questionnaire, and Grosvenor House achieved eight out of ten, which was one of the highest out of all the venues that they used.

I was once flown to America to prepare for another CEO function called the Lawyers' Bar, which they planned to hold in London. But first I had to give the organiser, Mr Haynes, a site inspection at Grosvenor House. They were spending £750,000 on this one event, so he was a tough man and wanted to look around everywhere. When he saw an empty whisky bottle outside a fire escape, he was not happy. I was tempted to say that perhaps Princess Margaret had left it, but decided against it! He then said that the service at breakfast was terrible, and pointed out all kinds of faults. He even said that our lifts were too slow, as he did not want to have to wait more than thirty seconds. So I really had to convince him that Grosvenor House could come up to scratch for his event and promised that we would deliver. I later told him that we had speeded up the lifts to suit his requirements, although this was actually found to be impractical and we changed nothing. He told me how much better the lifts were now that they were faster!

He was initially not impressed either that he was being shown around by the Deputy rather than the General Manager, but when we began chatting about our lives I gradually noticed a change of attitude. Mr Haynes revealed that he used to be a pilot in the American Air Force, so I told him that my father was in the Royal Air Force and we started to discuss military matters. As we walked through the corridors below stairs, I pointed out where I had once worked when washing up. I saw no reason not to be honest and I think Mr Haynes, like many Americans, liked the fact that I had achieved something with my life. In England we prefer the underdog.

Mr Haynes invited me to fly to Boston on my own for five days to see their event at first hand and take notes. It was like visiting the White House, because as I flew in, all I could see was a large white building. It was a magnificent venue, and I attended cocktail parties and dinners just to see for myself what was required for their London visit the following year. I learned a lot about working with clients, being professional at all times, the importance of punctuality, and always being prepared to answer any question thrown at you. It brought me into a different dimension as a manager. My visit coincided with a running race for CEO members, for which I was entered as an outsider. I came second in the race out of 200 runners and won an engraved silver tray, and was awarded another for being the first non-member past the winning post.

When they finally came to London a year later, I was treated like royalty. Wendy and I were taken out to dinner at an expensive restaurant and to the theatre to see the musical *Miss Saigon*. When their own dinner finally came to be held in the Great Room, after a year of planning, we had a Baron of Roast Beef carried in while a military band of guardsman marched behind, and gave them what they perceived to be a typically British event. There were 900 people present and they absolutely loved it, giving a standing ovation.

I became experienced at entertaining important corporate clients in a bid to gain their custom and outdo rival hotels. These companies were bringing in five to ten million pounds' worth of business to London, so I used to find out what kind of entertainment they had previously experienced in other parts of the world and told them that Grosvenor House could top it. Having the Great Room was a unique asset to us, as no other hotel could accommodate such huge numbers at a single function. I would take potential clients to society events, such as Lady's Day at Royal Ascot, with each client being given £50 with our compliments to place a bet. They were called 'the incentive market', where representatives or agents from top American companies would be entertained in the hope of attracting their custom. The incentive group was once given a private box for the Grand Prix motor racing at Silverstone with Sir Jackie Stewart. We really wanted to impress them and gain their business, so we laid on a magnificent five-star picnic-style buffet, accompanied by a three-piece jazz band.

The Great Room happened to be empty that same evening, which was very rare, so I brought the clients back to the hotel for dinner. After a champagne reception outside in the middle of Park Lane, where a waiter in tails held up the traffic so that they could cross the road, I led them back into the Great Room to eat.

I had a very long single table set up on a platform for twenty diners, made the lighting very dim, filled the room completely with dry ice so that it looked as if the table was floating, and had a violinist play while we ate. At the end of the meal I got up and made a speech, thanked all the potential clients for coming, and finished by saying that we had all had such a lovely day together at the Grand Prix that I wanted us to have just one last bit of fun together. 'Tonight,' I said, 'we're going to bring racing to you.' I waved my hand and at that second the lights came on and a black curtain was raised. Behind it was a full-size dodgem car track from a fairground. Their faces were an absolute picture! Nobody could believe it. They all rushed into the cars like excited children and were soon driving around banging into each other. Other hotels might offer a singer, but I was determined that Grosvenor House was going to make an impact. The company representatives never stopped talking about that night. The dodgems had cost £10,000 to book, but it was worth it in the long run, as no other hotel could top that.

I gave many potential clients tours of the kitchens too, which always fascinated them. They saw the pastry section, the fish and meat preparation, even the chef's office. They loved seeing the boiler house, containing thirty enormous boilers each thirty feet long, like the engine room of the *Titanic*. I showed them the best apartments and some of the top hotel rooms too. I made sure that the route I took was absolutely spotless, without so much as a single tray left in the corridors. These show rounds did much to attract new business.

'I remember working here as a teenager, I used to run down that corridor and nick a pastry,' I would tell them. 'Nobody could catch me, and I'd eat it behind the lockers.' They all laughed and loved it, because it showed a human side to the hotel. But I was just being honest.

Many staff helped me in my role as Deputy, such as Andrew Coy the Director of Banqueting. Andrew had previously worked at the Café Royal, the Savoy and the Ritz in charge of food and beverage, and knew the job inside out. He was brought in to sort out the banqueting side of Grosvenor House because he was very high-profile and Lord Forte and Rocco knew that there was room for improvement in this area. Guests were then paying £80 a head for a meal, plus drinks, their accommodation, and car parking (then £37 a night), and you might have 1,500 guests in a single night at a function, so it was essential that everything was five-star standard.

Previously the job had been had been that of 'Banqueting Manager', but because of Andrew's expertise he was given the title 'Director of Banqueting'. He was a workaholic and really moved the business forward, increasing revenue every year by ten per cent. Andrew was not afraid to speak his mind, so did not always see eye to eye with Tony Murkett, but he got things done. In a five-star hotel in Park Lane you have to be tough to achieve a professional result. Like me, Andrew paid attention to detail, which can make all the difference between the success or failure of an event, and he was considered to be the best Banqueting Manager in Europe. That is why many years later I hired him as General Manager of my own hotel.

Some of Andrew's experiences in hotels have been extraordinary. It was while working at the five-star Savoy Hotel in the Strand that on Valentine's Day in 1987 he had to cater for the wedding of Mark Thatcher, son of the then Prime Minister. The wedding was being organised by Britain's best-known toastmaster, Ivor Spencer, who had been the Savoy's resident toast-master for some twenty years before going solo. He telephoned Andrew and told him that a marriage ceremony was taking place in the Savoy Chapel, which would be followed by a reception at the hotel, just a short distance away. But he refused to say whose wedding it was.

Andrew began planning the lunchtime reception in the hotel dining room, and that same day already had a Bar Mitzvah lunch party booked into the River Room. A couple had previously been to see him to discuss the ceremony, looking as if they were the mother and grandfather of the Bar Mitzvah boy. Later the apparent grandfather telephoned and revealed that he was in fact the father.

'You probably noticed how ill I am,' he said. 'In fact, I am going to die very soon. So I won't be able to make my son's Bar Mitzvah.'

'Oh, of course you will!' replied Andrew encouragingly.

'No, I won't. I am going to die, and I want you to promise me that when I'm gone, and my wife calls you to cancel the Bar Mitzvah, that you won't cancel it. Keep it booked in, because she will change her mind.'

'I'm sure it won't happen, but I promise you that I will keep the booking in the diary for that Saturday.'

'And I would like you to stay by my wife throughout and look after her.'

'I shall never leave her side.'

'Thank you. Now I can die a happy man.'

Two months later Andrew received a letter from the wife, saying that her husband had died and that she wanted to cancel the booking. He wrote back saying that he would in fact keep the booking open, just in case she changed her mind.

Ivor Spencer continued to remain mysterious about the identity of the wedding party for that same day, other than that 250 guests would be attending. Eventually the bride and groom were brought to the Savoy to discuss arrangements, but Andrew did not recognise Mark Thatcher and his American bride-to-be, so was still none the wiser.

'The Prime Minister will of course be present,' Ivor Spencer announced casually during the course of the discussions.

'You're very lucky to have the Prime Minister coming,' Andrew commented.

'She *is* my mother,' said Mark Thatcher.

Shortly afterwards, Andrew received a telephone call from 10 Downing Street, summoning him to a meeting with Margaret Thatcher to discuss the reception arrangements.

'Now, on this special day, I want you to remember that I am the groom's mother,' she said gently, as they sat alone in her Downing Street sitting room.

'Yes, Prime Minister.'

She immediately slapped him on the leg. 'I just told you, don't call me Prime Minister. I'm the groom's mother!'

'Yes, Mrs Thatcher.'

Each time he inadvertently called her Prime Minister, he was swiftly admonished.

'Don't call me Prime Minister! I'm the groom's mother!'

Later he was invited to a party at 10 Downing Street, given by the Conservative Association.

'This is the man who is running my son's wedding reception,' Margaret Thatcher kept telling people proudly.

'Yes, Mrs Thatcher,' Andrew would agree.

One of her aide's took him to one side and warned, 'Don't call her Mrs Thatcher. Call her Prime Minister.'

'Oh no,' said Andrew, 'to me she is always Mrs Thatcher.'

Just before the wedding day, the Bar Mitzvah boy's mother called, saying that she wanted the lunch to take place after all.

'You did say to me that you would keep the booking.'

'That's no problem,' Andrew lied, having forgotten by then that one of her late husband's stipulations was that he remained by his wife's side throughout, to look after her and not leave her for a moment.

To cap it all, on the day itself, news came that Mark Thatcher's life had been threatened. The Savoy was closed completely, a dozen Special Branch policemen with Sten guns suddenly appeared in the hotel kitchen, and snipers climbed up on to the roof. Roads were closed and even the milk could not be delivered because of road blocks. But the events went on as planned, with the wedding reception downstairs and the Bar Mitzvah party upstairs, and Andrew ran continually back and forwards between the two, so that he seemed to be at both events at the same time. Now that's what you call dedication to duty. And when both functions were over, he then had to put on a Valentine's Ball for 650 people in aid of the Red Cross that same evening. All in a day's work, of course.

At the wedding, while the guests filed in to their tables, Mark Thatcher said they had decided that Grace would not be said before the meal, so the starter could be served straight away. As Andrew lined up his staff, Margaret Thatcher passed by and said out of the corner of her mouth, 'Mr Coy, the Bishop of London will say Grace.'

'Yes, Mrs Thatcher.'

The staff stood and waited for the Bishop to rise.

'There's no Grace,' hissed Ivor Spencer.

'There is now!' said Andrew.

Andrew Coy started work at 8 a.m. each day. He had metal tips on the soles of his shoes, and I could always tell when he had arrived by the sound he made walking along the stone floor. He would be in his black tails; I would be in my navy-blue suit.

'Good morning, Mr Kirby.'

'Good morning, Mr Coy.'

'Can't stop, Mr Kirby, I have a meeting.'

He hated being late for anything and always had his watch set ten minutes ahead of everyone else's. If he had a meeting at 9 a.m., he knew then that he would never be late. Behind the scenes we used to tease him, of course, by asking him what the time was! There was always a healthy banter between us.

'Mr Kirby knows sod all about food and beverage,' he used to tell people, 'but he knows everything about bedrooms.'

In any successful hotel, you always have to be ahead of the game. Every year I had an annual review and Tony Murkett agreed with Andrew that my main area of weakness was food and beverage. So I was sent to Canada for two weeks to see how successful hotels there were operating, and to look particularly at where our service and food could be improved. I realised then that we had to keep coming up with new ideas to survive, and to pay particular attention to health and hygiene.

Trusthouse Forte had their own laboratory, where staff could discover the horrors that can occur without due care. It was almost like a museum, as they would show you a loaf of bread with a mouse in the centre, a bottle of wine with a cockroach at the bottom of it, deadly spiders found in a crate of bananas, all items that had been delivered to hotels.

One food item in particular has caused more problems than any other in my career: eggs. The Conservative MP Edwina Currie invoked nationwide fury in 1988 when as Junior Health Minister she declared that most British egg production was infected with salmonella. It sparked outrage and the resulting controversy led to her resignation. But I personally think Edwina Currie was right. I have known of numerous cases in hotels where raw or undercooked eggs have caused illness. Just by handling an egg shell, members of the kitchen staff could unwittingly have salmonella on their fingers, which might then contaminate other dishes. 'Always wash your hands after touching an egg' became a standard phrase in hotel kitchens. Fortunately chickens are now kept in much better conditions and the problem has reduced.

Of all the events that I organised at Grosvenor House, one particularly stands out, as twenty guests suffered from severe food poisoning afterwards. A raw egg was found to be the cause and Grosvenor House was fined £25,000 as a result. And the event? It was the Undertakers' Ball. They almost became their own clients.

9

A Three-ring Circus

Marriage is a three-ring circus: engagement ring, wedding ring, and suffering.
Anonymous

I hate weddings!

Over the years I have organised more than 19,700 weddings in hotels and have seen it all. Tears, tantrums, drunkenness, feuding families, and that is just at the planning stage. On the big day itself there can be collapsing cakes, bolting horses, a fainting best man, quarrelsome in-laws, belligerent photographers, the bride tripping over her long dress and ending up flat on her face . . . you name it.

The largest that I was involved with was a half-million-pound wedding for an Arab prince in January 1994. The Great Room at Grosvenor House was transformed into a Spanish castle made from imitation stone, with the staircase end of the room raised so that guests at the back would be able to see the cabaret; five hundred bottles of Dom Perignon champagne were drunk, and the menu included blinis and beluga caviar. Michelin chef Michel Roux from Le Gavroche Restaurant designed the menu, and veal for the main course was brought over from France. Michel Roux and four of his own chefs cooked for the top table of ten guests, and twenty Grosvenor House chefs cooked for the other 640 guests.

One of the most lavish and expensive weddings that I ever arranged at Park Lane was that of a wealthy Saudi Arabian sheik. The Great Room was made to look like a stately home with £100,000 spent setting up a magnificent staircase as a centrepiece. The flowers cost £40,000, and this was in the mid 1980s, and no expense was spared on the entertainment provided by singers and dancers. Inevitably there was the finest caviar, the best champagne, and £50,000 was spent on drinks alone. Six hundred guests

149

were in attendance and 150 bedrooms were booked for those that needed to stay. Altogether the bill came to in excess of £1 million, at a time when the average wedding cost £1,200.

The smallest wedding that I have organised was for just six people. The civil ceremony was held in the hotel and was undertaken by two registrars. Apart from the bride and groom, there were two witnesses and two other guests. The six had dinner afterwards, and the bill for the whole event was just £400 pounds.

Probably the most original wedding reception in the Great Room was when the immaculately uniformed Head Waiter, complete with white gloves, suddenly made an announcement at the end of the meal. He was Australian and said that he was heading back to his homeland. As it was his last day, he declared that he wanted to sing for the guests before he went. While he was speaking, the manager came in and began remonstrating with him. Bewildered guests looked on as the two began to argue, and it was not long before the chef appeared and joined in the fray. Suddenly all three burst into song and began singing opera with the rest of the staff. They were all professional opera singers posing as waiters for the day, and had been booked to surprise and entertain the wedding guests. That was a very classy act.

The strangest wedding of all was the one that we did without the groom. Three days before this particular wedding, the couple had a major row and split up. As everything was paid for and organised, the florist, the cake and the reception, the bride was determined to go ahead with her big day and enjoy herself. So she arrived in the bridal car, wearing her wedding dress and veil, carrying a bouquet, and the reception went ahead exactly as planned, but with only her side of the family and friends present. All that was missing was the groom and his family. They had a wonderful time. Afterwards, the bride and a girlfriend shared the honeymoon suite. So nothing went to waste. Talk about a day to remember.

Few weddings in hotels are without their problems. I've known brides forget their dresses, grooms forget their cufflinks, and even both forget their passports. Chauffeur-driven cars have been sent back to their homes on the morning of the wedding to collect items, especially passports – otherwise the couple would not have reached their honeymoon destination. One couple staying at Grosvenor House were so large that they broke the bed on their honeymoon night. They were discovered drunk and giggling on the mattress, which had collapsed between the struts.

At one wedding the toastmaster lost the best man. He could not be found anywhere, so I searched around and eventually discovered him in tears in the gentlemen's toilet. He had been overcome with nerves and was too frightened to make the speech. Although he had a written speech in his hand, he claimed he had no idea what to say. I had been about to go off duty and was expected at a restaurant, but the man was so confused that I took him down to another bar, away from the wedding guests, and gave him a stiff talking-to in the hope that he would pull himself together. He still refused to go and make the speech. My patience was wearing thin by this time, as I was now late, so in the end I gave him a double brandy for courage. He walked back into the wedding reception and I heard him deliver a pretty good speech. What he did not realise was that I had given him a fifty-year-old brandy, a double at that time cost £64, and I put it straight on to his bill. I was annoyed that he had ruined my evening, but at least it helped him make the speech.

The room fell silent when one best man rose to give his speech. It was a warm summer's day and he was clearly becoming hot under the collar. Halfway through the speech, he fainted and hit the table with a gigantic crash. He did not hurt himself, and I took him outside for some fresh air and an expensive glass of brandy to make him feel better. I dusted him down, straightened his tie, and as he returned to the reception, I asked, 'Shall I charge the brandy to your account or the wedding account, Sir?'

'Oh, mine.'

'No problem, Sir.'

Another £64 glass of brandy sold.

During another wedding, I was called to an incident by a member of staff. It was a trendy wedding for a young couple, who arrived in American stretch limousines. The best man and bridegroom were wearing top hat and tails, gold cravats, and pretentiously carried silver-topped walking canes. They may have looked the part, but as soon as they opened their mouths it was clear that they were anything but aristocrats, and had no idea about civilised behaviour in public. When I went to see what was wrong, I found four young guys in the toilet together. They had taken a picture off the wall and were sniffing cocaine powder off the glass.

'And what are you guys up to?'

'What's it got to do with you, mate?'

'I'm the General Manager. Pack that up now and get out of the toilets, or I will call the police and have you thrown off the premises.'

They ran from the toilets like scalded cats, back to the wedding reception. Every time they saw me, they looked very wary, worried as to what I might do. It gave me great satisfaction. I was not prepared to have drug-taking blatantly going on in a public place.

We now have a saying in the hotel trade about some weddings, which we call 'new money', where the couple or their parents may have the cash for a lavish function, but have absolutely no idea about how to behave. So many times I have seen couples trying to have sex in all manner of places once they had consumed alcohol: in fire exits, refuse areas, maids' cupboards, closed restaurants, and not just couples either, but sometimes threesomes and foursomes. We used to keep personal items such as razors and shaving foam at reception for guests but, at this type of wedding, guests were always coming to the desk and asking for condoms. We began supplying them, but at double the price.

The new money weddings began having trendy cakes, too, such as croquembouche (a high cone of profiteroles bound with caramel), which is very difficult to cut. The bride and groom would insist on cutting them like a traditional wedding cake, often with disastrous results. Worse still are the pyramids of fairy cakes, each one looking as if it was made by 'Mr Kipling' with a cherry in the middle – also impossible to cut. Others had tacky cakes, maybe with a naked man and woman wrapped around each other in icing. Sometimes, even a traditional iced fruit cake could spell disaster, when a couple tried to cut through a cake as solid as a slab of concrete and the top tier inevitably hit the floor.

Weddings can be such wonderful events, but organisation is the key to success. For my part, it all begins with a telephone call or email from one of the happy couple. Once I know the date of the wedding, if the hotel function room is available and can accommodate, then I arrange a preliminary meeting to discuss requirements.

You never know who is going to turn up; they are just a name on a piece of paper until that point. The worst is if a 60-year-old man arrives with a 30-year-old woman. They *might* be the bride and groom, but they *could* be father and daughter, so it is important to tread carefully. I once asked a pregnant woman when her baby was due, only to discover that she was not pregnant at all. She just had a fat tummy. Sometimes it will be only the bride and groom, but often the bride's mother will be there to put her oar in too. That is always a recipe for disaster. Halfway through the discussions there is bound to be an argument.

'Oh, we can't have that! That won't look right at all.'

'Well, I want it like that. It's *my* day.'

'And I hope Susan isn't coming.'

'Of course she is. I've sent her an invitation now.'

'You'll just have to un-invite her.'

'I can't do that!'

'Don't sit her near me then, I don't even want her on the same side of the room.'

This happens eight times out of ten. At this point, I tend to ask if they would like some coffee or tea, so that I can escape for a few minutes. I have hardly known a single wedding when there hasn't been a family feud of some kind, which nearly always comes out in our interview. I feel like a psychiatrist sometimes, offering counselling and mediation. It is whilst discussing the table plan that the bad blood really begins to show. 'We can't sit Bill next to Mary, otherwise there'll be a row. And the Simpson family will have to be separated. If they're all at one table, things will really kick off.'

Invariably either the bride's or the groom's parents will have divorced and remarried, which brings in the awkward question as to where ex-husbands and ex-wives are going to be seated, with all the animosity that entails. If discussions get too heated, I firmly but politely ask the mother of the bride to calm down and let her daughter have a say. In my experience too, ninety-five per cent of the suggestions will be made by the women and five per cent by the men. I think men tend to agree with whatever the women want for a wedding, just to keep the peace.

So many people want to interfere when a wedding is being planned, and I will later get telephone calls from parents saying that they will pay for the honeymoon suite, but they don't want the couple to know, or that they want to provide the champagne. On most occasions it would be much better if they all liaised with each other to avoid complications and duplications.

Cost is, of course, a major issue.

'How much are you looking to spend on the reception?' I ask dubiously.

'We are on a tight budget,' is invariably the reply. Having said that, they gradually let slip that the wedding dress has cost £2,000; they have hired suits for the groom and best man (often top hat and tails, which the men hate wearing); there are bridesmaids' dresses, flowers, a chauffeured Rolls-Royce or a stretch limo (I hate those tacky cars so much and get embarrassed when they pull up outside the hotel – especially when they are pink!). The car alone will probably cost £400, just to be driven a short distance from the church to the reception. Then there is the unavoidable photographer, who is generally a nuisance, and will have cost in excess of £1,000. Finally they will announce that they are having a honeymoon in Tahiti, Barbados, Hawaii or the Bahamas. Yet, as far as the reception is concerned, they are on a tight budget and start to quibble over a penny or two on a bottle of wine.

Experience has taught me that, once a definite booking has been made, the money should always be paid in advance and this saves endless quibbling after the event. This has become common policy in hotels. At a Park Lane hotel, a wedding reception for a hundred people can easily cost more than a suburban house, so it is important to be sure of the money.

Once I know how many people are expected, then we can begin to discuss the food to be served. I will show them a choice of menu for the main meal, plus a buffet menu if they are having an evening function as well. Often they want a dance after the main wedding reception, with food and drink available for guests.

'This seems expensive – I'm not sure if I like this menu,' one of them is bound to say.

'It is not cheap, catering for so many people.' They usually haven't given any thought as to how much it actually costs to give several hundred people a three-course meal.

'Do we have to give them a drink when they sit down?'

'Well, it is polite and expected. Guests will also need to have a glass of champagne to toast you both.'

'Are you sure?'

'It is traditional.'

'For the evening buffet we have about another 120 guests arriving. How many should we cater for?' It is a question that they consistently ask, and I know full well that they don't want to pay for all the guests. 'I think we should only have food for half that amount, what do you think?'

'I'm sorry,' I always say, 'that's really not going to work as you could easily run out of food, which would be very embarrassing. If your budget is tight, then cater for seventy-five per cent of your total number of guests.'

Once they have an idea of the type of menu they require, I invite them back to sample the dishes. I will have the chef prepare two starters, two main courses, and two puddings, so that the bride and groom can actually taste the food beforehand and will know exactly what it is going to look like on the plate. There are so many weddings where dishes are chosen simply from a list on a menu, which might sound delicious by name, but the couple are then disappointed on the wedding day itself when they taste the food for the first time and find that it is not what they had expected. If they can meet with the chef, sample the food in advance and taste a few wines, then it cuts that problem out.

During the tasting, however, they will suddenly become food experts and connoisseurs of wine.

'Oh, that's not very nice! I don't like that,' they might say after sampling a very good Chablis. Then they will rave about an ordinary house white. Many women will go for a rosé, but spurn a decent Pinot Grigio in favour of Zinfadel. Vintage champagne will be pushed aside because they prefer the taste of Cava. Usually this is when couples have outstretched their budget and cannot really afford a five-star hotel reception and are trying to save money.

No matter how contemporary the wedding theme, the couple nearly always opt for a very conventional menu. Melon is probably the most popular starter of all, particularly at summer weddings. Paté is the second most popular choice, and smoked salmon third. We try to avoid soup because of the potential for spillages. Chicken is the general option for couples on a tight budget, and roast beef or lamb if they are happy to spend more. We steer them away from duck, as that is difficult to cook for a very large party because some people like it very pink and rare, while others want it well cooked. Children rarely want to eat the same as adults, and even at a wedding reception we will be asked to provide fish fingers and chips.

Traditional crumbles, such as rhubarb or apple, are a recurring option for dessert. We use circles of plastic drainpipe, cut to size, as the moulds when making a pudding such as this en masse. Crumbles will be served with a homemade ice cream and a coulis. Fruit salads are common, in an attempt to find something that the majority will eat. Profiteroles are a perennial favourite too, which we serve in the shape of two swans, back to back.

Menus at wedding receptions have really changed little over the last fifty years. Today, however, we seem to be plagued with allergies – wheat, gluten, nuts, eggs . . . In the old days we would have 500 people at a wedding reception, all eating an identical meal, with maybe two vegetarians. We never used to hear about anyone having an allergy, but today we have so many guests that cannot eat this or that. Out of an average hundred people there will now be ten vegetarians and a dozen with allergies. We need to know their name and exactly where they are seated, so that the waiter can serve the correct meal. Someone can actually die if given the wrong food. I know of a 21-year-old man with a nut allergy who died after a dinner, just because the chef had used a nut oil in the preparation of a curry. If someone has a nut allergy, chefs know not to put nuts in a dish, but now have to think about what might be in the cooking oil. I have even had a guest recently that was allergic to olive oil, whose face would swell if she ate it; so planning the menu does get tougher each year.

At Grosvenor House we used to have huge buffets looking like a display of jewels, with a whole dressed salmon, thinly carved roast meats beautifully arranged, chickens, salads, rice dishes, new potatoes, and so on, which took hours to set up. The food could be arranged on mirrored glass to add to the effect, and would be laid out on long trestle tables covered with white cloths.

We used to put crates underneath the tablecloths to raise the food up to different heights. It appeared immaculate to the guests, but fortunately they could not see how it all looked from behind. There were huge ice carvings in the shape of swans, urns cascading with fruit, or sometimes they were in the form of a large shell filled with fish. They were supplied by a specialist company and looked absolutely stunning, but we had to store them, which was no easy task because of the size of the box. They weighed a ton and it took three people to lift them into place. And they could easily be dropped or knocked whilst getting them out of the box, and then we would have to find a way of putting a swan's beak back on. We had to get the timings exactly right too, because if brought straight out from the freezer the carvings looked white and frosty, rather than clear and sparkling; if we got them out too soon, they would melt and disintegrate. The ice carvings would be displayed on a tray with a lip all around it, which we disguised with a tablecloth, and there was a drip hose into a bucket hidden underneath table to catch the water as the ice gradually melted. We used to place them at the back of the table, with a half-moon-shaped table in front, so that guests could not reach out and touch them.

I try and steer couples away from a buffet at the main reception, as that can turn into a nightmare. You have to invite the top table up first, then other tables in order, and by the time the last guests have helped themselves to food, the top table will be finished and waiting. No matter how big the buffet table, it always becomes a long-drawn-out affair because people take so long to choose what they are going to have. Also the preparation for a buffet is labour-intensive and time-consuming for the staff, and there is an unavoidable amount of wastage, with sacks full of food thrown away at the end. So I always advise them to opt for a three-course sit-down meal, which makes life easier for everyone involved.

Then they will have suggestions for the table flowers. Some of the arrangements are terrible and a real waste of money. I have seen many tacky floral decorations, including plastic roses, glass vases with battery-operated sparkling fairy lights inside, imitation ice made of rubber, and glass goldfish bowls with a single plant inside, because they feel it looks 'trendy'. I am all for progress, but sometimes the tables look atrocious.

'Aren't they beautiful!' they will say.

'Oh, they're really lovely,' I lie through my teeth and just hope that they don't realise. 'They look absolutely super.'

Sometimes the decorations will include huge helium-filled balloons, often heart-shaped at the top table, which look really tawdry. The balloons gradually burst, usually during the speeches, and I even had one wedding where a long ribbon on a balloon was set alight by a candle. I watched the flame moving up the ribbon, like a cartoon bomb, and just waited for the bang. The best weddings are usually those of the more mature couple marrying for the second time, who tend to have a much more tasteful and sophisticated celebration.

The worst is the pink wedding! They have pink tablecloths, pink napkins, pink flowers and pink bows everywhere. It looks like Barbara Cartland's boudoir. Then they arrive in pink outfits and a pink limousine . . .

Some want little bags of sweets on every table for the guests. And most want gifts for the children. They think that if they give all the children colouring books, this will keep them quiet during the meal, but it never works. Children just get bored and end up running all over the place, irritating other guests. I cannot stand children at weddings; they are a pain to everyone. They are always noisy and invariably start crying, and then scream throughout the speeches. My advice would be: do not allow kids to weddings. They should be banned. I will ask the couple beforehand how many children are coming.

'Oh, we have six. No, eight!'

'What age are they?'

'Between two and seven.'

'How nice . . .'

'Oh, and another twenty will be coming in the evening.'

I know then that the whole affair will be turned into a kindergarten, with children running everywhere and dominating the whole event. They are always bored stiff at weddings, either falling asleep by 7.30 p.m. or else becoming grizzly and fractious. They throw food around, play in the guest lifts and have tantrums if they don't get their own way. It can be horrendous. Some dress two-year-old boys in miniature suits and ties for the event, which is another recipe for disaster, as the child is bound to play up.

Sometimes Granny, a friend or the mother-in-law makes the cake and it is usually terrible. There is a fashion now for chocolate wedding cakes, which crumble as soon as they are cut. Others bring three tiers each made out of a different recipe: a sponge cake, a fruit cake and a chocolate cake. The bottom tier is always the sponge, and it never dawns on them that it won't bear the weight of a heavy fruit cake above it and inevitably the cake topples or leans like the Tower of Pisa. Some collapse altogether. Many never think about bringing the pillars to support the separate tiers, and so we have to supply them at the last minute. We put the pillars on and assemble the cake, then watch as the pillars gradually sink into the sponge.

On one occasion when a wedding party became ill after the reception, the Environmental Health Officers inevitably came and took samples of all the dishes produced in the hotel kitchens. Everything we had provided turned out to be fine. The source of the food poisoning was the one item that the wedding party had provided themselves. The Trojan horse was their homemade wedding cake. Today we keep a slice of every wedding cake for testing, just in case a similar problem arises

Cakes often feature figures of the bride and groom in icing on the top, which never look anything like the couple at all. I had a wedding recently where, halfway through the speeches, the figure of the bride fell off the cake, and I watched open-mouthed as the bridegroom slowly sank deeper and deeper into the icing. When he was up to his tummy I had to leave the room and kill myself with laughter, pretending I had a bad cough.

Occasionally you have a very trendy, contemporary-style wedding, but the grandmother has made the cake. It looks so old-fashioned and out of place, but nobody dare say anything as they cut through inches of royal icing. Then they never know how to cut the cake.

'Shall we cut the bottom tier . . . no, maybe the top. Oh, I'm not sure. What do you think, Neil?'

Few people want to eat wedding cake anyway after a three-course meal. We throw so much away. I suggest that after the cutting of the cake ceremony, they should let the chef cut up the bottom tier and put it on the evening buffet, and keep the top tier for family and friends.

Next, the subject of bedrooms will come up.

'Is the honeymoon suite included in the price of the wedding?'

'No, I'm sorry, it's not.'

'OK. May we see the room?'

'That's no problem.'

The bride and groom to be are always very concerned about the bedroom, even though they will be using it only for one night. Some don't like the wallpaper, the curtains, or even the layout of the room. I generally think to myself, they're only in there for about ten hours or less, what does it matter? It is just not practical to make major changes. So then I will show them another room decorated in a different colour scheme. Some couples behave in such a prima donna way, when most of them have been living together for years anyway. Lots of them ask for a four-poster bed, which I can understand if they want a romantic time, but why do they want to change the wallpaper? I couldn't even afford a honeymoon suite when we got married.

Once these details have been sorted, I will then walk the couple through the route that they will take on the day and go through the timings from the moment they arrive. Many like to walk down a red carpet and then stand to greet their guests one at a time. I show them where the coats will be taken, the champagne served, and where the photographs can be taken.

Photographers can ruin a wedding. Sometimes I have to be quite tough with them, as they think they rule the roost. All they care about is taking as many pictures as possible, which of course is their job, but they have no regard for the timings of the meal, the fact that we have to get the guests seated, that the chef has food sitting in the kitchen, and the staff are waiting to serve.

'What about the bread rolls? When shall we put them in the oven so that we can serve them hot?'

'Sorry, they're running fifteen minutes late.' That is guaranteed to upset the chef.

'We've got a quick turnaround – there's a dinner for 125 tonight. Why the delay?'

'Because the photographer is a selfish bastard, that's why.'

Then when the pictures are all taken and the guests can finally sit down to a meal that is past its best, the photographer will probably rub salt in the wound by asking for something to eat.

'Chef, can I have a sandwich for the photo man?'

'Tell him to f*** off, I'm busy! Tell him there's a wedding party to feed.'

Chefs usually make them wait at least half an hour as a way of getting their own back. They know that this really irritates the photographers.

There are some professional photographers who will agree to meet up beforehand, visit the venue and run through the schedule, but they are few and far between. I usually allow photographers one hour, then everyone is called into the dining room regardless. Often they object, but it is the only way to keep to the schedule. I've had many a run-in with photographers.

Bridesmaids and the best man are regularly an obstruction too, mainly because they have no idea what they are actually meant to do. I always meet with the best man and tell him the time that everyone has to be seated for the meal.

'Do you want to call the guests in?'

'Oh no, I can't do that,' he'll say, 'I'd be far too nervous.'

I end up having to do some of the best man's duties for him.

The next problem will be the speeches after the meal. The speakers at any wedding breakfast seem to be so nervous when they first arrive. One day someone is going to have a heart attack before making a speech, their blood pressure must be so high. I always say to the bride and groom when I first meet them: do the speeches before the meal, then all the speakers can relax afterwards and enjoy the meal. But only a few do.

Some of them take themselves off beforehand to gather their thoughts, and many a time I have had to go looking for the groom, best man or father of the bride. When I tell them that they have ten minutes before the speeches start, they look at me as if they really hate me. Often they say, 'Just give me five minutes, please.' Then they wander off. Some end up in the bar; others smoke themselves silly with cigarettes.

I had one wedding where the groom was so nervous that he was literally shaking with fear. After about three minutes his mother had to step in and finish the speech for him. Afterwards he went up to the honeymoon suite and was immediately sick. He had to have a shower before he could rejoin the wedding party. What a state to get yourself into over a speech! He had been living with his 'bride' for seven years anyway, and they had a child, so it was a pathetic reaction.

'You did really well,' I lied to him afterwards.

Sometimes the best man will make an embarrassing and completely inappropriate speech, more suited to a stag night than the wedding reception. If he is one of the bride's ex-boyfriends, then a bit of jealousy creeps in and he can make her feel uneasy. Or if a friend of the groom's, he can begin to relate stories of past conquests or sexual misdemeanours that have everyone looking uncomfortable.

I had another wedding where the bride and groom said that they were just going for a quick cigarette, five minutes before the speeches. Ten minutes later, there was no sign of them. I searched the lounges and bars and couldn't find them anywhere. How could we have the speeches and toasts without the bride and groom? The only place I hadn't looked was the honeymoon suite. I went up to the floor with my master key and was just about to knock on the door, when I heard the two of them inside making love. She was howling like a bitch on heat. So I went back downstairs to reception, and telephoned their room.

'Have you finished your cigarettes?'

'Oh yes, Neil, just coming.'

No, I thought to myself, you already have!

Since the smoking ban, we now have to have a comfort break for the guests before the speeches so that people can go outside for a cigarette. I announce that the speeches will be in five minutes, but there are always some that cannot get back in time. Then they just have to pop into the toilet, delaying the speeches even further. Sometimes we even have to delay serving the food because three people on a table will be outside having a cigarette and we can't serve just half a table. I hate weddings!

During the meal there are always mobile phones going off. Some people just have no respect today and will have their telephone conversation regardless, even if it is during a speech. You would think that they might have the common sense to turn them off. If a child starts screaming during a speech, nobody seems to take them out either, even if they are drowning out the speaker. And some speeches are just far too long, often with enough pages to fill a book. Occasionally you get a father-in-law who has done a little public speaking and will drone on and on with the most boring of speeches, and often telling totally irrelevant stories. I always say to them: keep it short and sweet. As my hero Winston Churchill used to say: the mind cannot absorb more than the backside can endure.

Then there is the issue of the guest book. The bride often wants all the guests to sign a book as a lasting record of the day, but it is always a pain. No one wants to be the first to sign. Usually I have to beg someone to be first, then I ask them to pass it around the table. It is a simple enough instruction, but no, I have to track it down later and make sure myself that everyone has signed. Which is a chore that I can do without in the middle of a wedding reception. Men never want to write in it and just hand the book over to their wife or girlfriend. I can never help noticing either that the handwriting and spelling of most of the young people attending is atrocious these days. Only half the guests ever sign the book. I've had a couple of weddings where children have got hold of it and used it as a drawing book to scribble in. I've had to furtively tear pages out while nobody is looking.

Once the reception is over, often running twenty minutes late because the photographer took far too long, there is the problem of getting everybody out of the dining room. At Grosvenor House we might have had 900 to 1,000 for a wedding breakfast, and then have to quickly turn the room around for a different function with another 1,500 guests.

'Please take all your belongings with you and make your way to the function room downstairs, many thanks.'

You would think that they were all deaf from the response such an announcement provokes. Jackets, handbags, cameras, babies' pushchairs, the small gifts of thanks that the bride and groom have just given out . . . all get left behind. As staff start to clear the tables in preparation for the next function, they have to ensure that all the disposable cameras left on the tables aren't thrown away. There is a great fad these days for bringing disposable cameras to weddings. Children get hold of them and take pictures of the ceiling, their fingers, up their noses . . . goodness knows what the photographs look like once they are developed.

The floral decorations on tables rarely get taken either and are simply thrown away. It seems such a waste of money. The couple could have spent a little more on a higher-class menu instead, or a better- quality wine rather than just the house red. If there are any wedding presents left behind, or envelopes with cash in them, I put all these in the Honeymoon Suite. I do that myself so that no one can be accused if anything goes missing. Couples often have a gift list at a major department store for their presents these days so that they get exactly what they want and no duplicates. When we got married, Wendy asked for orange kitchen equipment. Although people knew what we wanted, there was no list as such, so we ended up with three orange dustpan-and- brush sets, three orange washing-up bowls and drainers, three orange plate racks, three orange pedal bins, and three orange brooms. I hate orange! So the shop gift list is a much better option, although my favourite approach is that of the Greeks. We had a Greek wedding at Grosvenor House and guests pinned cash to the bride's dress. Ten-pound, twenty-pound and fifty-pound notes were pinned on to her. I thought that was a marvellous idea, although I longed to pin a twenty-pound note on and take ten-pounds change!

The worst part of a wedding can be the evening function. The bride and groom usually have the first dance, but sometimes forget to tell the DJ their favourite song. So the DJ has to spend time rummaging around to try and find it, while everyone waits in an embarrassing silence. At the buffet they will have told us that they want to keep the top tier of the cake and have the bottom tier cut up for the guests. But just before the chef cuts it up, the mother-in-law will announce that the bottom tier is to be kept and the top one cut up instead. I then have to go back to the bride for confirmation.

'Oh, take no notice of my mother,' she will say, 'cut up the bottom tier. She's an interfering cow.'

By this time, with the main part over, the toasts and speeches done, people relax and have a drink. Additional friends arrive at the end of the day. They are all sober to begin with, looking very smart, but as the evening wears on you start to see a different person. After a few drinks, some can hardly put two words together. Their faces change colour. They don't want to pay for the drink and become belligerent.

'That's f***ing expensive!'

'It's the same price as when you arrived to buy your first drink.'

'Can we have a tab?'

'Are you staying here?'

'Yes.'

'OK, you can start a tab. Which room are you in?'

'642.'

'I know that you are not in 642. Now, which room are you in?'

'Oh, sorry, I forgot. It's 364.'

'Give me your proper room number, that's if you are actually staying here?'

'Just give me a drink!'

They are not staying at the hotel at all and just want to charge their drinks to someone else's account.

They begin to get aggressive and abusive; many are sick in the toilets if you're lucky and on the floor if you're not; food from the buffet will end up being thrown all over the place, and couples that have just got married start arguing with their other half. All because of alcohol. And where do they put it all? Some have their first drink even before the church ceremony. I have even seen brides fall out of their limousines at the reception, drunk after consuming a bottle of champagne on the car journey between the church and the hotel. Great for business, but their bodies must take days to recover. I have even heard toasts where the wrong name has been used, simply because they've had far too much to drink.

'Please raise a glass to my new son-in-law, John.'

'It's David!'

'Sorry, David . . .'

There will be smashed glasses as the evening progresses, sometimes fisticuffs if a family feud ignites, and guests urinating in the corridor. And how brides go to the toilet, I shall never know! Many have such huge dresses. I see them going into the disabled toilets because they just cannot fit into the ordinary Ladies', often taking a bridesmaid in to help them. Gone, too, are the demure virginal-looking brides, as many wear dresses showing an enormous amount of flesh and a huge cleavage that the dress can barely contain. Sometimes, by the end of the evening, the material cannot stand the strain and they burst out. Bridesmaids generally tend to look much more glamorous than the bride, although I have often had to help bridesmaids out to their taxis at the end of the evening because they have been just too intoxicated to walk. If we could have alcohol-free weddings, there would be far less trouble.

Because they are staying at the hotel, the bride and groom seem to be the last to go to bed. Often out of their minds with drink. No chance, I think to myself, of any romantic love making. The bottle of champagne and strawberries in their room are really unnecessary. There is absolutely no way most of them could drink it; they are so drunk already. Then there are always the few dozen people who just won't go to bed and will be there until 3 a.m., drinking very little by this time. The Night Manager on duty always receives complaints from other guests trying to sleep above. They have either been disturbed by the noise, or have had an inebriated wedding guest trying to open their door because they have gone to the wrong room. In spite of all that they have consumed that day, the wedding guests will frequently still call room service in the middle of the night for a club sandwich because they are hungry!

Next day is clean-up time. The toilets can be particularly disgusting after a wedding and staff have to wear a special uniform with long gloves and a face mask to protect them. There could be cigarette ends everywhere and food embedded in the carpet. Confetti is another bone of contention. Hotels have tried to stop conventional paper confetti, as it is such a mess to sweep up, so now rice is thrown instead. It might be more environmentally friendly, but it has hardly landed before pigeons descend like a scene from Alfred Hitchcock's *The Birds*. This creates further mess. There is so much work involved putting everything straight after the event. Meanwhile, guests will be late for breakfast or wake up long after check-out time, then query their bills and deny that they have had extra food or drinks.

And out of all the couples that get married, nine times out of ten you never see them again. It reminds me of when I used to regularly attend our local church on Sundays. There would be christenings, for which up to forty or fifty people would arrive whom I had never seen in church before, and they never came back again. Rarely do couples even write a letter afterwards saying how wonderful everything was. They might say thank you to us on departure, but a letter or card would be a nice for all the staff that have worked so hard to make a memorable day for them. And wedding parties never tip the staff either. All that back-breaking work and yet not a single gratuity.

I have seen some extremely happy weddings, with couples very much in love, which is wonderful to see. Unfortunately I've also seen too many marriages that do not last. The shortest endured for just three months before the couple split. I always send anniversary cards every year, enquiring when the couple are going to visit us again for another function. I feel that this a personal touch if people have happy memories of their wedding day, and a great marketing ploy for the hotel to encourage people back. Mostly I hear nothing at all. Some come back to celebrate a major anniversary, but from time to time I receive a reply stating that the couple have separated. And sometimes the weddings don't even happen in the first place. The couple have a major row, decide that they are incompatible and cancel just a couple of weeks before the big day. Then so much planning and preparation simply goes to waste.

I HATE WEDDINGS!

10

Princes and Lords

Where wealth accumulates, and men decay;
Princes and lords may flourish.
Oliver Goldsmith, *The Deserted Village*

The pungent smell of fresh paint lingered in the air and irritated my nose. In the background I could hear a man brushing up the pile of the carpet until it was a uniform height; no chance now of tripping over the decorative brass fitments set into the floor, and any small holes were completely disguised. Downstairs the silverware was being polished to within an inch of its life for a mirror finish. This could mean only one of two things: either Lord Forte was on his way, or a member of the Royal Family was visiting Grosvenor House.

I looked in my diary. Princess Diana was due to visit the hotel for a charity lunch. Although royalty came regularly, I always got a bit nervous when dealing with them. The Queen once took over the whole of 90 Park Lane for a private birthday party, and the guest list was like a *Who's Who* of British royalty, with the Duke of Edinburgh, Queen Elizabeth the Queen Mother, the Prince and Princess of Wales, the Duke and Duchess of York, the Princess Royal and Prince Edward, amongst her guests. Imagine the planning and security that went into that!

Princess Diana's visit had required an extra prayer meeting. I gathered together the Banqueting Director and his team, the Head Housekeeper, the Head of Security, the Front of House Manager, the Head Chef, the Back of House Manager, and the Maintenance Manager. Every area had to be covered thoroughly. Nothing could be left to chance:

'Good morning, everyone. As you are all aware, we have a very high-profile charity lunch coming up in the Ballroom with 450 people attending. It must

run like clockwork. Banqueting, how are things going?'

'*We have ensured that all silver, cutlery and glassware is spotlessly clean. The menus have been checked with Kensington Palace, and all has been approved. We will also be catering for fourteen veggies, so there's a separate main course for them. The table plan is here. The microphone has been tested and is in good working order.*'

'*Thank you, Andrew. Now Her Royal Highness does not want any wine to be offered to her, only Evian water. And that must be still, not sparkling. I only want you, Andrew, to attend to her, and nobody else. You must ensure that the water at her meal is checked by you personally. We don't want anyone spitting in it, or trying to poison her while she's under our roof. And I would also like you to be there when her food is put on the plates.*'

'*OK, Mr Kirby.*'

'*I don't want anybody touching her food except the Head Chef in the presence of the Banqueting Director, understood? All staff serving at tables must be in white gloves. And please ensure that we use new gloves from stock. All uniforms must be spotless too. No stains, please.*'

'*I will personally check before they go in.' (I can always rely on Andrew to make sure that everything is looking at its best.)*

'*Security, the toilets must be checked every fifteen minutes on the morning, with someone in there at all times, just in case Princess Diana uses the loo. No one must go back into the Ballroom once it's been searched on the day, otherwise they have to do it all over again, and I'll get a telling off from the police.*

'*Maintenance, has the kitchen been looked at for faults?*'

'*Gas, oven, hobs are all in working order.*'

'*And is the air-conditioning OK?*'

'*Yes, it is, Mr Kirby.*'

'*Please make sure that all the chandeliers have been cleaned. I know they're not due to be done fully for another month, but we don't want any cobwebs hanging from them.*'

'*We've arranged for an outside company to come in and clean them overnight.*'

'*That's great. Now, you all know your responsibilities for this very important function. Please all report back to me if there are any problems, so I can be happy that we will be ready on the day.*'

Straight after the meeting I do a tour of inspection with the Maintenance Department of all the areas that Her Royal Highness will see, from the front of the hotel on Park Lane, her route to the Ballroom, and the Ballroom itself.

'These toilets need painting, I want them done in the next twenty-four hours so that there's not too strong a smell of paint, and the carpets could do with a clean in here too. Look, one of the toilet seats is broken. Imagine if she sits on that one! Come on, guys. I'm disappointed that these items have not been picked up before now. They should be done irrespective of whether Princess Diana's coming or not.'

'Sorry, boss.'

'When they're finished, please call me and we'll have one more look around, just to make me feel comfortable. More attention to detail is needed here, boys, please.'

Before I knew it, the day itself had arrived and I stood waiting at the Ballroom entrance on Park Lane. One thousand five hundred guests for a St George's Day lunch were pouring into the Great Room entrance just forty feet away, and I hoped that they wouldn't get wind of Princess Diana's visit. That would worry security if hundreds of onlookers suddenly appeared unexpectedly.

Soon I got the call that I had been waiting for. Princess Diana was just three minutes away. Two minutes thirty seconds passed and I saw her convoy coming up the opposite side of Park Lane. I could feel my heart beginning to flutter. The police outriders came to a halt as the maroon Daimler with its gleaming paintwork pulled up silently outside the Ballroom entrance. Princess Diana was seated on the side nearest to me and I could see a lady-in-waiting beside her. I was not allowed to approach the car until her bodyguard had got out from the front seat and opened her door. When the Princess had *both* feet on the ground – that was my cue to step forward and greet her.

Feeling my legs turn to jelly, I walked towards her with my outstretched hand. It was often said that she was so photogenic that photographers could not take a bad picture of her, but I thought she looked even more beautiful in the flesh.

'Good afternoon, Your Royal Highness. My name is Neil Kirby. I'm the Deputy General Manager. Welcome to Grosvenor House.'

'It's very nice to meet you, Neil. I'm so looking forward to my lunch here. How many are coming today?'

'Four hundred and forty-eight, Ma'am. Two can't come due to illness.'

'Oh dear, nothing serious I hope?'

'No, Ma'am, just colds.'

I escorted her through the Ballroom entrance.

The Princess had been to Grosvenor House many times, looking particularly sensational at the Red Dragon Ball in 1983 and the America's Cup Ball in 1986, and this day she seemed very relaxed, almost flirtatious.

'Are you very busy?'

'Yes, Ma'am, we have a St George's Day lunch for fifteen-hundred in the Great Room.'

'That should be fun.'

'Yes, it's an annual function here.'

'Do they get very drunk, Neil?'

'Yes, Ma'am, very.'

'But they all enjoy themselves.' She giggled and gave her familiar 'shy Di' look.

'Are you making a speech today, Ma'am?'

'Oh, am I supposed to be making a speech?' She looked momentarily startled. 'I haven't been told.'

'No, Ma'am, I was just asking.' I was worried that I had said the wrong thing. I was only making polite conversation.

'If I need to make one, Neil, can I call on you?'

'I get quite nervous when I do speeches. What about you?'

'I get *very* nervous.'

All too soon we reached the door of the ballroom. Inside the guests were already seated at their tables, eagerly waiting to receive her. I wanted to continue chatting, but knew that I had to get out of the way. It was not me that they had come to see.

'I will see you at the end of the lunch to escort you back to your car, Ma'am.'

'Thank you, Neil, it is kind of you to make me feel so welcome.' Maybe she said that to everyone, but she sounded genuine.

'Thank you, Ma'am. Enjoy your lunch.'

So far so good. Now it was important to get the Princess and her entourage seated so that the first course could be served as soon as possible. The kitchen had only thirty minutes before the 1,500 people in the Great Room sat down to eat, so the Banqueting Director and his team had a tough job to do. Nothing could be allowed to go wrong. Within minutes a crisis below stairs began to unfold.

Bleep, bleep.
'Mr Kirby, a chef has cut his finger very badly. He is nearly fainting, and looks very white.'
This is all I need.
'OK, tell him to hold his finger above his head.'
I run as fast as I can to the front desk.
'Reception, call an ambulance, immediately please.'
Ten minutes go by and there's no sign of the ambulance.
'They said that they are very busy, Mr Kirby. Should we send him by cab?'
'Yes all right, we have no choice. Someone must go with him though. And we need another chef to replace him. We can't be a chef down.'
I call his wife to explain what has happened, then rush down to the kitchen. The chef has a deathly pallor.
'Right, chef, you've cut your finger, you're going to be OK.'
'But there's the lunch . . . Princess Diana, Mr Kirby.'
'It's all right, we'll soldier on.'
'There are another twelve-hundred in for dinner tonight as well.'
'We'll be OK.'
I walk him upstairs towards the waiting taxi.
'Main course just going out!' shouts another chef below.
Life in the kitchen carries on as normal.
The taxi rank is at the front of the hotel, so this means walking him through reception. Goodness knows what the guests think, seeing a chef covered in blood, his finger up in the air. Some people probably won't have lunch now.

Bleep, bleep.
'Reception here. Guests are having problems with their key card. It's not letting them through to 257 section doors.'
'I'll deal with it.'
I hate those bloody key cards – every day we get about six of them fail. It's so irritating for our guests to go all the way to their rooms, only to have to come back for another key card. I call for our computer man.

'He's gone home, Mr Kirby.'

'OK, I'll ring him at home.'

It takes thirty minutes to get him back to sort the problem out.

'Chef has called from the hospital, Mr Kirby. He needs six stitches in his finger. He won't be back at work for five days.'

'All right, we'll cope.'

I make my way back to the Ballroom. As I pass the Great Room I can hear that the St George's lot are well and truly pissed, all singing 'Land of Hope and Glory'. I've never seen so many men in their late sixties or early seventies so drunk. But even so, they are very well behaved.

A second later one falls on the floor and cracks his head open. There is blood everywhere. Another ambulance called. This time it actually arrives and he goes off to hospital. I call *his* wife and explain. Then it's back to the Ballroom, where the charity lunch is coming to an end.

Princess Diana was on her feet and had decided to say a few unplanned words. 'I would like to thank you all for coming here today. Without your support, our charity just would not succeed. Also I would like to thank Neil and his team for the wonderful meal and service today.' A round of applause followed. Her event at least had gone without a hitch, and I felt great as I walked her out.

'Many thanks for your kind words, Your Royal Highness.'

'It's a great pleasure, Neil, and I hope to see you again.'

'Thank you, Ma'am.'

A momentary pause in the traffic, and then her car pulled out into Park Lane as silently as it had arrived. I felt sorry to see her go, but I heaved a huge sigh of relief.

Although notoriously suffering from eating disorders, whenever Princess Diana was at the hotel she always ate three full courses without leaving anything. What her fellow guests did not know was that she was served smaller portions than everyone else, and she would never take a bread roll. When her plate was returned to the kitchen, the staff knew which was hers and inspected it thoroughly to see if anything had been left. Princess Diana always refused alcohol, would never have coffee, and drank only mineral water. She insisted that it was Evian and would drink no other. Like every member of the Royal Family who came to the hotel, I noticed that the

Princess never went to the toilet while she was with us. Royalty seem to have cast iron bladders.

In 1990 the Princess arranged a lunch at Grosvenor House in honour of her gynaecologist, Sir George Pinker, who was retiring. He had delivered nine royal babies, including Prince William and Prince Harry, and had been the Queen's surgeon-gynaecologist for seventeen years. It was a ladies-only lunch and Princess Diana invited 1,200 women, all of whom had one thing in common: George Pinker had delivered their babies. As he ate his lunch, I stood on the balcony looking down and could not help wondering what he was thinking. He was the only man present and knew every single one of these women in a very intimate way, including the Princess, two queens and a duchess. I know exactly what *I* was thinking, 'Just think of all those fannies he's seen!'

One lady paid for the whole event so that all the money for tickets went directly to the charity Birthright, of which Diana as Princess of Wales had become the patron in 1984. Through her patronage more than £5 million was raised for the charity. Lady Wolfson of Marylebone was chairman of Birthright and came for a trial meal with the organiser. After the tasting session, the organiser said that it was not quite right and made some suggested changes. They came back later for a second meal, when more slight alterations were suggested. Then a third . . . until in the end we cooked six trial meals before she was happy. The sixth menu ended up being exactly the same as the one we had started with in the first place! With 1,200 rich ladies present at the meal, it raised a fortune for the charity, so it was all worthwhile. But we could not help smiling at the long procedure in selecting the menu.

Princess Diana's father, Earl Spencer, and stepmother, Raine, used to stay in the apartments. He was very shaky by this time after a major stroke and had to be physically supported by his wife. After his death she married a French count and returned to the hotel with her new husband, Jean-François de Chambrun. Lord Charles Spencer-Churchill, younger brother of the Duke of Marlborough, was a relative of Earl Spencer's and so obviously mixed in the same circles. Rocco employed Lord Charles as the PR man for the whole of the Forte Group of hotels and gave him a grace-and-favour one-bedroom apartment. His job was to encourage the cream of society into the hotels, which was how Princess Diana's family came to rent an apartment. Through his contacts in the French Jockey Club he managed to get Trusthouse Forte to sponsor the prestigious Arc de Triomphe race meeting. He also had many US connections, including the Vanderbilts, so was able to attract American 'royalty' to Park Lane. Like Lord Forte, Lord Charles was always immaculately dressed, but at six foot six he towered over his diminutive boss. Hotels were really a home from home for Lord Charles, maybe because he was born at the Dorchester Hotel during the war.

Sir Edward and Lady Rayne were another couple that Lord Charles Spencer-Churchill brought to the apartments, and they had a London base with us. Edward Rayne was then head of the famous shoemakers, H&M Rayne Ltd, based in Old Bond Street, who made shoes for the Queen, the Queen Mother, and the Princess of Wales, and held the Royal Warrant. Marlene Dietrich, Vivien Leigh and Ava Gardner were among their many famous clients. Lady Rayne was absolutely beautiful. She always told me that she had discovered the club sandwich when on a visit to America, and brought it back to England. I looked after them while I was still Apartments Manager. Sadly he was killed in a fire at their home, when he went back inside to retrieve some paintings and was overcome by fumes. She was absolutely broken-hearted.

The Prince of Wales came to Grosvenor House many times, particularly for functions associated with The Prince's Trust. While I was Deputy Manager he visited for an environmental conference in our 86 Park Lane meeting rooms. I met him at the door when he arrived and walked him to the conference, where he was due to make a speech, and then later I escorted him to the Great Room for a presentation and lunch. This involved about a half-a-mile walk along various corridors.

'I'm just going to take you to the Great Room, Sir,' I said.

'This is a long hike.'

'It keeps me fit, Sir, and I'm used to it because I run marathons.'

The Prince momentarily stopped absolutely dead in his tracks. It made me jump and I wondered what I had done wrong.

'Do you run marathons?' he asked animatedly.

'Yes I do, Sir.'

'Is it bad for your knees?'

'Well no, actually it's not. In fact, it has strengthened my knees since I've been running. I've done about twelve of them.'

'How interesting.'

'I damaged my knees playing soccer, but they're much better now that I run. The only people that do damage are those that are overweight.'

'That's very interesting, and what's your fastest time?'

'It was 2 hours 53 minutes, Sir.'

'And is that good?'

'I came around 800th out of 32,000 runners in the 1985 London Marathon.'

'That's very good, very good,' he replied as we finally approached the Great Room. 'It's very nice to meet you.'

'Thank you, Sir.'

The Prince was almost late arriving at the lunch, so fascinated did he seem by my knees.

The Prince was wearing a grey double-breasted suit, with a blue shirt and a pink tie, set off with a pink handkerchief in his top pocket. He was very smart, but as a former valet myself I could see that the creases in his trousers weren't as razor sharp as I would have done them, with my seven-pound tailor's steam iron, and his lapel was bubbled where the lining had not been ironed properly. The valet had not pressed them from the front *and* the back, which gives a rolled lapel instead of a flat crease. Maybe that is the way the Prince likes his jackets.

Camilla, Duchess of Cornwall, came several times to Grosvenor House while still Mrs Parker Bowles. Contrary to the poor press comments that she was receiving at the time about her appearance, she was immaculately dressed, wearing very high-quality clothes. Obviously she was not then undertaking royal duties, as she does now, but used to lunch privately with friends in our 90 Park Lane restaurant or have afternoon tea in the lounge. The last time I saw her, she drove up in her own car at the Reeves Mews entrance at the rear of the hotel. I was in the Accounts Office looking out over the courtyard, and could see that she was wearing tailored brown trousers, teamed with matching brown shoes, and a fashionably long brown cardigan, but I noticed that the years of cigarette smoking had taken its toll on her skin. Strange to think that if I was still at Grosvenor House today, I would be meeting her officially at the front entrance and greeting her as 'Your Royal Highness'.

* * *

Prince Philip is the only member of the Royal Family that I ever remember having second helpings of food. He didn't actually request more himself, but was offered it by the chairman of the function he was at. Normally you just would not offer royalty more food. The main course was *salmon en croûte* with a champagne sauce. The kitchen staff cut up the *salmon en croûte* straight from the oven, plated it and sent it out to the diners, throwing away the end piece into the bin. As all the guests came to the end of this course Andrew Coy, the Director of Banqueting, walked past the top table and asked if everything was all right.

'Wonderful,' said the chairman enthusiastically, then leaning across to Prince Philip asked, 'Would you like a little more, Sir?'

'Oh, I wouldn't mind,' said Prince Philip.

'Right,' replied Andrew, far less enthusiastically. Back in the kitchen, the end piece of *salmon en croûte* had to be retrieved from the bin, covered in champagne sauce, and was served to the unknowing Prince. I bet it was the only time he was ever served food straight out of the rubbish.

Princess Anne attended a function in the late 1980s when a particular cheese called Lymeswold had suddenly become very popular. She often used to have cheese at a lunch or dinner, and she liked fresh fruit as well, but royalty usually have exactly the same menu as everyone else present. So if strawberries and cream are on the menu, then that is what they will have. But at a ladies' lunch Princess Anne suddenly said that she fancied some Lymeswold.

'That's fine, Ma'am,' said the Banqueting Director, and went to the kitchen to fetch some cheese.

'I don't buy in that pasteurised muck,' shouted the chef, and so someone had to be sent out to a cheese shop around the corner to buy some Lymeswold and run back to serve it to Princess Anne.

'Your cheese, Ma'am.'

'Thank you.'

After that, we kept a larger selection of cheeses in stock just in case a member of the Royal Family was with us. Princess Anne always refused the wine, however, and only drank Coca-Cola, which we never ran out of.

When I was flown to Cannes for a CEO Club event, my Director of Banqueting, Andrew Coy, was with me and he ended up manhandling Princess Anne! She was due to make a speech and had to use a radio microphone, which meant that a small pack had to be attached to her. Andrew had to go up the back of her dress to thread the wire through, which resulted in a wonderful press photograph of the Princess with a big grin on her face. Andrew didn't wash his hands for days!

Prince Edward visited us many times through his various presidencies and patronages. He would attend, for example, the National Youth Theatre Annual Ball as their patron (since 1987), and the Lord's Taverners Ball during his year as President (1993–94). His father, Prince Philip, occasionally came too, as the Lord's Taverners' 'Twelfth Man'. The first Lord's Taverners Ball at Grosvenor House was in 1951, with Princess Elizabeth and Prince Philip in attendance, so there has been a long association with the hotel. It is one of the UK's leading sports and disabilities charities, and cricket's official recreational charity. Andrew Coy used to go to their offices in Queen Anne Street, where the President of the day presided over meetings, and discuss arrangements for the Lord's Taverner's Ball, held each November. Lulu sang one year at the Ball, far too loud and the guests all complained about the volume. Rory Bremner performed the cabaret once, mimicking some of the guests that were there, so it was always a very entertaining function to put on. Prince Edward, like his father and sister, is a particularly witty speaker and something of a practical joker. At the Duke of Edinburgh's Award thirtieth anniversary banquet, the Prince staggered slightly when he rose to his feet to make a speech. As he spoke, his words were slurred and his eyes appeared to be glazed. Honoured guests looked at each other uneasily, as their International Trustee appeared to be drunk. The glassy stare changed in an instant to a wicked glint and Prince Edward roared with laughter. 'I thought that would get you worried!' he beamed.

Princess Anne once began by deliberately reading completely the wrong speech after a dinner, and wickedly watched the guests' discomfort. Then she grinned, ripped the speech up and said, 'Sorry, that was yesterday's!' She then gave a witty impromptu speech without a single note. People still remember the time when Prince Philip set fire to Sir Harry Secombe's speech with a candle while the former Goon was still reading it. There are times when royalty just want to have fun.

It was not only members of the House of Windsor who visited, but international royalty, world rulers and heads of state. The King of Jordan, the Prime Minister of Japan, and Chief Ajao were among the VIPs that stayed.

The Sultan of Brunei and his huge entourage came regularly, and, as one of the wealthiest men on the planet, absolutely no expense was spared. It is said that his home has 1,788 rooms and he owns between three and six thousand cars. I once had to organise a birthday party for the Sultan of Brunei's son. Batman was very popular at that time and, at the Sultan's request, a set was built in the Ballroom with a huge wall, through which a full-size replica Bat-mobile would crash. I arranged for a fibreglass car to be supplied by a film company for the day. It took two days to build the set, for which I charged the clients £10,000 a day. The prince was eighteen and we were instructed to supply eighteen birthday cakes. In the end only one slice was cut out of just one cake – the rest of the cakes were given away. At the party there were only around a hundred guests, and the Saudi Royal Family loved karaoke and all kept singing loudly and very badly.

At another birthday party for one of the Sultan's daughters, we had to secretly fill her suite with over five hundred helium balloons, so that every inch of the ceiling was covered. We could only bring them up in the staff lift a few at a time, already blown up, and inevitably they would start bursting if we weren't careful.

The King of Saudi Arabia's brother came to stay in the late 1980s. He took over the whole of the sixth floor and there were confrontations between his own security and the hotel's security staff. News reached me that they had chained and padlocked a fire exit near the Saudi Prince's suite, which I could not allow for safety reasons. I sent my security men up to sort this out, but they had to tread carefully as it was a big contract to us, bringing in £270,000 a week, and they were staying for six weeks. In the end they called in the local police to resolve it and there was a big tussle with the Foreign Legion security men, who resolutely refused to unlock the fire exit, and the police backed off. But they did eventually see sense and removed the chain, maybe realising that even royalty could be burned if a fire broke out.

I never ceased to be amazed by the sheer wealth of the many Arab princes and sheikhs that stayed with us. They loved carrying cash, with wads of fifty-pound notes and never any small change. When I was a valet, I knew that their suits were handmade from Savile Row at £2,000 a time, with shoes at £400. Today those suits would be £3,000, and the shoes £1,500 a pair. I saw Rolex watches that had then cost in excess of £20,000. They had custom-made bullet-proof cars which set them back £450,000, and the breathtaking amount of gold and jewellery that they wore was simply priceless. I have never seen so much extravagance in my whole life, and they would think nothing of spending £250 on a bottle of wine and £3,000 on drinks at a single meal. They happily paid £4,000 a night for a suite, which was on a room-only basis. Masses of caviar and smoked salmon would be ordered, and a lot of it would later be thrown away uneaten, so there was an enormous amount of wastage.

Whenever they had been out shopping, five or six black limousines would pull up outside and they would emerge carrying Harrods carriers, and Marks and Spencer's bags – the Arabs just loved shopping in M&S. It would take the luggage porters up to an hour to carry all the shopping up to their suites.

It was not just the Arabs; I also used to hear from chauffeurs what the rich British ladies had been discussing when they were driven out for a shopping expedition to buy new clothes and jewels. 'Barbados, darling, for our holidays and then we're off to Hawaii. John has just bought a new Bentley, he picks it up on the day before we go. Such a hectic time, darling.' It was always 'darling' this and 'darling' that – so much snobbery. I grew to hate it and became even prouder of self-made men like Sir Sean Connery and Sir Jackie Stewart. Sir Sean was the son of a cleaner and a truck driver, and his first job was as a milkman in Edinburgh; Sir Jackie started out as an apprentice mechanic in his family's garage in Dunbartonshire. Both achieved their wealth and status through talent and sheer hard work, and never took any of it for granted. That, I admired.

At Grosvenor House we had royalty of our own, of course: the Forte family. One minute I would be saying that a new carpet was needed in a particular area, only to be told that no money was available for it, and then the next a new carpet would suddenly be laid because Lord Forte was due to visit. The Area Director would have got it in the neck if Lord Forte had seen a fraying carpet or, heaven forbid, a hole. Later we would get a reprimand for blowing the budget on replacement carpets, even when we had been told to buy them in the first place. You couldn't win sometimes, and often it was worse than having true blue-blooded royals visit.

Security was always a major issue whenever royalty or politicians were present, particularly after the bombing of Brighton's Grand Hotel during the

Conservative Party Conference in October 1984. Whenever Prime Minister Margaret Thatcher came to Grosvenor House we would have snipers on the roof, rooms would be meticulously searched and then sealed afterwards. If a member of staff inadvertently entered a room after the security men had been in, it had to be searched all over again and the sniffer dogs had to be brought back in.

After the Brighton terrorist attack, we would receive an average of three bomb threats a day. Often major functions had to be cancelled. Even if we were sure that it was a hoax, there were times when we just could not take a risk and thousands of pounds were lost. Sometimes I would contact the police after a bomb threat and they would ask me if a code word had been given. If it was not a coded warning, I was told to ignore the threat and carry on as normal. I then lived in a constant state of fear, just waiting for the bang. Even doormen were not allowed to park their own cars in the hotel forecourt in case bombs were placed underneath. When Charles Spencer-Churchill arranged a party with a guest list that included the Queen and the Prince of Wales, the security was incredible. Not an inch of the rooms used were left unsearched, right down to heating grilles in the walls, which were checked out by sniffer dogs and then sealed with tape.

I was at work on Tuesday 20 July 1982 when a nail bomb in a blue Austin car exploded in Hyde Park opposite the hotel. Two soldiers from the Household Cavalry were killed as they marched from their Knightsbridge barracks for the daily Changing of the Guard ceremony. Another died later from his wounds; twenty-three people were injured in the blast and seven horses were killed or so badly maimed that they had to be put down. Two hours later another bomb exploded in Regent's Park, killing six more soldiers of the Royal Green Jackets and injuring a further twenty-four people. The final death toll was eleven people and the IRA admitted responsibility. Just a month before, a gunman linked to the notorious terrorist Abu Nidal had shot and crippled the Israeli ambassador to London in an attack outside the Dorchester Hotel in Park Lane, so tension was already high.

I heard the bomb go off across the park and our windows shook with the vibration. Within a short time there were sirens blaring, ambulances everywhere, and Central London came to a standstill. Staff could not get to work, and those already at the hotel could not get home; guests could not get in or out of the hotel either. We were suddenly living through very frightening times. Soon a bomb at Harrods famous department store would kill six people and injure ninety more, and nowhere in London would feel safe.

Although security tightened, hotel occupancy in London dropped. At Grosvenor House the regularity of bomb threats meant that often I had to make the decision whether or not to evacuate the whole building. It was a huge responsibility, as so many lives could be at stake. If a warning came without a coded message, we just had to hope that it was a hoax. Sometimes the hours passed interminably slowly as we waited and waited, never knowing if any moment would be our last. Heads of department would do a thorough search and report back.

'We haven't found anything suspicious, Mr Kirby.'

'OK, let's all wait, there are three minutes to go.'

We waited. The seconds ticked by and then silence. No explosion. Everyone went back to their departments, learning to keep a stiff upper lip. The persistent threats went on for some years and many staff resigned from the hotel, as they just couldn't cope with the strain of having to come to London each day and facing the risk of a bomb going off at any time. I can't say that I blamed them.

Living in Surrey, I travelled to work every day via Victoria Station, then on a bus up to Park Lane. On the morning of 18 February 1991, as the bus dropped me off in Park Lane, I heard a dull thud. A bomb had gone off at Victoria Station, killing one person, maiming thirty-eight others. Although warnings had been given before the detonation, photographer David Corner went back to the scene and lost his life. The IRA had planted the bomb in a waste bin that I had passed some twelve minutes earlier. Since that bomb, you still don't see waste bins in any of our major stations.

Tony Murkett, the General Manager of the day, came to our 9.30 morning meeting to calm us all down. We decided to increase the security even more, both around and inside the hotel, so that our staff and guests felt more at ease in their minds. We were doing our best to ensure that they were safe, but there was still a very uncomfortable feeling in our hotel and I'm sure all over London. I don't think people who hadn't experienced terrorism really realised what everyone went through. Absolutely no one was safe and there was great relief when it eventually all died down. For several years the numbers of tourists dropped greatly, particularly visitors from America. We lost some £10 million in revenue due to the problem. Add all the other businesses up in London that were in the same position, and losses must have run into billions. At Grosvenor House alone we also lost over three hundred staff who had to take time off due to stress, and some did not return. In many ways life was never the same again.

11

Running Twice as Fast

Now, here, you see, it takes all the running you can do,
to keep in the same place. If you want to get somewhere
else, you must run at least twice as fast as that!
Lewis Carrol, *Through the Looking-Glass*

I lay back in the bath, convinced that I was going to die. The heat in New York was unbearable and Rocco Forte had practically carried me across Central Park to the Westbury Hotel after I had collapsed with dehydration. I was due at a dinner party downstairs in the restaurant, but at that moment I couldn't have cared less. If I even made it out of the bath, it would be a miracle.

On the surface Rocco Forte and I were like chalk and cheese. He had been born in the elegant seaside resort of Bournemouth and was educated at a public school near Bath, before going on to read modern languages at Pembroke College, Oxford. A far cry from my council-estate upbringing and very basic education. Yet he and I had much in common. The Fortes had to build up their multi-million pound empire from scratch, and Charles Forte had been determined that his only son, Rocco, would start work at ground level rather than go straight in at the top. To earn extra pocket money during his school holidays Rocco worked in several of his father's establishments, waiting at table and, just like me, was even a washer-up! There was no priority treatment either. When he once accidentally smashed a stack of plates, he lost a week's wages to cover the breakage. Rocco has a very dry sense of humour, and when a belligerent guest once reproached him, saying that she was going to write a letter of complaint to Mr Forte because she knew him very well, Rocco replied wryly: 'I think I know him better.'

At the age of sixteen Rocco undertook a period of training in the wine cellars of the Café Royal in London's Regent Street, which his father had owned since 1954. Nobody knew who Rocco was and one day a wine merchant told him that, if he was ever looking for a full-time job, there was a place for him in the cellar. Needless to say, he did not take up the offer. When his father eventually handed over the chairmanship of Forte plc to Rocco in 1992, the multi-billion pound business comprised of 940 hotels and 600 restaurants, not to mention Thorn EMI, three West End theatres, the Empire cinema in Leicester Square, the publishing company Sidgwick & Jackson, and the catering facilities at twenty-four European airports. But having experienced work behind the scenes at first hand, at least Rocco knew what it was like to get his hands dirty.

It was while I was still working in the apartment block at Grosvenor House and became his private valet that I really got to know Rocco Forte. When I began to press his suits in 1981, I happened to be training to run in my first London Marathon. I had just competed in the Manchester Piccadilly Marathon, for which Rocco had sponsored me, and had become excited at the prospect of running in London.

One day I went to put my key in his door but found that the lock wouldn't turn. This was rather unusual, so I rang the doorbell and Rocco opened the door himself, still wearing his dressing gown. This was equally unusual. As I went in to his flat, I could see that he had a scar on the top of his forehead, near the hairline. He then told me that he had crashed his Porsche while turning off a slip road to go towards Lord Forte's farm at Ripley, in Surrey. The car had skidded on a patch of oil and had ended up in a ditch. Although his injuries seemed minor, Rocco suffered from blinding headaches after the accident and is still deaf in his left ear and wears a hearing aid to this day. Many times while pressing his suits I almost flattened his tiny hearing aid, which he would accidentally leave in a pocket.

'How did you get on in the marathon?' he asked, as he showed me into the flat. I told him how I had done in Manchester and said that he owed me £50 in sponsorship money. I added that I was now training for the 1982 London Marathon.

'I'd like to train for that myself,' he said.

That was the moment that Rocco Forte and I agreed to become running partners. He took about six weeks to recover from his accident, and then we started training in earnest. We went on to run in eight marathons together

– seven in London and one in New York – and trained regularly in Hyde Park and Green Park, with Rocco setting our routes.

I first discovered that I was a good runner while I was still at school. At the age of eleven I became the South London Cross Country Champion, a position I held every year up to the age of fifteen. I also ran in the All England Cross Country Championship, and always seemed to be faster than my peers. Although I was classed as a junior, my speed put me in line with the intermediate group. In a race at Brockwell Park, as I approached the finish, stewards kept trying to usher me in a different direction.

'You're finishing in the junior section!' they shouted.

'But I *am* a junior,' I answered back.

They couldn't believe it, as I had beaten all the senior boys. When I was cross country racing they used to put a hare in the race, and I could beat the hare.

At the time my real interest was football, and I gave up running when I became a youth player for Crystal Palace and Charlton Athletic. I did not take it up again until I was twenty-nine and watched the very first London Marathon in March 1981 on television. I thought it was fantastic and just knew that I had to give it a try. Marathons were popping every-where in Britain, and I entered the Manchester Charity Marathon that autumn with 9,000 other runners. I told Wendy that I hoped to run it in four hours, but to my amazement I did it in 3 hours 14 minutes. I was shivering with cold afterwards and Wendy was nowhere to be seen, because she had not expected me to finish so quickly. A message had to be sent out over the tannoy: 'Will Wendy Kirby please come to the finishing line – Neil's freezing!'

A marathon is now set at 26 miles 385 yards (42,195 metres) but that is a fairly recent ruling. Legend has it that the distance was originally based on a run made in Ancient Greece by a long-distance foot soldier called Pheidippides. He ran 25 miles from the battlefield at Marathon to Athens with news that the Greeks had conquered the invading Persians. In the first modern Olympic Games held in Greece in 1896, a marathon of 25 miles was held, based on the legendary distance that Pheidippides had run. But the 26 miles 385 yards that we have today actually came about partly through the influence of the British Royal Family. In July 1908 the Olympic Games were held in London for the first time and the starting line of the marathon was intended to be in Eton High Street, exactly 25 miles away from the

Olympic Stadium at White City in Shepherd's Bush. The British Olympic Association then decided that, as the Princess of Wales (later Queen Mary) and her children would be watching the runners set off, it might be a nice idea to begin the marathon at Windsor Castle instead, although this would add an extra mile. A special spot was chosen for the Royal Box on the East Terrace diagonally opposite the starting line, which measured exactly 26 miles from the Olympic Stadium. Queen Alexandra, consort of King Edward VII, was to be at the finishing line in Shepherd's Bush, and a lap of the track to end at her Royal Box added a further 586 yards to the race. Finally, so that the Queen would have the best possible view of the finish, the direction of running was altered to clockwise on the inner lane, which reduced the distance in the stadium to 385 yards. The distance from the Royal Box at Windsor Castle to the Royal Box at White City therefore totalled 26 miles 385 yards, which became the established length of a marathon.

This extra distance proved too much for some in 1908, especially as the heat that day was over 80 degrees Fahrenheit. A five-foot-two moustachioed Italian named Dorando Pietri 'hit the wall' just before entering the stadium for the final lap and fell five times as he struggled to complete the marathon. As the crowd of 75,000 spectators cheered, umpires physically pushed him over the finishing line. His timing was 2 hours 54 minutes 46 seconds. Irish-American Johnny Hayes reached the line a minute later and was ultimately declared the winner. After complaints, Dorando was officially disqualified because he had been helped over the line. But Queen Alexandra was so impressed with the little Italian's efforts that she invited him back to the stadium the next day and presented him with a gold cup of his own. Dorando was hailed as an international celebrity as a result and the 'Queen's Cup' became a national treasure in Italy.

I ran in the Windsor Half Marathon once and saw Queen Elizabeth II and the Duke of Edinburgh on a hill looking down on us, both of them on horseback, so there is still royal interest to this day. Princess Diana fired the starting pistol at the 1987 London Marathon to set the runners off, and in 2004 Prince William ran in the London Mile in aid of Sports Relief. 'I've been training for about two minutes,' he joked before setting off, 'I've had a good run round the block.'

In April 1982 Rocco and I entered our first London Marathon, for which the entry fee was just £5. It felt strange at first when Rocco and I began training, as he was still my boss and I continued to call him 'Sir'. I had to run on his right-hand side because of his deafness in the left ear through the accident. Everybody at Grosvenor House knew that we were running together, and this led to tension in some areas, from the General Manager downwards, as they saw me as Rocco's friend. The bosses at Trusthouse Forte were also conscious of the situation, so it placed me in a slightly awkward position. My loyalty ultimately was to Rocco, so if we were out running and he started asking me questions about the business, I felt duty-bound to tell him the truth. He might ask me about that week's occupancy, or the room rates being charged for a big function.

'Mmm, we could do better, you know,' he would say. If he later told the board something that had reached his ears, they guessed that I was his source of information. As the years went by, some directors wanted me out of Grosvenor House altogether because of my relationship with Rocco, which they saw as a threat. Even though the knives were sharpened behind my back, I never gossiped about work and only told Rocco the straight-forward facts that he asked for, so I got through it.

Sometimes management would pump me for information in reverse.

'How's Rocco? What's he got to say about Grosvenor House?'

'Oh, nothing,' I could say truthfully, because Rocco gave little feedback. But I felt uncomfortable about the situation, as if people looked upon me as some sort of spy. It caused jealousies even with lower orders of staff.

I formed a Trusthouse Forte running team, made up mostly of Grosvenor House staff, and I designed the vests that we wore. We had the company name printed on the front, but I needed a slogan for the reverse. I happened to see a box of Marathon Matches which had the catchphrase 'Best in the long run', which I thought was perfect. So we had that as our slogan, cour-tesy of a box of matches, printed on our shirts and tracksuits. In the 1987 London Marathon there were around fifteen runners wearing blue Trusthouse Forte shirts, so the company really stood out.

Even though there was a Trusthouse Forte team, Rocco and I continued to train on our own. When we first began training together, he still had his office at Grosvenor House and so his secretary would ring down for me whenever he wanted to run. When the company headquarters moved to High Holborn, I used to get a call from Sheila his PA: 'Rocco wonders if you would like to go running tonight?'

'Yes, no problem,' I would say, as I always kept spare kit at the hotel. I then had to run from Grosvenor House to High Holborn as fast as I could to meet him. It took me about twelve minutes through the backstreets of London and, after signing in at the security desk, I would make my way up to the first floor where Rocco's office was, and sat puffing and panting in my running gear until he was ready. He was always late because he was a very busy man, but he would eventually change into his shorts and we would be off. Our regular route was down past the Waldorf Hotel in Aldwych, past the Savoy Hotel in The Strand, through Trafalgar Square and into The Mall, before doing speed sessions and circuits around Green Park, for which I set the timings. Then we would run to Hyde Park, around the Serpentine, and back to the Royal Albert Hall, where he would go back home to Lowndes Place and I would return to Grosvenor House.

Speed sessions were a major part of our training, so important when running long-distance marathons. I was lucky in that I was very fit, had great lungs, and never seemed to be out of breath or tired. Even as a child I could run around all day without tiring. So I taught Rocco how to breath properly (in through your mouth, out through your nose, until you get fitter and then it is the other way round) to keep the blood cool and slow the heart rate; the correct running posture (always looking down and never straight ahead); how to keep his hands relaxed to avoid tension, and some of the tricks of the trade. Vaseline, for example, is an important part of any runner's kit. You must put it between your toes, around your ankles, in your groin and crotch, under your arms, everywhere that might suffer. I once ran a twenty-mile race at Wimbledon and ended up with bleeding nipples because I forgot to put Vaseline on my chest. My white T-shirt looked as if I had been stabbed in the heart. Vaseline on the feet is essential and prevents blisters. Organisers of the London Marathon estimate that runners get through 88 pounds of Vaseline before the race.

Often I would get a call at weekends if Rocco wanted to run. This meant a train journey for me from my Surrey home in Sanderstead, and a taxi ride before we could meet up. Rocco would have decided the route, sometimes going over the bridges of London, maybe through Battersea Park, often running twenty miles at a stretch, sometimes even twenty-two miles. I always had to carry £2 in the pocket of my shorts because Rocco would get thirsty and, like royalty, he never ever carried money. I used to buy us each a bottle of water and a Mars Bar, and off we would go again. Once we went to Lord Forte's farm at Ripley and were running along the Surrey roads when Rocco suddenly announced that he was thirsty. Ahead of us was a Little Chef restaurant.

'I can't go in there,' said Rocco, sounding like the Prince of Wales. It dawned on me then that he owned the Little Chef chain. 'I'm not going in, because they'll recognise me.'

'It's all right, I'll go in.' I walked into the restaurant, reaching for the £2 in the pocket of my shorts. I ordered a couple of juices to take out, and when I went to pay, the bill came to £3.

'I've only got £2 on me,' I confessed. 'The drinks are for Rocco Forte. He's just outside.'

'Oh, yeah, yeah,' said the assistant, adopting a pull-the-other-one expression.

'He is, honestly! He's just outside.'

In the end I could only afford one drink and I took it out for Rocco, pretending that I had already drunk mine inside. I was dying of thirst for the rest of the run.

Rocco began to suffer with his Achilles tendon. In the 1985 London Marathon I was desperate to run my fastest time, but he unintentionally held me back. Rocco was on strong painkillers to ease the pain and really should not have run at all. He got to around seven or eight miles and the pain became so bad that he had to pull out. I then went on to run my fastest time ever, 2 hours 53 minutes 1 second, and so broke the three-hour mark, which every amateur marathon runner wants to do. When I reached the finishing line, I was amazed to see Rocco there to meet me. Whenever we ran together his chauffeur used to wait at the finish, ready to drive us back to Grosvenor House, where there was usually a buffet for runners. This time Rocco had pulled out early, yet he still managed to be at the finishing line.

'Well done, that's a fantastic time,' he congratulated me.

'How did you manage to get here?' I asked, knowing that his chauffeur wouldn't have known that he'd dropped out and would be waiting for him at the finish.

'I had to get on a tube,' he said. 'I had no money with me, but because I had my runner's number on, they let me have a free ride.'

It conjured up a wonderful image of this millionaire, wearing only shorts and a vest, travelling for free. It was probably the only time in his life that he had ever used the London Underground.

Rocco and I trained very hard and he was a dedicated runner. He really used to push himself and carried two small dumb-bells while training to strengthen his upper arms. Rocco used to visit the Grosvenor House gym to build himself up, he cycled a great deal too, and had a rowing machine at home, so he was an incredibly fit man. He ran his first marathon in 3 hours 28 minutes. I had already achieved 3 hours 14 minutes by then, and began to run wherever marathons were taking place in an attempt to break the three-hour mark, running in Guildford, Birmingham, Farnham, Richmond and Manchester. In 1983/84 I was running four or five a year, and managed the Winchester Marathon in 3 hours 11 minutes and the Sutton Marathon in 3 hours 6 minutes. In my worst ever marathon Rocco beat me by ten minutes.

We had flown to the States for the New York Marathon in September 1985. Rocco owned various hotels there, including the Waldorf and the Plaza Athenae, and was going over on business anyway. About eight of us travelled with him from Grosvenor House for the race; Rocco did a tour of his hotels, ending up with us all at the Westbury, whose General Manager was running in the marathon as well. On the day of the race two stretch limousines arrived to drive us to the starting point. I got into one with Rocco and found myself sitting awkwardly. When we reached Staten Island, the starting point, I felt a sudden sharp pain in my back as I got out of the car and was in agony. I had never had any kind of back problems before, so was rather concerned as I could hardly walk.

'I hope you're going to be all right.' Rocco sounded rather irritated. I was his running partner – he was used to having me by his side and he was clearly concerned that I might not be up to it.

In New York everything was so well organised for the marathon and there were massage facilities available for the runners. They immediately gave me a banana for energy, then a fantastic massage. Rocco kept popping in to see if I was going to be fit to run, and eventually the pain eased and we set off for the start of the race. It was September, the humidity was 92 degrees and unbearable. In the previous year's marathon an Italian runner called Orlando Pizzolato had stopped three times because of the heat, but he still went on to win.

I decided not to go mad. I was really excited about being in New York and taking part in this wonderful event, and made up my mind that we would run at an average speed and just enjoy it. My back was still a little sore, so this was not a day for targets or trying to break our record. It was a misty morning and we set off at a very gentle pace. After barely a couple of miles I began to feel very strange, and sweat started pouring from my hands. I thought maybe I was coming down with flu or a virus of some kind.

'I feel a bit funny,' I said to Rocco as he ran beside me.

'It's the humidity, just the humidity.' He was very focused on the run.

Seven or eight miles into the race I started to feel even worse. The sun had emerged by now and the heat was insufferable, but I felt that I should continue for Rocco's sake. After thirteen or fourteen miles, however, I had just had enough and told Rocco that he should go on without me.

'No, keep going, keep going,' he urged.

Normally I would be the one encouraging him not to give up; now it was the other way round.

At nineteen miles I felt that I could not run any further and would have to walk. I could not understand why Rocco was not suffering from the heat; other people were pulling out all along the route because of it. Maybe it was his Italian blood that enabled him to cope with such weather. I discovered later that one runner had sadly dropped dead at fourteen miles. If I'd known that at the time, I would have withdrawn altogether. I told Rocco to go on ahead, and he reached the finishing line without me. Orlando Pizzolato won for the second year in a row. I achieved my slowest time ever of 3 hours 42 minutes, when normally it would average 3 hours 10 minutes. By the time I reached the finishing line, I felt really ill. I drank some water to try and rehydrate myself, but as we stood there with our medals everything seemed to spin.

'Are you all right, Neil?' Rocco grabbed my arm as I vomited up the water I had just drunk. I was in a near state of collapse through dehydration, and he virtually carried me across Central Park and then into a taxi to the Westbury Hotel, which he owned.

'I'm giving a dinner party for us all later on,' Rocco had said earlier in the day, 'so I want everyone down in the restaurant.'

In my room, I lay back in the bath feeling like death. I had never suffered from anything like it before and my whole body seemed to be shutting down. A runner can lose one litre of sweat per hour during a marathon, and drop four or five kilos in body weight, which is purely water loss. These days several hundred thousand bottles of mineral water are given out along the route to counteract the problem of dehydration. Drinking too much water, however, can be just as bad as not drinking enough because it dilutes the sodium in the blood, which can lead to vomiting and seizures. The recommendation now is 120–170 millilitres of fluids every twenty to thirty minutes, and to drink only when you are actually thirsty. Some runners tank up on water and then become ill. The London Marathon was sponsored by Mars from 1984 to 1988 and one year they gave us all litre-cartons of thick orange juice before the start of the race. Most runners vomited it all back up as soon as they began running, as a concentrated acid drink was not a good idea.

The heat that day in New York was intolerable, and from then onwards the New York Marathon was moved to November when it is cooler. I could feel myself drifting off in the bath, when the sound of the telephone jolted me back into life.

'Are you coming down, Neil?' It was Rocco.

'Oh, I'm sorry, Sir. I'm just getting out of the bath.'

'We're waiting for you.'

I have never felt less like getting dressed up and going down for a dinner party, and once there I couldn't eat a thing.

'Are you all right, Neil?' Dennis Hearn, the Deputy Chief Executive of Trusthouse Forte, looked concerned.

'I feel terrible, Sir,' I admitted.

I had discovered the hard way that heat did not agree with me. When I returned to New York to run again in November 1991, there were no problems at all and I completed the marathon in 3 hours 17 minutes.

The atmosphere at the New York marathons was fantastic. The route took us through Brooklyn, Queens, the Bronx, Manhattan and many places that I had previously seen only in the movies. But it was much tougher than London because of the hills.

I eventually got Rocco down to 3 hours 11 minutes by 1989. He always wanted to get under three hours, but never managed it. After Rocco took over the chairmanship of Forte plc he no longer had the time to dedicate to marathons, and our running partnership ended. Instead he went into triathlons (swimming, cycling and running), representing his age group in the 2001, 2002 and 2003 World Triathlon Championships. In July 2005 he took part in the first Iron Man event in Klagenfurt, Austria, finishing in 11 hours 40 minutes and coming second in his age group. When I saw Rocco at Lord Forte's memorial service in 2007, he was looking incredibly fit and toned. He was then aged sixty-two, but could easily have been forty-five. I always admired him when we were running together, the multi-millionaire and the former council estate boy. Living a genteel life of luxury, he nevertheless learned how to spit in the gutter like the rest of the runners.

Over the years Rocco has raised substantial amounts of money for charity through his sporting activities, and I find myself that helping a charity is the spur that keeps me going. As you 'hit the wall' in a marathon at around eighteen miles, when the glycogen that provides energy is sapped, your muscles throb and you feel as if you are running through wet cement, it is the thought of not letting the charity down that is the motivation which prevents you giving up. Sporting events are marvellous opportunities for fundraising and one year the Trusthouse Forte running team managed to raise over £50,000 for a charitable house near Wimbledon for ex-hotel staff that had fallen on hard times and were now homeless. I was later chauffeur-driven there with Rocco, we presented them with a huge cheque and had afternoon tea in the grounds. It felt good to be able to help, yet at the same time it was sad talking to former housekeepers, porters and hotel staff who had hit rock bottom.

At each marathon or half marathon I have been able to raise a few thousand pounds for charity myself, and I am thrilled that it has now amounted to over £200,000. The 2010 Brighton Marathon was my twenty-eighth full marathon, and I have run in 169 half marathons too, so the money gradually adds up. One year I had signed up for the London Marathon and read in the London *Evening Standard* that the Queen had given a home on the Sandringham estate to the Leonard Cheshire Disability charity. Park House was the childhood home of Princess Diana and it is where she was born in July 1961. The idea was to turn it into a hotel catering specifically for people with disabilities, and it would be fully equipped for their needs. It sounded like a very good cause to me, and I contacted them immediately. I was aiming to raise £2,000 at the London Marathon, which I discovered would purchase a special bath for the disabled with an electronic hoist, so I offered to donate the money to the new Park House Hotel for this purpose.

I ran the marathon and managed to raise the £2,000 that I had pledged.

I personally handed the money over to the charity one afternoon, had a cup of tea with them, and thought no more about it. The months went by and the telephone rang one day at my Sanderstead home, and a caller invited Wendy and me to the official opening of Park House Hotel. This was followed later by a formal invitation, which said that the Queen would personally perform the opening ceremony. There was panic in our household and Wendy had to go out and buy a new outfit and a hat.

On the day itself in 1987 we drove past crowds of people lining the route at Sandringham, through some very ornate gates and up to the impressive Victorian house. We waited in a marquee on the lawn while the Queen had a private tour of the sixteen-bedroom hotel with Leonard Cheshire, then she joined us in the tent for refreshments. Her Majesty wandered around, looking very relaxed with a cup of tea in hand, and spoke to each of us before we all went into the hotel for the official opening. The Queen said a few words, unveiled a plaque, and then it was our turn to tour the hotel. As we walked past a bathroom I was aware of a woman inside demonstrating how the disabled facilities in there worked and to my total astonishment there was a plaque outside, saying that the bath and hoist had been 'Donated by Neil Kirby'. I could hardly believe it! It was fantastic, though, to have an opportunity to see the final result. Often you run, raise sponsorship money, you pass it on to a worthy cause and then forget all about it. But this time it was good to be able to see for myself what had been done with the money. I have to admit to a small thrill, too, at seeing my name on a plaque in a building that the Queen had just opened.

Anything that I have managed to achieve, however, is a mere drop in the ocean when compared to Sir Jimmy Savile, who few people could beat for fundraising. It is said that he helped raise over £40 million for charities connected with the disabled, and he had a particular interest in Stoke Mandeville Hospital where he once worked as a porter. I met him initially through running, and we ran many times in London, Bolton and Manchester, although not together as I was much faster than him. We did the Camberley Half Marathon, too, and he was always good fun and had a ready quip. In November 2007 he was mugged by a fan in a Leeds hotel, who made off with his glasses. 'I thought it was marvellous!' he said, 'It was just like old times.'

He had a flat in Regent's Park and I invited him to Grosvenor House for lunch a few times. He also came and advised me when I was refurbishing the Health Club and tried out new equipment for me. Once he brought a beautiful girl to lunch with lovely blonde hair. I thought she must be his stunning new girlfriend, but when she went off to the ladies' room he told me that she had only weeks to live. The poor girl had cancer, and the blonde hair was a wig. He was such a kind and generous man.

During one memorable London Marathon, Rocco was running on my left as usual when he suddenly announced loudly that he needed to go to the toilet.

'OK, Sir,' I replied, but had no idea what to do about it. There were not many conveniences along the route, but we ran as quickly as we could towards the nearest 'Gents'. The world and his wife seemed to be queuing outside and it would have taken forever to wait, so we carried on running. He was clearly in some discomfort.

Relieving yourself during a race is usually not a problem for men, who can easily nip behind a tree. I was once in the line-up at the start of a race when a man urinated into a plastic cup and passed it along the other runners. There were cries of, 'Don't drink it!' as the cup was handed from one to another. But Rocco's need was much greater and he could not just go behind a tree with thousands of spectators watching. Eventually we saw a petrol station up ahead, so we took a detour towards their toilet. By this time Rocco was like a cat on a hot tin roof and could hardly contain himself. He ran anxiously towards the door and pushed firmly on it. It was locked. Someone else had beaten him to it and he had to wait. I was sure that there was going to be an accident. A runner finally emerged and Rocco shot inside like a bullet from a gun. Within seconds, however, he was out again.

'I'm not going in there,' he said, 'there's no toilet paper!'

So we were off again in search of facilities. Personally, I would have used the garage toilet and to hell with the consequences, but Rocco was clearly not used to roughing it. Two miles down the road we finally found a portable toilet set aside for runners.

'We've lost about four minutes on our time now,' I rebuked him as he came out. But he certainly looked relieved.

'I went to the toilet, you know,' he told everyone afterwards, when explaining why our timing was not as good as it might have been. 'We lost about four minutes, didn't we. Was it four minutes?'

'Yes, Sir, four or five minutes.'

I will never forget that marathon when Rocco was caught short.

For many years, even when in management, I continued to be Rocco's private valet and undertook other duties at his home. At a Grosvenor House buffet after the 1985 London Marathon, Rocco met my wife Wendy and stood watching my children running around enjoying themselves. It must have looked like a happy, domestic scene because he turned to me and said, 'Neil, it's about time I found myself a wife.' In February 1986 he married the beautiful Aliai Ricci, daughter of an eminent Italian neurologist, and eventually they had three children Lydia, Irene and Charles. Aliai did not like the housekeeper that Rocco had been employing. One evening they held a dinner party at Rocco's house to celebrate their engagement, with Lord and Lady Forte and Aliai's parents as guests, and I was called upon to wait at table. It was very important that everything went smoothly, and I was just serving the pre-dinner drinks and canapés when we all heard a huge crash from the kitchen below. The housekeeper had dropped the main course on the floor.

I went in to clean up and found her in a huge panic. Trying to calm her down, I scooped all the food up off the floor and put it back on to the serving tray as neatly as I could, and went back up to the dining room.

'Don't worry,' I told Rocco and Aliai, 'there was plenty of extra food.'

I then brought in the food on its silver tray, and the guests all helped themselves, not knowing that it had been scraped off the floor.

After that episode, however, Aliai quickly sacked the housekeeper.

'Oh Neil, I need someone to clean,' she said desperately one day.

'What about my wife?' I suggested, saying the first thing that came into my head.

'That would be good.'

I then had to break the news to Wendy, who was three months pregnant with our son David at the time. For six weeks Wendy went to Rocco's house to clean, once taking our young children Nicola and Neil with her, driving all the way from Surrey to Central London and back again. Despite her 'bump', Wendy cleaned the toilets and baths, ironed laundry, and kept the house spotless until the Fortes found a new housekeeper. Aliai was always extremely kind and used to nip around London on a bicycle with a little basket in the front to do her shopping. When Wendy and I recently became grandparents Aliai, now Lady Forte, tactfully told us that we didn't look old enough. It is a common enough phrase, but I was more than happy to believe her.

Early in their marriage, Aliai was having tea with her mother one day and I was pressing Rocco's suits downstairs. I suddenly heard a bloodcurdling scream. Their young daughter, Lydia, then aged about eighteen months, had climbed up on to the coffee table, upsetting a pot of scalding hot water all over herself. I ran into the room, and the scene was awful. The child's skin was falling off like dripping candle wax. I shall never forget her screams as they carried her to the ambulance. Some surgery was needed, but she grew into a beautiful girl with no obvious scars from that horrific afternoon.

After 1993, when Rocco gave up marathons, I said that I would never run another. That year I had competed in my twenty-fifth marathon, I had achieved my ambition of breaking the three-hour mark, and I thought that it was a good time to retire. I continued to run regularly in half marathons, and twice did the twenty-mile race around Wimbledon Common, but was persuaded out of retirement to run in the 2005 and 2007 London marathons by the Chase Children's Hospice near Guildford, which seemed such a good cause and was desperately in need of funds. It was very hard to refuse. I have now run in thirteen London marathons and the camaraderie is still wonderful. And if it is raining, we all have a laugh as we line up at the start wearing black plastic bin bags for protection. Unlike many sports, there is no rivalry; it is all good-humoured and people share water and a joke. If anyone starts to flag, other runners always urge them to keep going, and it can feel very emotional.

Over forty of us now run for the Surrey-based charity Chase Hospice Care for Children, wearing distinctive yellow shirts donated by Michael More-Molyneux of Loseley Ice Cream fame. The shirts have our names printed on the front, so total strangers will shout, 'Come on, Neil!' as I run by, because they can see my name. The More-Molyneuxs sadly lost a twelve-year-old son, Christopher, in a tragic accident and in 1997 donated land on which a hospice was built in his memory. Michael More-Molyneux gives a lunch party for the runners each year, when a team photograph is taken for posterity. He and his wife used to run themselves up until 2007. Forty runners can raise around £150,000 between them for the hospice, so it is well worthwhile.

I still love running to this day, even in the wind and the rain, because of the freedom that it gives me. It not only keeps me fit, but when you work long hours in hotels, it is essential to escape and find space to recharge your batteries. I frequently go for a fourteen-mile run whenever I have a break, and there are no telephones, no emails, and no guests can get at you. Running also gives me a chance to think and solve problems – maybe because it clears the mind and helps you focus.

Even as a valet, I used to be at the hotel by 6.45 a.m. and would not finish until around 7 p.m. Sometimes five nights a week I would meet Rocco at High Holborn at about 7.30 p.m. for a ninety-minute run. By the time I got back to Grosvenor House, had showered and changed, then set off to catch the train from Victoria station, I would not actually get home for dinner with Wendy until 11 p.m. So running was a major part of my life and swallowed up virtually every free moment that I had.

In 1994 my life took another unexpected turn that not only meant even less time at home, but propelled me towards my goal. My mind immediately went back to 1967 when I was just fifteen and a half and had seen that smartly dressed man in a navy-blue suit walk through the basement area where I was washing up.

Now, 26 years 385 days later, I was that man.

12

Let Us Count Our Spoons

If he does really think that there is no distinction between virtue and vice, why, Sir, when he leaves our houses let us count our spoons.
Samuel Johnson, Letter 14 July 1763

By 1994 I had been sailing along happily as Deputy Manager for four years, with Tony Murkett as the General Manager. We were aware of some rumblings going on at Head Office because sales figures were not what they could be and more income needed to be generated from Grosvenor House. Tony called a meeting one day in June, as the Operations Director wanted to come and speak to us about some changes that he wished to instigate within the group.

Forte had divided their empire into groups: Posthouses, Little Chefs, Happy Eaters, Meridian Hotels, Grand Heritage Hotels (four-star and country house hotels), and Exclusive Hotels (the luxury five-star establishments). A new Operations Director had been appointed for Exclusive Hotels worldwide, which included Grosvenor House and the Hyde Park Hotel in London, the Westbury in New York, the Plaza Athenae and George V in Paris, the Ritz in Madrid, Sandy Lane in Barbados, and all their luxury five-star hotels. Grosvenor House was considered to be their number-one hotel overall, as the single biggest profit earner within the company. We had weathered the economic recession of the early 1990s, and now the company wanted it to be even more profitable.

The new Operations Director arrived and to my astonishment had clearly decided that Tony Murkett was no longer the right man for the job. I had always got on very well with Tony and it was really down to him that I had climbed the ladder to be Deputy Manager, so I had much to thank him for. At the meeting, with all the heads of department present, the Operations

Director suddenly announced that Tony Murkett would shortly be leaving the hotel.

'He's done a great job for us,' the Operations Director went on, as if he was sorry to see him go, but Tony was really being pushed out against his will. 'And Neil Kirby will be appointed acting General Manager,' he continued. You could have knocked me down with a feather; nobody had forewarned me. All eyes turned in my direction, as suddenly I was their new boss. I had gone into that meeting as Deputy and came out as General Manager.

Tony Murkett left immediately the meeting ended. His departure was as sudden as that. Bang, he was gone. Tony had been a good General Manager; he had strengths and weaknesses, like all of us, but he was very popular with the staff and a hard act to follow. He had started in hotels as a waiter and worked his way up to the top position, so knew the industry inside out. He went on to become Managing Director of the Sloane Club and in 2006 became owner of America's historic Hotel Northampton in Massachusetts. An official statement simply said: 'Mr Murkett is leaving to pursue opportunities outside of Grosvenor House and Forte.' No one was prepared to give a clear explanation as to why he had been pushed.

I rang Wendy to tell her the news, as my colleagues patted me on the back. They all knew where I had started in the hotel business and were behind me one hundred per cent. It was gratifying that Grosvenor House profits rose in the three months that followed. Even Rocco congratulated me on the promotion.

'Look after the place for me,' he said.

The Operations Director and I did not start off on a very good footing. Not knowing that I was going to be appointed General Manager, I had booked a much-needed holiday for Wendy, myself and the children, in Florida. I had been going through the stress of my mother's illness and operation at the time, although was unaware that she was actually dying, and I was not prepared to let my family down.

'But the holiday's already booked and paid for,' I pleaded, when he insisted that I cancel.

'We'll pay you money to cover your expenses,' was his response, 'but you cannot go on holiday.'

'I'm going, and that's it,' I said. I was not prepared to be dictated to.

He was not at all happy. Maybe it was the wrong approach on my part, but I refused to budge and flew off to Florida as planned. A temporary manager was flown in from the Burg Hotel in Switzerland to hold the fort during my absence. I returned to Grosvenor House in the top job as General Manager, my dream had finally been achieved, and it should have been a time of great personal rejoicing. Instead, I came back to England to my mother's deathbed. Just as I had reached the heights in my career, I experienced the depths in my personal life.

By a strange coincidence, I had already been using the General Manager's office for four years, and so had no need to move. As General Manager, however, I was given the use of apartment 34. While Duty Manager, I had often slept on a Z-bed in my office after working late, so this was certainly a step up. The use of this two-bedroom apartment at Grosvenor House was one of the perks of the job, and some general managers really took advantage of it. One even installed his wife and daughter in it. He lived off the restaurant menu and ordered anything that he wanted, and consumed wine and champagne as he wished. He was not what you would call a hands-on General Manager and I rarely saw him in the hotel.

I worked under thirteen general managers in twenty-eight years, and two or three of them had their families living in the apartment for free and would host lavish dinner parties at the hotel's expense with waiters and waitresses attending to their needs. They ordered the most expensive champagnes and wines. All their laundry would be done for free and, whilst this was allowed as a perk, they abused it by sending absolutely everything to the laundry, even their socks. The company was settling massive bills for their laundry and dry cleaning. One particular General Manager had a house in the country and used to steal Grosvenor House towels for his bathroom at home. He would turn up for work on Monday mornings with a huge bag filled with his family's dirty washing to be laundered at the hotel's expense. When I was a valet I had to count items of laundry before they went out, to be certain that we received the same number of items back. I used to see, amongst this General Manager's laundry, children's socks, his wife's bras and many personal items that really should not have been included.

Another General Manager's partner got drunk at the staff Christmas party one year. I don't know if they had a quarrel because of it, but his partner smashed down their apartment door that night. It was a solid wooden door too.

Some general managers were extremely unpopular with the staff, and when they called for room service to their apartment upstairs, waiters often spat in their tea and coffee or added something unspeakable to their food. It was the staff way of getting their own back for poor treatment. This type of General Manager rarely pulled his weight at work and expected to be treated just like our rich paying guests. One even insisted that we rang the doorbell of his apartment twice before we entered. What really annoyed me was that they expected everyone to attend to their needs immediately, even if it meant neglecting a guest. To my way of thinking, the customer should always come first.

When apartments were being refurbished and some of the elegant antique furniture was replaced with more modern pieces, a lot of the old furniture disappeared out of the back door of the hotel and into the homes of general managers. Lorries and vans would turn up, and the furniture was whisked away.

Over the years a number of my colleagues were dismissed for stealing, which some did in a very inventive way. When steaks and smoked salmon kept disappearing, no one could work out who was responsible or how it was done. Everyone who worked in that area was stopped and searched over a period of many months. The culprit was a chef, who had been searched many times without anything ever being found on him. He travelled to work on a motorbike, and nobody thought to search his biking gear. He hid the food in the lining of his crash helmet and, although he got away with theft for a long time, he was eventually caught.

The theft of food was always a moot point with the staff. It seemed such a shame that so much first-class food was thrown away, and it would have been no loss to the hotel if staff had taken it home for themselves. But they had to watch helplessly as smoked salmon, caviar, roast duck and pieces of beef were thrown in the bin. Occasionally some people wrapped food into a piece of cellophane and tried to smuggle it out, but the company looked upon it as pilfering. I suppose a line had to be drawn somewhere, and you could easily have had staff walking out with all kinds things, so the company policy was unyielding: leftover food had to be destroyed. But when many people are starving in the world, I hated to see so much food go to waste every single day. Even today it irritates me when guests have a rack of toast at breakfast and eat only half a slice, or order a full English breakfast and leave most of it. The rest has to be thrown away and it seems such a waste of good food.

In the 1960s and 1970s when floral arrangements were left over after a banquet, staff were always going home at night with bags filled with flowers. By the 1980s, however, so much was being stolen from the hotel, management had to make the blanket decision that absolutely nothing left the building. Flowers were then generally thrown away after a function, as the next event organisers would bring in their own arrangements. But occasionally staff members asked the Head of Housekeeping if they could have some of the flowers, then a requisition was issued and the blooms left the hotel legitimately, and with the correct paperwork to prove that they weren't being stolen. Food and beverage, however, were never allowed to be taken home by the staff. Some got round this by consuming it on the premises, then it went home in their stomachs.

Alcohol was a big source for stealing and swindling. As there were mini-bars in all the rooms, staff restocking them used to hide miniatures in their pockets, even though there a big risk of being caught. Staff were routinely stopped and searched at random as they left by the back door, so thefts such as this were frequently uncovered. Because of the way in which functions were organised in the Great Room, seating two thousand people, and the ballroom, seating up to five hundred, vast quantities of wines and spirits were left over at the tables once a function had ended. Because these had been paid for by the guests, staff were legitimately allowed to help themselves. I will always remember Mr Christmas, who worked back of house, as he would drink what was left over in all the glasses before he washed them up. He became an alcoholic and eventually died of cirrhosis of the liver.

Large hotels in general have much to answer for, sadly, because they create thousands of alcoholics. The wages are often low and drink is so freely available. The temptation for some people is just too great and I saw many members of staff whose lives became ruined by alcohol.

When Charlie, Norman, Mike and I, were the four valets of the apartment block, we often held meetings over a glass of whisky, although never actually paid for it. Company apartments had their own well-stocked drinks cabinets, which contained the highest-quality wines and spirits, vintage ports and single malts, which we had to continually keep topped up for their clients. The companies had no idea how many bottles were in there or how often they needed replacing, so it was very easy to walk out with half a bottle of whisky or gin, hidden in a laundry bag, to share with the other valets later. Nobody was any the wiser. We never stole from individuals, only the large companies that we felt could afford it. Occasionally we had a cigar too. I hardly smoked, but these were free, so I didn't look a gift horse in the mouth. We four sat in the valets' service apartment, each with a glass of whisky and a large cigar, and discussed the important subjects of the day. Usually it was our tips and how we were coining it in.

Wine waiters who worked in the function rooms had many ways of making themselves some extra money. They used to top up partly empty or completely empty wine bottles, resell them the next day and keep the cash for themselves. Their system was to funnel wine into bottles that had already been opened and paid for, and then present this to the customer as a newly opened bottle. Being the time before credit cards were used, most transactions were in cash. Bills were always handwritten by the wine waiters, if made out at all, so there was ample opportunity to defraud both customers and the hotel. Cash went straight into their pocket. They were instantly dismissed if caught, but most were too clever to be found out. Each wine waiter looked after two or three tables at a function, with ten guests per table, so there was money to be made there. Although staff were frequently searched on the way out, nobody thought to search them on the way in. Wine waiters used to smuggle bottles of spirits and wine into the hotel, which they then sold to the customers. Obviously this did not show up during stocktaking, and the waiters were able to pocket the money without it being noticed.

If a table of ten guests or more were having a meal, as they became more inebriated throughout the evening, they often lost count of how many bottles of wine they were drinking. Sometimes a waiter would craftily remove a full bottle of wine from their table with the empties when they weren't looking. The guests would later decide that supplies were getting low and they needed more. 'Another bottle of wine, waiter!' He would then bring back the wine he had removed earlier, so the guests paid twice for the same bottle.

Eventually the hotel realised just how much money they were losing through scams such as this and put a new system in place. From then on, waiters had to issue numbered requisition dockets in the function rooms. When a customer ordered drinks, the waiters had to take the appropriate docket to a central place to be presented to one of two dispense bar managers, who were seated behind a wire-mesh security screen. This worked well for a while until the wine waiters began conspiring with the bar managers. It took another two years before those managers were found out and dismissed. The security department then searched the lockers of all thirty function-room wine waiters at night and found enough alcohol to fill a tanker. Each locker had a dozen or more bottles, which had been smuggled in to sell on to the customer. Security lined it all up in the corridor and there must have been three to four hundred bottles of wines and spirits. All thirty wine waiters were dismissed.

People do not always notice how much they are spending once they have had a few drinks, until they receive the bill when they check out. The classic response is: 'I don't remember spending all that money on drinks. It can't be mine.' We always got customers to sign for what they had ordered, and could produce receipts with their signature on to prove it. At Grosvenor House they might query the drinks bill, and we would have to say tactfully, 'You did have rather an expensive port, Sir.' What they did not know was that the barman had a financial incentive to take as much revenue as possible, and could easily lead customers astray. He might recommend a superb malt whisky, but not mention that it was actually between fifteen and twenty pounds a glass. For a single bottle of whisky or gin even in those days guests could be charged £70 or more. If the barman had brought in his own bottles to sell, there was a good profit to be made. Often if guests paid for a round of drinks in cash, the barman would not ring the full amount up on the till and kept the cash for himself.

A conservative estimate is that Grosvenor House lost around £2,000 a day in revenue through theft of this kind, which works out at a minimum of £700,000 a year lost.

Sometimes guests used to hold cocktail parties in their suites before going down to dinner. The floor waiters would then clear up the suites, steal a bottle of whisky or gin, and hide it in the back of their tailcoats, which they had specially made for this purpose. I would often see waiters walking down the corridor with two bottles clanking in their tails. The bottles were sold to heads of department for ten shillings each, who then sold them back to the wine waiters for two shillings more. These were finally sold to the guests for maybe four or five pounds a bottle. Everyone was out to make a profit. If staff were not in a position to smuggle alcohol out or sell it on within the hotel, then they took the only remaining option open to them. They drank it! Many a time guests would ring down for the Duty Manager to complain that the miniatures of gin and vodka in their mini-bar contained water. After the early shift I would stand at the bus stop on my way home and would frequently see staff coming out of the hotel drunk. Many could hardly walk, they were so intoxicated. Around twenty-seven per cent of the revenue on mini-bar sales was lost every month – some through guests dishonestly claiming that they hadn't drunk it themselves — but at least ten per cent of it was staff theft.

Concierges often had scams going to increase their income. If a guest booked a chauffeur-driven car to another part of London, which might perhaps cost £100, the concierge would charge the customer £175 and keep the difference. Plus he would also receive commission from the car hire company in cash on top of that. When I was Deputy Manager, I was once approached by a car hire company who offered me £750 a month, cash in hand, if I would give them the contract to transport all Grosvenor House customers. I declined, but I knew then that the concierges were clearly making a packet for themselves, just through organising cars. We almost fired one concierge because Tony Murkett and I were only too well aware that he was involved in many similar scams and was fiddling a lot of money for himself. When we confronted him, he just looked at us disdainfully and said, 'Mr Kirby and Mr Murkett, you're a quarter of a million pounds too late.' Tony Murkett was seething, as there was nothing that we could do about it.

Concierges knew the rate that guests were paying and, if someone could afford £2,000 a night for a room, they had no qualms about overcharging them whenever they could, marking up the price of theatre tickets and so on. Many concierges had homes all around the world and were the highest earners on the staff. One day a guest went to catch a plane at Heathrow and when he arrived at the airport discovered that he had left his passport in a drawer at the hotel. He rang Grosvenor House in a panic, as he was desperate to catch the plane, and so the number-three concierge jumped on his motorbike and rode all the way to Heathrow with the man's passport. It was not a fast bike either, just a very ordinary motorcycle. The man was so relieved to have his passport that he gave the concierge a £1,000 tip.

Some banqueting managers were not above having their palms greased.

One, who must remain nameless, had a little scheme going with an outside events planner who was putting on functions in the Great Room. Often big firms employed an independent organiser or agent to arrange their lunch, dinner or conference at Grosvenor House, and the company would then pay commission to the organiser. If the company booked for another year and held the event again, it was known as a re-offer and no commission was charged. But one particular event organiser had a fiddle going. He charged commission on the rebooking and shared it fifty-fifty with the Banqueting Manager. So there was a nice little profit to be made for both of them.

Commission on just one job for 1,400 guests can amount to a tidy sum, probably around £20,000, and each time these two were pocketing it. Eventually it was discovered that the Banqueting Manager was receiving backhanders on many events, and was blackmailing his co-conspirator too, because he would say that the Great Room would be unavailable in future unless he received his cut. He was also charging clients for taking the chandeliers down in the Great Room, if that was what they required, but he pocketed the £1,200 fee. If tips were left at a function for the staff, this Banqueting Manager kept all the money for himself. He also used to put on an event for a particular company on a Sunday and would not allow anyone else to book the Ballroom on that date. The company paid £3,500 to hire the room, but supplied their own food and caterers, and he received his share of the profits. In the end his scams were found out and he was fired.

When Andrew Coy, my Director of Banqueting, took over the job he was determined to put a stop to any underhand practices. He called the crooked events planner into his office.

'Can you tell me why we will be paying commission on two jobs?' he asked. 'As a professional you will understand that we pay commission on new work, but not on re-offer work. I am sure that you have the best interests of your client at heart, and the Grosvenor House is one of your best venues. It would be a shame if we had to cancel the events.'

'Yes, I am a professional, Andrew,' he said, 'and you're a shit!'

Andrew thought that this was the end of the matter, but the shady organiser tried to do the same thing over a job for Wedgwood. To catch him out, the man from Wedgwood had a small Dictaphone under his jacket and recorded their conversation. Andrew then called him back into his office.

'We're both professionals,' he began, 'and I want you to explain this.' And he played him the recording. After that, Grosvenor House did not pay commission on re-offers.

Theft was everywhere. Money and personal items would be taken from guests' rooms by chambermaids. Some staff stole sheets, towels and even paintings off the walls. Today security is so much tighter, with electronic key systems which give only a limited number of people access to a room. At one period when theft of money from rooms was becoming more frequent, a trap was set up to find the culprit. A small camera was hidden on top of the curtain pelmet and wired to the room next door, where security men monitored all movements. A mini-bar attendant was seen to enter the room and take money from a briefcase, which security had planted in the room. He then tucked the money inside his sock. As he left the room, a security guard outside asked, 'Have you just taken money out of the bedroom?'

'Of course not, Sir,' the attendant replied innocently.

'What's that in your sock, then?'

The attendant was instantly fired and it sent shivers throughout the whole hotel. Modern technology was now being used for security purposes and staff had to be on their guard.

Grosvenor House was one of the first hotels to have electronic keys which recorded exactly who had been into a room. They were plastic, but shaped like an actual key. The introduction was for two reasons. First, it put a stop to staff theft, and secondly it gave peace of mind to the customers. A printout could tell security not only when the guest had entered the room, but which members of staff had been in too. It could not prevent theft completely but if, for example, drink was regularly disappearing from mini-bars, security would usually be able to see a pattern emerge. The thief would turn out to be the one member of staff that had been in all the rooms where items had been stolen. It was almost watertight.

When a linen chute was introduced to send dirty sheets and towels quickly from the floors down to the Laundry Room, it became an easy method for disposing of stolen objects. On one occasion paintings were disappearing from rooms and we could not work out how staff were stealing them, but I discovered that they were sending them down the laundry chute amongst the sheets and then collecting them later from the basement, before sneaking them out of the building through the loading bay.

One year we found that bottles of champagne were being hidden in a hamper of dirty linen. When a crate of champagne arrived in the loading bay, one member of staff was keeping a couple of bottles for himself and hid them temporarily in the hamper waiting to go to the laundry. Later he met up with the laundry van driver who was driving them out of the hotel and they shared the drink. He was fired once we discovered the scam.

If a room was being refurbished, builders would take out bags of rubble – but inside the rubble bag could be a picture or a small item of furniture, and these could be sent down in a rubble chute and then retrieved from the skip outside in the street. Chutes were very easy methods of removing items from the building and a headache for security, but we nearly always caught them in the end.

A perk of the job, rather than a cheat, was that purchasing managers used to receive many gifts from companies. Really they were intended as a bribe so that they could secure our custom, but we preferred to look upon them as gifts. It might be a Fortnum & Mason's hamper, a case of wine or spirits, theatre tickets for a West End show, an afternoon at the races, a weekend in Paris, an expensive meal in a restaurant, or straightforward cash in hand. The Purchasing Manager might, for example, be asked to buy 10,000 bars of soap for the hotel and would receive something from the supplier in return for the business. When you are buying in bulk for a five-star hotel, with hundreds of thousands of pounds' worth of business, suppliers desperate to get the custom will offer all kinds of incentives to the Purchasing Manager. I once received a car when I was in that position. I was buying uniforms for the staff from a company in North London. It was a big order, with new uniforms for the doormen, receptionists, butlers and so on. It was probably around £100,000's worth of business. Just before I placed the order, my wife and I were wined and dined by the company boss and I happened to say that I needed a car. A few days later a Vauxhall car arrived at my home.

Expenses were another area where staff members could swindle more money for themselves. Valets might press two suits but charge for three. Managers claiming for suits, which were a legitimate expense, often slipped in an extra one. Petrol miles could easily be increased when travel expenses were reimbursed. Just a slip of the pen and an extra nought could appear on a claim.

The only major fraud during my time was when an Apartments Manager and an accountant in the Credit Control Department colluded over the rents. They would collect rent money from the permanent residents in the Apartment Block but not put it all through the books. Inevitably they were caught and the Apartments Manager went to prison as a result. In some instances they had fraudulently raised the rents, entering only the legitimate rent rate in to the accounts and keeping the balance for themselves. With other guests they had offered a rent reduction if they paid in cash, and then some of the money was siphoned off into their own pockets. Altogether they stole around £20,000.

Something that always surprised me was that whenever general managers, banqueting managers, or people in high positions were fired, they always seemed to go on to better jobs somewhere else. I never understood how. Some just seemed to come up smelling of roses. We had to get references for people in the lowliest of jobs, yet unscrupulous managers that had been dismissed from Grosvenor House never let it hold them back in their career. A few were out-and-out thieves, yet I would discover that they had gone on to a high position in another hotel.

When I was in management we introduced security turnstiles at the Timekeeping Office for staff to go in and out of each day, as they clocked on and off, to try and cut down on theft. I used it as well, just to set an example to the others. Security did a one-in-ten airport-style stop and search, and this really reduced theft to practically nil, as staff never knew if they were going to be next in line for a search. Security called the police if anyone was caught stealing, and news of this quickly spread throughout the employees. It meant instant dismissal and nobody wanted a criminal record that might prevent them getting another job, so theft soon went down to zero.

As Manager and on the other side of the fence, I had to put a stop to any unlawful practices. Firing staff was always an unpleasant experience, especially if it was someone that I had known for years. One member of staff I had to dismiss was a waiter accused of fondling an eighteen-year-old student. She was working at Grosvenor House for three months during her summer break from university and had been coming down in the staff lift with him when he had touched her indecently. She burst into tears and ran to the Personnel Manager. There was a big investigation and, although the man denied it completely, he was fired. We listened to both sides of

210

the story and were positive that he was not telling the truth. He appealed and, as Deputy General Manager at that time, I had to interview him. The man brought his wife to the meeting and, as I questioned him methodically about the accusation, he broke down in tears and admitted that it was true. His wife hit him around the back of the head with her handbag and ran from the room crying. It was not a part of the job that I enjoyed.

The situation was more difficult when staff were incompetent rather than dishonest. We had one receptionist who continually made genuine errors and I often received complaints about his attitude too. Tony Murkett asked me to fire him, and so I called the guy into my office. After a short while I noticed a terrible stench. It was awful and not like anything I had ever smelt before in my life. I turned to Linda Woodhouse, the Personnel Manager, and suggested that we take a recess.

'What is that dreadful smell?' I asked her when we were alone.

'It's fear,' she said. 'Have you never smelt that before?'

I hadn't. The man was perfectly clean and it was not body odour or anything like that – it was just pure fear. I felt so sorry for him that I gave him another chance. Tony Murkett was furious, but I just couldn't bring myself to fire him.

I returned to Grosvenor House many years later for a dinner and was just checking in with my wife when I noticed that this same receptionist was on duty. He refused to speak to me, obviously remembering the fear that I had unintentionally induced. He hated my guts after that episode, even though I had spared him. Over the years I have now had to fire more than 2,500 staff for various reasons. Theft, fighting, bad behaviour, arguments and attitude problems, lack of ability and sheer laziness being the most common reasons and invariably they want to stab me in the back afterwards. I always say to employees when I first take them on that they must be team players and get on with each other. That is one of my Commandments, and it is the key to success in any hotel. It makes life better for all concerned if every member of staff works together, and the customer soon notices if a team doesn't gel. Here are my top Commandments for employees:

1. DO look after the guests – they pay your wages.
2. DO respect your colleagues.
3. DO look to create sales – then the profit looks after itself.

4. DO pay attention to detail at all times.
5. DON'T screw the guests.
6. DON'T steal tips from your colleagues.
7. KEEP away from the booze.
8. DON'T spit in the General Manager's food.

For a period we had problems when staff began to join a union, thinking that this made them immune to dismissal if they failed to pull their weight. Many at Grosvenor House joined the Transport and General Workers' Union, and one year all the chambermaids and waiters went on strike for more pay and in sympathy for the wine waiters who had been dismissed for selling their own wines and spirits. Those of us who were left had to make the beds, deal with the laundry, deliver meals on trolleys for room service, and generally take over their duties. I was out running with Rocco one evening and, as we came under the subway at Hyde Park and headed for the hotel, we saw a crowd of picketers outside Grosvenor House carrying placards saying 'Down with Lord Forte' and all kinds of derogatory statements. Rocco was furious, but I told him not to take any notice of them. They obviously saw us coming and refused to let us back into the hotel. He simply told them that if they weren't back at work by a certain date, then they would lose their jobs. They all came back to work.

Seeing his father insulted on placards made Rocco stronger in some ways, and determined never to give in to pressure from the unions. Although the basic wage was not high, management knew only too well that tips were huge in a five-star hotel and that the majority of the staff were doing very nicely, thank you. Lord Forte always paid well above the Catering Wages Act minimum rates anyway, which were reviewed annually, so there was little to gain from belonging to a union. When the unions took control of the Shelbourne Hotel in Dublin in 1983, Lord Forte simply closed it down. After a complete refurbishment, it reopened six months later with a large number of former employees, but not the militant unionists. Loyalty had to be to the Fortes rather than the unions. It was Lord Forte, after all, who was paying the wages and providing employment.

Not all staff members were rogues by a long chalk. Apartment 15A was the smallest in the hotel and was regularly used by the Banqueting Manager Robert Peel, as he usually worked into the early hours and often would not get to bed until 3 a.m. He was a lovely character and I treated Mr Peel like any other guest staying in the apartments. As a valet, I would clean his shoes, press his suit and collect any laundry to be washed. Once a month he gave me a £5 tip. Rather extraordinary when you think about it: staff tipping the staff. When Robert Peel left Grosvenor House he became Chief Executive of Thistle Hotels and eventually bought a chain of his own, which he called Robert Peel Hotels. He even bought up a couple of Forte hotels to add to his empire, and renamed them. He was a great hotelier, and I knew that I wanted to follow in his footsteps one day.

Jimmy Welsh was the Liaison Manager at Grosvenor House and was another lovely man. He taught me a lot about etiquette and the correct way to behave. As you walked into the hotel, his desk was immediately on the left of the door and he would look after all the VIPs that came to stay. Celebrities and their staff dealt with Jimmy personally and even rang him to make their booking, rather than book through the reservation system. He sadly died from cancer at Lister Hospital in London, where Wendy and I went to see him, and we later attended his funeral. He had a partner called Philip, who worked in the apartments, and after Jimmy's death Philip eventually entered into another relationship. I was horrified to read in the newspapers one day that Philip had been murdered by his new lover.

Linda Woodhouse, the Personnel Manager and later Director of Human Resources, was another who taught me a great deal, as it was an area of the hospitality industry that I knew nothing about until I became a manager. It was Linda who told me how to handle the staff. 'Don't lose your temper,' she might advise when I had to deal with a difficult employee. 'I know that you're desperate to fire him, but you've got to do it the right way.' She would tell me exactly how to go into a meeting, and the attitude to adopt to achieve the results I wanted. Linda eventually left the hotel and now runs her own successful human resources company, Woodhouse Independent, recruiting managers for five- and four-star deluxe hotels and quality restaurants.

Linda married an Italian waiter who worked at Grosvenor House. Relationships between staff were quite common. I met my wife Wendy there, of course. In the staff bar we would soon get to know who had fallen in love with whom, which people were dating, not to mention the staff members who were merely meeting for illicit sex. Some of the latter had wives and husbands at home. They were soon caught out and quickly resigned. With over two thousand staff, it really was like a village community and everybody's affairs quickly became the subject of gossip. No one could leave a bedroom without a chambermaid spotting them, so it was virtually impossible to conduct a secret relationship. But there was genuine joy when a couple ended up getting married.

Sometimes certain members of staff would have a fling with one of the guests. Room service waiters were the most susceptible, as they could be called to bring food to a room only to find a half-dressed predatory female guest waiting for them. The waiters were often young and attractive, and the ladies were nearly always in their forties or fifties. A waiter might go into the room with a food trolley, and not come out again for fifteen minutes. They used to joke that it was their black tailcoats that attracted the ladies and some confessed to having sex without even taking their tails off. Mini-bar attendants visiting rooms to restock the bottles were equally inclined to have their wicked way with a guest if the opportunity arose.

Occasionally guests tried to seduce a member of staff against their will, and that could cause problems. Chambermaids usually prop the room doors open with a heavy weight and a 'Cleaning in progress' sign so that they do not find themselves shut in a bedroom with a guest. We had one occasion where a girl was cleaning a room and a guest in his sixties locked the room door so that she could not escape, and put his arm up against the wall so that she could not get by him. He then started touching her, and she burst into tears and managed to flee the room. We immediately called the police and, although he denied it, we made him leave the hotel.

When an overweight American arrived at the hotel one night, he was rather the worse for drink and had to be helped out of his taxi. He had a beautiful girl with him, who asked Paul, one of the night doormen, if he would help the man to his room. She gave Paul the man's key card and they went up in the lift.

'It's very kind of you,' the girl thanked Paul as he manoeuvred the man on to the bed. The American was completely comatose and snoring his head off. 'I don't know what I'm going to do now,' the girl said, 'How am I going to get my money?'

'Money?' Paul looked surprised.

'Yes, I'm a prostitute.'

'How much was he going to pay you?'

'Three hundred pounds.'

Paul reached into the man's pocket, took out his wallet, which was filled with cash, and gave the girl her money. She then started to kiss him, and one thing led to another. So Paul put his top hat to one side and had his fun at another man's expense! I wonder how the American felt when he woke up in the morning? The girl was long gone by then.

The Health Club, where people would inevitably take their clothes off, could occasionally be a venue for some extra exercise. One night, after the club should have been locked up, a male guest was discovered with one of the female employees in the pool. Both were naked and making love under the water. The cleaners usually came in to the Health Club at midnight, but on this particular occasion turned up an hour early and surprised the couple, who obviously thought they had the place to themselves. We fired the girl, but I don't know if the pool was cleaned afterwards.

As General Manager, I like to think that I had a good relationship with the staff overall. The valets seemed happy to press my suits and polish my shoes, and generally looked after me. It was no secret that I had once been a valet myself, and I used to give them tips and the occasional drink, which they appreciated. Maybe I gave them something to aspire to as well: I was living proof that a valet could go on to become General Manager.

With so many people working under one roof there was always a great deal of jealousy and backstabbing amongst the staff, but when I reached the top job I genuinely felt a sense of warmth from the workforce, quite simply because I had started at the bottom. Unlike many of my predecessors I had not arrived at Grosvenor House as a manager, and this seemed to avoid an 'us and them' situation. Yes, I was the big boss, but at heart I was still considered to be one of them and that was what made all the difference. Although I was now in my smart navy-blue suit, I would still sometimes go down and have my coffee with the maintenance men and the workers below stairs. This allowed me to ask them their opinions and get their feedback as to where improvements could be made. They felt that they could talk to me, which improved staff morale, and they knew that I cared. Ultimately we kept to my Commandments and worked as a team.

There was only one area of the hotel where staff could be a total law unto themselves. Just one small group of employees who were such a vital cog in the wheel that they considered themselves to be masters of all they surveyed. Today they have celebrity status too, and can be even more difficult to deal with. I always used to take a deep breath before I entered the kitchen and confronted them – the chefs.

13

The Devil Sends Cooks

God sends meat, and the Devil sends cooks.
English proverb

One morning, while I was still a kitchen porter, one of the chefs came in with a cigarette hanging from his mouth. He walked over to the corner of the kitchen where there was a mop in a bucket, picked up the mop, unzipped his trousers and relieved himself in the bucket. Another chef came in just a moment later and said, 'You'll get into trouble with the Manager if he catches you smoking.' I thought to myself: never mind the cigarette, what about the contents of the bucket? Fortunately that particular chef did not remain employed at Grosvenor House for very long.

Chefs can be some of the most difficult and demanding of employees, and often behave as if they own the hotel. Today's celebrity chefs, such as Gordon Ramsay, shown on television shouting at kitchen staff with liberal use of the 'F' word, have not necessarily helped the situation. Many chefs now feel that this is the way that they should behave and try to emulate the likes of Ramsay, not for their undoubted cooking skills, but for their hot-tempered behaviour in the kitchen. When I bought my first hotel, it was not long before I sacked all four chefs, and I have sacked even more since then, either because I have been unhappy with their attitude or they were uncomfortable with the high service standards that I expect. I want five-star quality at all times.

My first encounter with chefs was in 1967 when I began work as a kitchen porter. We were known by everyone simply as KPs. Between the seven kitchens at Grosvenor House there were 112 chefs, and in those days around seventy per cent of them were French. The remainder were mainly English, although there were a few Italian and Spanish chefs too. There were many language problems because English was obviously not the native tongue of most chefs, and if they shouted out, 'Four smoked salmons, four roast ducks . . ', there could be mayhem if the waiters and waitresses could not understand their accents. All the chefs would shout and scream at the same time; there was no air-conditioning and so they all became very hot-tempered in the sauna-like heat from the ovens and hotplates. In the summer it was absolutely horrendous, and the air became blue with the foul language in various lingos. *Hell's Kitchen* really is an appropriate term for the environment in which they had to work.

When chefs were in a bad mood, the kitchen porters, waiters and waitresses bore the brunt of it. If anything went wrong, it was never ever the chefs' fault. A hotplate, where finished dishes were placed ready to go out to the diners, divided the kitchen like the Berlin Wall. With chefs on one side and waiters on the other, the hotplate formed a barrier over which abuse would be regularly hurled. If a guest complained that his chicken was cold, a chef would scream at the waiter for not serving it quickly enough, even if the waiter had served it immediately. If a customer complained about the taste of the food, it would still be the waiter's fault. So there was a lot of bad feeling across the divide and ninety per cent of the chefs were very unpopular.

If the General Manager or the Banqueting Manager happened to walk through the kitchen, the chefs changed immediately – they were cool, calm and looked as if butter wouldn't melt in their mouths. 'Good morning, Sir. Yes, the team are doing a wonderful job.' Five minutes later, they would revert to being screaming banshees. The chefs really only cared about themselves. They rarely mixed with any other members of staff and even sat separately in the staff canteen. As a result, the kitchen was always a very difficult department to manage. Once main courses were served, the chefs would often go home, leaving the desserts to the pastry department, and they certainly never cooked breakfasts. That was way beneath them to be frying eggs and bacon. We had to employ special breakfast chefs for that.

I believe a lot of the bad attitude from chefs stemmed from the fact that they did not deal directly with the customer. Very occasionally fifteen or twenty chefs would be brought out at the end of a very big function and would receive applause from the guests, but it was rare and most of the time they were in a world of their own where they ruled the roost. If there were any problems, it was the waiting staff who were on the frontline and bore the full impact of the guests' anger, even if the chef was really to blame. Today things have changed and often kitchens are upstairs and food is cooked in full view of the guests. There is no dividing wall and I think this makes chefs feel much more in touch with the guests and they receive immediate feedback from the customers.

The chefs that I admired were the eight that worked in the staff canteen. They prepared and cooked more meals for staff than the main kitchens did for customers, probably around 4,000 covers a day. It wasn't à la carte or Michelin-star food – they were never going to achieve any awards or AA rosettes – but I felt sad that they were forgotten about and received little recognition. They were treated as staff serving staff.

As General Manager in any hotel, my first port of call was always the kitchen. And I knew exactly what I would encounter even before I entered the door: immaturity, selfishness, arrogance, bad attitude and bullying. Running a successful kitchen should be all about teamwork. I have never tolerated bullying of any kind, and on no account would I ever employ a chef who feels that he is a god and can treat the rest of his staff in a tyrannical fashion. Many times I have seen chefs reduce waiters, waitresses, and even receptionists, to tears. The young commis chefs were particularly bullied, and I once went into a kitchen and found a chef throwing tomatoes at a kitchen porter.

'What on earth do you think you're doing?'

'Oh, I'm sorry, boss . . .'

'Well, sorry isn't good enough. You're throwing food around the kitchen, and at a member of my staff too. *My* staff, note, and not *your* staff, because I'm the General Manager. You've got an attitude problem, my boy. Now get in the office at once – I will not tolerate bullying and you're a bully.'

I gave him a stiff talking to, made him apologise to the kitchen porter and clean up the mess as well.

Chefs were not only bad-tempered with the staff, but they were always arguing amongst themselves as well. Actual physical fights could break out and chefs would need to be separated. Pots and pans could be thrown at the wall in a fit of rage, and I've even seen knives flying through the air.

Sometimes I had to inform chefs that complaints had been received about their food.

'Take it on the chin,' I would tell them, 'but make sure you get it right next time.'

I would then go out into the corridor, count to five, and return.

'What was that, gentlemen?' I would ask. I knew without a shadow of a doubt that they would have said something insulting about me under their breath. They looked at me as if to say, 'He's a cunning old fox, that Kirby.'

'You have a lovely day, won't you.'

'Yes, Mr Kirby.'

I used to make a point of calling in at the kitchen twenty or thirty times a day, and invariably I would catch one of the chefs having a crafty cigarette. 'You're not on a break, and I am employing you to do a job,' I used to say firmly. Often I received their resignation within two days.

As a youthful kitchen porter I was hot-tempered and not prepared to be bullied by chefs, but by luck I was a good footballer and this saved me from abuse. One of the chefs was goalkeeper for the Grosvenor House team and considered me to be their star player, so the chefs left me alone at work. I saw them bullying my mates verbally, which I hated, but if anyone stood up to them then the chefs would retaliate by spitting in their food. I used to eat in the staff canteen, where I knew that the food would be untouched. Late at night, once the chefs had gone home, and we had finished washing up and mopping the floors, we often used to wheel a banqueting table into the kitchen. We laid it up with a white tablecloth and candelabra, drank leftover wine and ate food that we had hidden under the hotplate, and raised two fingers to the chefs. We cleared up afterwards, and nobody ever knew of our midnight feasts.

Sadly there are still too many browbeating cooks in hotels and restaurants throughout the world, but fortunately their day seems to be coming to an end. The reality television shows that have given chefs their prominence have served only to highlight the fact that a belligerent attitude, and reducing staff to tears, does not always get the best out of people. You only have to look at some of the less volatile chefs, such as Raymond Blanc and Gary Rhodes, to realise that you achieve far more with honey than with vinegar. Firm and in control, yes, but aggressive and unpredictable, no.

In my kitchen today, Head Chef Michael Titherington is of the modern school. Quiet and unflappable, he has introduced his own inimitable style of cuisine and oversaw the development of the new à la carte restaurant which I launched in 2007. That year he became the first chef to give a cookery demonstration via the internet directly from the hotel kitchen, so that potential diners could see him prepare a dish from scratch before ordering. When customers are arranging functions, Michael will sit with them and go through menus, make suggestions, and even give them food tastings so that he can fulfil their requirements and make the event special. If we've had a big lunch or a dinner function, I will always bring Michael out at the end of the meal and introduce him, so that guests can see the chef responsible for the food they have just eaten, and he is always applauded. For me this is important. Instead of slaving away anonymously in the kitchen, which can be unrewarding, I like my chefs to feel involved from the very beginning when the menus are selected, right through to the end when they can see the guests' appreciation.

In my early days at Grosvenor House it was still silver service, with vegetables in tureens served individually at the table, and it seemed to take for ever to feed 1,500 people at a function. Banqueting was a difficult area to work in, as there would be so many complaints that the food was cold by the time the guests had everything on their plates and could actually begin eating their meal. The temperature of food is probably still the biggest complaint in hotels or restaurants, especially when there is a large number to serve. Lack of seasoning is another gripe, but these days, with so many people suffering from medical conditions such as high blood pressure, it is far better not to add too much salt to dishes. Chefs often feel insulted if guests think they need to add salt and pepper anyway. Slow service is a common criticism too, but this often stems back to the kitchen, because if the chefs don't have the food ready on time then the waiting staff can't serve it. The waiter gets a complaint from the customer, but will often get abuse from the chef if he passes the complaint on. It is *never* the chef's fault, of course. Timing is always an issue, and guests eat at different speeds. The waiter cannot say, 'Hurry up and eat your soup, the chef has your main course ready,' if a guest is a slow eater. But he will receive the complaint if the main course then ends up being cold or overcooked. Equally a fast eater might carp because the next course isn't ready quickly enough for him. Pity the poor waiting staff, always stuck in the middle between the customer and the chef.

Guests ordering room service often complained that food was cold by the time it reached them, especially breakfasts. In the late 1970s hot-boxes were introduced so that dishes arrived in a container at the right temperature. The hot-box was placed under the cloth-covered table from which they would sit and eat. Sometimes guests would ring down and say that they had not received any food and reception had to point out that it was in the hot-box. Then we had the opposite problem, as guests burned their hands removing food from the box and would complain that it was *too* hot! The Duty Manager had to go up to the room with treatment for finger burns.

In overall charge would be a Head Chef, who by the 1980s had the fancy title Executive Chef. Head Chefs tended to spend most of the day sitting in their office dealing with ordering and paperwork. Some over the years received backhanders from suppliers, gifts at their homes, and brown envelopes containing cash from butchers, fishmongers, greengrocers and purveyors of all manner of foodstuffs to ensure that they received the Grosvenor House business. Orders were not small, as a banquet in the Great Room might require 1,500 portions of lamb or turkey from a butcher, and so just one day's supply of meat could be very lucrative. At the end of a year, millions of pounds' worth of food would have been purchased.

When Trusthouse Forte took over, they put an end to any shady deals with food suppliers and introduced a Group Purchasing Department. Although we ordered our own quantities at Grosvenor House, the Group Purchasing Department stipulated which suppliers we were to deal with. Dried goods, for example, could only be ordered from one company. This reduced the backhanders, but then head chefs demanded a bigger salary in recompense for their loss.

Many head chefs did not pull their weight and had quite a cushy lifestyle, allowing other members of staff to wait on them. Admittedly they had a big responsibility on their shoulders but, like some of the general managers, a few abused their position.

As the head chefs were responsible for the quantity of food purchased, there was an enormous amount of wastage through over-ordering. They had to cover themselves so that food never ran out, and they also had to allow for the occasional culinary disaster, but if they needed 1,500 portions of meat for a function, they would usually order 1,600. This often meant that a hundred portions of lamb or turkey would then be thrown away as surplus to requirements. When management began to complain about the quantity of food in the bin, perhaps noticing that thirty steaks had been thrown away, chefs simply added the extra food to the huge stockpots instead to conceal the waste.

Head chefs were not beyond making mistakes either and from time to time they *under*-ordered. The ramifications of that were dire. If there was too much food, the customers were obviously unaware, but they soon noticed if there were not enough portions to go round. The excuse would be that the delivery was late arriving, but it was invariably because the Head Chef had ordered the wrong amount. With the ordering they had a large pad, about two by two foot in size, which had all the food items listed and the chef would just fill in the amounts required, but they did not always get it right. Eventually the system was changed and large walk-in fridges were installed so that food could be prepared a day in advance, then there was no danger of not having enough.

There were still occasional functions where guests were given the wrong food. Once a week there would be a meeting between the Head Chef, the Banqueting Manager, and the Food and Beverage Manager to discuss requirements but errors could still be made. The Banqueting Department was very streamlined and extremely detailed lists were drawn up for major functions, with meticulous timings and numbers to be served, which were passed on to the kitchens to try and avoid slip-ups. Chefs used to have to write out all the menus by hand in those days, and the typists could never understand their writing, so that could lead to mistakes. One menu listed a starter as 'Duck and Porn Terrine'. A guest quipped, 'Yesterday we had Spotted Dick, and now we have porn.'

All chefs burn themselves – it is an occupational hazard – but in the 1960s a kitchen could be a very dangerous place to work. One Christmas Day I had a female chef trip at the top of some stairs with a jug of boiling brandy sauce. It shot all over her face and the skin immediately started to peel off. It was horrifying. The poor girl had to be rushed to hospital and later needed skin grafts. The incident really upset the staff and put a dampener on the whole of Christmas that year. Many staff slipped if food had been accidentally spilt on floors and would smack their heads against the floor. One poor guy slipped one day on some grease and, in trying to save himself from falling, reached out for the nearest object and put his hand straight in a deep fat fryer. His injuries were appalling. Another unlucky man chopped the end of his finger right off. Cut fingers were very common and each week we would have two or three chefs with deep wounds, because there was so much pressure to get the food prepared for the large banquets. There were three restaurants to be catered for, the hotel lounge snacks, 24-hour room service, plus the function rooms, so chefs had a lot to cater for. If you have 800 meals to get out quickly, followed by a dinner for another thousand, speed is of the essence and accidents inevitably happen.

As a kitchen porter, I used to wash all the dishes by hand. In later years, dishwashing machines were introduced, which greatly reduced the workload, but cooking pans used by the chefs were often so dirty with baked-on food that hand washing was still the only way to get them really clean. The boys washing up had to wear thick rubber aprons to try and keep themselves dry, but the chefs would never tell them when a pan was still red hot and many a time a washer-up would burn their hands. A thoughtful person would warn you to take care because a pan was hot, but not the chefs. They were bastards sometimes.

The ovens were very old-fashioned in the 1960s and had to be stripped and cleaned overnight. Although the gas had been turned off, they were still too hot to handle for over an hour afterwards. We had to take them apart and they were so full of grease and dirt that a paint scraper was needed to remove the burnt-on food. There were no chemical cleaners, and we just had to wear gloves and scrub them down with hot soapy water, using bent wire coat hangers to get into hard to reach areas. The chefs didn't care if pans boiled over or fat spilled inside an oven; they weren't the ones that had to clean it. They used to kick and slam the oven doors too, and the maintenance men were always having to replace broken hinges. In the twenty-first century we have wonderful Rational Steam Combi Ovens, which are so much cleaner and have revolutionised catering, but in my kitchen porter days it was sheer elbow grease. Today we also have electric induction hobs, which look like black glass and you can place your hand on them without getting burned. Only the pan gets hot. At cookery demonstrations, chefs place ten-pound notes on the hob and they are not destroyed. It is a very clean and efficient way of cooking, and any spillages can easily be wiped off.

Out of all hotel employees, there is a greater incidence of alcoholism and drug-taking amongst chefs than in any other department. This is probably because of the great pressure that they are under. Celebrity chefs Jamie Oliver and Heston Blumenthal support the Ark Foundation, an anti-drink and drugs charity for people within the hospitality industry, in the hope of bringing about more public awareness of the problem. The charity's founder, Michael Quinn, the first-ever British Head Chef at London's Ritz Hotel, almost lost everything, including his life, through alcohol abuse. He now does all he can to warn youngsters about the stresses of hotel work and the dangers of alcohol and drugs. His charity is now affiliated to Hospitality Action, which helps people within the industry that have fallen on hard times.

We once hosted a function for Russian delegates and had to serve Beluga caviar from a huge urn carved out of ice. It was a beautiful ice sculpture from a specialist firm, costing several hundred pounds, and the chefs spent hours decorating it with fresh fruit so that it looked absolutely magnificent. The gimmick was that the sculpture contained vodka, which the delegates could pour into glasses from a small tap. The idea was that they put the caviar on their knuckles with a pearl spoon, and once this was eaten they had a shot of vodka. The chefs watered the vodka down so that they could drink half of it themselves. Once the event was over, they were eating the remaining caviar and knocking back the vodka like there was no tomorrow. It is this easy access to alcohol that has been the downfall of many chefs.

Poor hygiene was another area where chefs could cause problems in the 1960s. If one suffered with diarrhoea or sickness and still came to work, then the bug could spread amongst the staff, and even on to the guests. Today they have to stay at home if they are ill and are not allowed back until they are fully clear. Environmental health officers could come into hotels and take swabs from the chefs if guests had caught something and complained. Often if someone had a vomiting bug they would blame it on the food. 'It must have been something I've eaten,' is still a common response to an upset tummy, but it is much more likely to be a virus than the actual food. Once, after environmental health officers had done tests at Grosvenor House, the results revealed that four or five of the chefs had not washed their hands after going to the toilet. After that incident, hygiene greatly improved.

Personally, I never eat prawns at a buffet as they have such a short shelf life and can easily cause stomach upsets. Three hours is the maximum time that prawns should be out, then they have to go straight in the bin. In the past chefs did not know this and any prawns left over from a buffet went back into the fridge. Later they might be used for a prawn sandwich, by which time unseen bacteria had developed and the trouble would begin. Within five hours whoever had eaten them would be rushing to the bathroom. When you think about it, prawns have been caught somewhere, put into a bag for a few hours before being frozen somewhere else; later they are removed and travel by lorry to the hotel or restaurant and might sit in a loading bay for half an hour, before being transferred to yet another freezer. Eventually they will be defrosted and can then sit on a buffet table for hours. And if not consumed they might end up a day later in a prawn sandwich. So I steer well clear of prawns.

Another regular hygiene problem with lazy chefs was that they used to just wipe chopping knives on their apron or a cloth rather than wash them. If they used the same knife to cut meat or fish, and then prepared a vegetable or salad dish, the food was contaminated. Often vegetarians complained that they could taste fish in their vegetable dish, and this was because the chef had not washed his knife. Chopping boards were another source of cross-contamination, as the same board would be used for everything. Today boards are colour-coded, so a red board is used for meat, green for vegetables, white for onions, leeks and garlic, and blue for fish. They are made of polyethylene, which is easy to clean and does not absorb odours. Food stored in fridges now has to be rigorously dated and scrupulously separated too, so that blood from raw meat doesn't drip down on food below. Food handling is a minefield, but rightly so because chefs are playing with lives. Just one mistake and they can poison hundreds of people.

In the past, hotel kitchens have been plagued by cockroaches, which could sometimes fall into the food. Mice can be a problem, and some hotels near the River Thames had rats. The pest control companies had almost a full-time job keeping the place clean. If a mouse managed to reach the grandeur of the guest areas upstairs, there would be hell to pay, but we were used to them in the staff corridors in those days.

Careless chefs frequently burned food, especially potatoes, and gravy and sauces became the way of disguising mistakes. We once had a garden party where a whole pig was meant to be roasted on a spit, but the chef did not begin cooking it early enough and the meat was raw. It was impossible to serve it, as the guests would have been ill. As General Manager I was summoned to the organisers, who were really upset and all I could do was offer them their money back. That was a disaster, simply because the chef had not got his act together. Sometimes chefs sent meat out raw deliberately. If a guest ordered a rare steak, it would be given barely thirty seconds each side and then go out on the plate almost blue. It made me feel ill. Many times, however, a guest would say that a steak had not been cooked as ordered. The chef would do nothing with it, just send the same steak back out again on a clean plate with fresh garnish, and the guest would then say that the steak was now perfect.

If a guest complained about a dish, chefs did not take very kindly to it and would spit in their next course. The waiting staff were unaware of this, but as I quietly washed the pots and pans I used to see all that went on. Upsetting the chef led to reprisals and a particularly difficult guest would not know that his bacon had been rubbed along the floor before it went on his plate. On one occasion a chef was so irritated by a constantly complaining guest, who found fault with everything, that he urinated into a plastic cup and poured some of it into the man's soup. It gave a whole new meaning to pea and ham soup! I had to keep quiet about what I saw then; otherwise the chefs would have ousted me out of a job.

Once I was in management, it was a different story. Seven out of every ten staff whom I have fired during my career have been chefs, and the kitchen is probably the one department in a hotel where there is the biggest turnaround of staff. At one time it averaged ninety per cent a year. If I look at a chef's CV and see that he has hopped from job to job, then I would be very wary about employing him. Only recently I interviewed a chef and saw that he had worked in fifteen different establishments in fifteen months. I did not give him a job. One chef I fired was a real wimp, totally inflex-ible to the way the hotel worked, and quite unsuitable for running a busy kitchen. I had the tissues ready even before he came into my office, as I just knew that he would burst into tears, and he went off snivelling.

Cookery has moved forward in recent years thanks to television programmes, and what celebrity chefs have achieved is better working conditions gener-ally for chefs everywhere. Prior to this era, many chefs worked in appalling conditions in the dungeons below stairs. Today, most hotel and restaurant kitchens are air-conditioned, work surfaces are stainless steel, and chefs often use steam ovens to cook and do not even break out in a sweat. Some even buy in ready-prepared vegetables so there is no *mise en place*, or production line chopping food, and life is much easier for the chef than it used to be.

Some people do not realise that working in a restaurant kitchen is very different to cooking in a large five-star hotel. The restaurateurs of this world are not under the same pressure and don't have to get 1,500 diners served at the same time. A celebrity chef's restaurant might serve perhaps 200 people in an entire day. The food is cooked in small portions à la carte, and the guests are prepared to wait and make an evening of having dinner, so there is far less stress than having to cook for large numbers as in a hotel situation.

Food is now big business and customers will pay an arm and a leg to eat at the most fashionable restaurants. Celebrity guests want the best and are prepared to pay for it. In April 2008 Hollywood film actor Johnny Depp stayed for four nights at the luxury Copperleaf Boutique Hotel in Appleton, Wisconsin, during the making of his movie *Public Enemies*. One night he entertained nine friends to dinner at a nearby bistro, Flanagan's Wine Review, spending more than $6,000 on food and wine. To show his appreciation, the actor left a $1,500 tip. Proprietor Pat Flanagan said, 'Johnny Depp is welcome here anytime!'

Because chefs did not come into contact with guests, they obviously did not receive tips either, and I think this has always rankled with them. It was another reason for divisions and bad feeling, as it was always the waiting staff that received gratuities and the chef did not see a penny of it. 'We've done all the work preparing and cooking the food,' they used to grumble at the waiters. 'All you've done is take it to the table, but you get all the money.' I have changed that system and now have tips pooled and shared between the waiting staff, the chefs, and the kitchen porters, which keeps everyone happy and there is no argument about it. One group cooks the food, another serves it, another washes up the dishes, so I feel that they should all be treated equally.

Traditionally staff in hospitality have been paid low wages on the basis that they make it up in tips. Today we have a basic minimum wage, plus holiday pay, and so gratuities are genuinely an extra bonus for good service. Some greedy hoteliers and restaurateurs used to keep the tips for themselves and not pass them on to staff. This particularly happened in establishments where a ten per cent service charge was added to the bill. If someone had a £20,000 bill for a wedding reception, an additional ten per cent service charge was no small amount. In September 2009 the law changed and states that, if customers leave a cash tip, it must be given to the staff. But if they give a credit or debit card tip when paying the bill, the hotelier is allowed to keep it if he wishes. This is a retrograde step in my mind and not a practice that I follow, as I want my staff to have their dues.

Strangely, as food in restaurants and hotels has become more expensive the portions have become smaller. I first experienced this change in style when Nico Ladennis took over the Grosvenor House's 90 Park Lane restaurant, and I think that today customers are often grossly overcharged for small amounts of food in restaurants, and pay over the odds for wine too. With the world economic recession of 2009 I think many restaurateurs found it coming back to haunt them and had to reduce prices to encourage custom. Browns Hotel in London, for example, began to offer lunch at £20 when two years earlier it would have been £50, so maybe the credit crunch helped put things back into proportion. As many restaurants and pubs closed each week during the recession, it became a struggle for survival.

One of my biggest bugbears is food critics. One day they might be on television as a presenter, and the next they suddenly feel that they know all there is to know about food and that they are in a position to be a food critic. Most have never worked in a kitchen in their life. They might have cooked for half a dozen people at home, but put them in the Grosvenor House kitchens and they wouldn't have a clue what to do and would not last five minutes. I have no time for this type of critic.

I have often wondered why so few chefs have bought their own hotels. Some have ventured into the industry, such as Raymond Blanc with Le Manoir aux Quat' Saisons in Oxfordshire, and Michael Caines with the historic Royal Clarence in Exeter, Devon, and his partnership with Andrew Brownsword in the creation of the Abode chain of hotels, but my theory is that many don't simply because it is such hard work. Yet there is more money to be made long-term in hotels than there will ever be in restaurants, because rooms always make more profit than food. Maybe chefs in general lack the right temperament. Guests would not want a Gordon Ramsay–style manager telling them to 'F*** off!' if they complained about dust in their room or requested an extra pillow.

Because of my experiences with chefs over the years, I have tried hard to mould mine in a positive way. I always let them know what an important part of the team they are. The Head Chef, the Head Housekeeper, the Head Receptionist, the Head Kitchen Porter, the Restaurant Manager, are all of equal significance, none is more important than the other and each has a job to do and their own particular area of responsibility. 'You don't have to love each other, you don't have to marry each other, you don't have to go out drinking together . . .' I tell them at meetings, 'but when you're at the hotel, try and work together as a team, and you'll come to work a much happier person.' I find then that they go that extra mile. I also make sure that the customers see my Head Chef, Michael, and if he is out front in the public areas of the hotel then he is also being seen by the receptionists, the Restaurant Manager, the housekeeping staff, and so on. He is such an important player in the team that I don't want him hidden in the dungeons, and if a guest says, 'I had a really good meal last night', and compliments him on his cooking, then he gets to feel good about that too.

A hotel is really only as good as its staff, and it is vital to treat them well. If mine begin to play up, then they know that their days are numbered. But if they do well, then it does not go unnoticed and they are rewarded with regular pay rises. So they know exactly where they stand with me, and 'firm, but fair' has always been my motto. One of my pet hates is staff that cannot be bothered, and the worst possible thing that any of them can say to me is, 'It's not my job', when something hasn't been done. Teamwork is paramount.

As General Manager at Grosvenor House, if the chefs made a mistake, the buck stopped with me. But it is a problem that I have overcome today. If a guest receives a rare steak when he asked for it to be well done, for example, I now head straight for the kitchen and calmly call the chef responsible.

'Come with me to the restaurant.'

'Why, Mr Kirby?'

'Come and tell a guest why you served him a rare steak when he ordered it well done.'

'Oh, I can't do that, Mr Kirby. I can't go in there.'

'Come on . . .'

'Oh no, Mr Kirby, please. Please don't make me go in there.'

'All right. But now you know what it was like for that waiter or waitress. They got the rough edge of the customer's tongue. Would you want to be out there and have your head bitten off like that?'

'No, Mr Kirby.'

'Well, get your act together and serve the food properly next time.'

I remain firm and never lose my cool, but I think it's only fair that they take responsibility for their mistakes. If only I'd had the courage to do that with the chefs at Grosvenor House all those years ago.

14

Miracles Take a Little Longer

All saints can do miracles,
but few of them can keep a hotel.
Mark Twain, *Notebook* 1935

An Arab guest was checking out of the hotel one morning and, as he leaned over to speak to the receptionist, a very smartly dressed man walked by and casually took the guest's burgundy-leather briefcase. Inside was a quarter of a million pounds in cash, which was never recovered. The thief cleverly turned his head as he passed the security camera so that, although his crime was recorded, he could not be recognised.

Theft from hotels is commonplace and professional thieves haunted Park Lane. Immaculately dressed to blend in with genuine guests, they are typically artful opportunists, and on this particular occasion the bag thief really struck lucky. He walked out through the revolving doors so nonchalantly that nobody would have looked twice at him. He probably stepped into a taxi and was gone in seconds.

Guests are not beyond reproach themselves and habitually pilfer from hotels, often the smallest and relatively valueless bits and pieces too. Facecloths and napkins are stolen more regularly than any other item. At Grosvenor House we used to buy over 100,000 facecloths a year because so many disappeared, or guests had used them to clean their shoes and thereby saved on a valet charge. New linen napkins continually had to be purchased to replace those that went missing from the restaurants and function rooms. Books for the guests' use systematically disappeared. Financially, small items just had to be written off as an occupational hazard.

In recent years unscrupulous guests have become more audacious. Some have been known to simply walk out of a hotel carrying the 42-inch plasma

TV from their room. One man removed a marble fireplace from his room at the Four Seasons Beverley Wilshire Hotel in California, and at a Holiday Inn in the United States a couple managed to load the entire contents of their room into a removal van that was outside in the car park. At Grosvenor House a guest once stole a large fourteen-bulb crystal-glass chandelier from a suite. He must have known what he was doing, as he unscrewed the live wires without being electrocuted. We used to joke that it must have been one of the Trotter family from *Only Fools and Horses*. When we tried to track the man down, we discovered that he had given us a false address.

A study of one thousand British hoteliers revealed that women are more likely to steal items than men, and towels and bathrobes were the most likely items to be stolen. When slippers were introduced for guests, these vanished into their suitcases as well without being worn. Some guests even take items that are of no apparent use to them, such as TV remote controls which work only in that particular hotel. A popular trick is filling vodka and gin bottles with water, and whisky bottles with cold tea, to pretend that they have not consumed any drinks from the room's mini-bar.

'Did you have anything from the mini-bar, Mr Smith?' a receptionist might say to a guest checking out after breakfast.

'No, nothing at all.'

Later that morning the mini-bar attendant would say, 'Mr Smith's gone, and he's had six Becks, four whiskies and two vodkas.'

So we used to send the bill on. Occasionally we would get a letter back denying that they had drunk it and blaming the staff. All we could do then was write it off.

Five-star hotels with richer guests are certainly not immune from theft, and occupiers of £700-a-night rooms have been known to depart with higher-value items such as DVD players, statuary, paintings, bottles of expensive wine, and even bedside lamps and radio-alarms. Some guests stole the pillows from their beds because they were particularly soft. At Grosvenor House we used to lose 20,000 coat hangers annually, particularly trouser hangers with clips and the padded hangers for ladies' garments; also 100,000 bars of soap and 10,000 shower caps a year. Sometimes items such as keys and remote controls reported as stolen would be discovered later in the laundry room, as items left on the guests' beds could inadvertently be sent down the laundry chute with their dirty sheets.

Some hotels embellish everything, from drinking glasses to linen, cutlery to plates, key fobs to menus, with their name or logo on the basis that, if items are stolen, at least they act as a means of advertising. We found at Grosvenor House, however, that anything bearing the hotel name – such as napkins, knives, bath-towels and bathmats – were more likely to be stolen than anything else. Over a thousand ashtrays vanished every year for that very reason. In the end we stopped putting the name on, because there was so much theft.

Any small objects such as ornaments and clocks have to be wired or screwed in place to prevent them being lifted, but paintings still get stolen from walls, especially in corridors. I currently have a bronze bust of Sir Winston Churchill in my reception lounge, and I have had the statue glued to a piece of solid black granite and the granite plinth permanently fixed to a table to try and thwart thieves.

I have actually witnessed customers stealing tips that have been left on a table in the restaurant for a waiter or waitress, especially in the function rooms. When people were up dancing in the ballroom, drinks would regularly be stolen from the tables during their temporary absence. I was once on the balcony of the Great Room looking down on the floor below and I saw a man take someone's bottle of wine from a table and transfer it to his own when he thought nobody was watching him. Some guests brought in their own drinks to try and save money, especially bottles of champagne. Then they had the cheek to ask for an ice bucket.

Guests departing without paying their bill is a hazard for all hoteliers. A very famous American band once stayed at Grosvenor House for a whole week, and then left without settling the account. Today many hotels take fifty per cent in advance on the guests' credit card and, if they leave without paying, the balance can also be taken from the card. Other hotels just take the credit card details to check its validity when the guest first books in, then if he or she does not pay, the hotel can simply claim what is owed via the card. Of course, you always get the dodgy guests who try and pay with a stolen credit card, but usually these have been reported by the owner and so payments do not get authorised. Sometimes these thieves, known in the trade as 'runners', are off before you can ask them to pay by another method, and hotels can lose thousands of pounds a year this way. But security on cards and prevention of identity fraud is getting much better every year. Hotels also pass on information to fellow hoteliers to warn them of any scams and give descriptions of swindlers. At Grosvenor House there used to be local policemen who dealt only with hotel crime, such as credit card fraud, bag theft and security issues.

The simple 'Do not disturb' sign, so common in hotels, could often be used by unscrupulous guests to their advantage. In hotel lingo 'Do not disturb' means exactly that; the guest must not be disturbed by anyone. This was very frustrating sometimes for chambermaids if they were prevented from getting into a room to clean, but if they entered then they might find a guest asleep, in the nude, having sex, or whatever, and it was actually written into their contracts that they were forbidden to go in if a sign was in place. But if it was past the time when the guest should have checked out, then it was permissible for the chambermaid to inform the house-keeper, who would then telephone the room to get the all-clear to open the door. Occasionally a guest might simply have forgotten to remove the card, but more often than not the guests had sneaked out of the hotel without paying. The introduction of credit card payments put an end to this type of trickery.

Five-star hotels seldom had single rooms in those days and so a person on their own would be given a double room, but paid a lower rate. This inevitably led to another type of deception, where a guest only paid for single occupancy but smuggled someone else in to share the room. They would have room-service breakfast, rather than go down to the dining room, and always asked for the tray to be left outside the door. We generally became suspicious if they asked for extra toast or an additional cup and saucer. Hotel staff were like detectives and could soon see that two bathrobes had been used in a room supposedly only occupied by one person. When they checked out, reception would say, 'Now there were two of you, weren't there?'

'Oh no, there was only me.'

'But two of you have been seen leaving the room. It's on our security cameras.'

Sometimes they confessed, while others brazened it out.

Some guests tried to escape because they had caused an expensive amount of damage to the room and did not want to pay for it. Burnt bedspreads were common, especially if a guest accidentally placed their travel iron on top of it. That could mean a £200 bill for its replacement. Couples had fights and we could find blood anywhere: on the bed, the curtains, the carpet, or the walls, which cost around £300 to clean up professionally.

One man had an argument with his girlfriend, kicked the door to her room in, leaving a big hole, and smashed the television on the floor in anger. The police arrested him, and he later came back to the hotel and paid for the damage. He confessed that he was drunk at the time, but he seemed a real wimp when sober. So much damage was drink related.

Many times we had customers come into the restaurant, have an expensive meal, then go off to the toilet and you never saw them again. We had this happen at Grosvenor House when four guests ordered two bottles of Dom Perignon champagne and the best food on the menu, running up a bill of over £400. One by one they pretended that they were going to the toilet or just popping out for a cigarette. The waiters noticed the minutes ticking by and eventually realised that the diners were not coming back. The best restaurants in the world now take a telephone number when a table is booked, and call the guests a few days beforehand to check that the booking is still required and, more importantly, that it is a genuine telephone number. But it is harder for hotel restaurants to do that when non-residents come in for a meal without booking. If there is a table of two or four, waiters have to be vigilant that the diners do not all 'go to the toilet' at the same time.

From time to time burglars used to climb up the drain pipes and in through an open window to steal items, but the most audacious thieves of all were the very well-dressed men and women who simply strolled into the hotel, went up to one of the floors in a guest lift and searched for a room with an open door. If a chambermaid was inside cleaning, they would pose as the guest staying in that particular room and might say, 'Oh, I've just come back to pick up a few things,' or maybe, 'I forgot my raincoat'. They would then quickly gather any valuable objects lying around, such as cash, chequebooks, cameras, jewellery, and depart as swiftly as possible. These thieves were so casual and convincing that the chambermaid would not suspect a thing. We put a stop to this by making sure that the chambermaids either locked themselves in the room while cleaning or, if they left the door open, to only allow anyone in that had the correct key card and could prove their identity.

It is not just objects that guests take that can be a problem, but also the items that they leave behind. Every six months we used to go through lost property at Grosvenor House and once found: 600 pairs of ladies' knickers,

750 umbrellas, 41 cameras, clothing of all kinds, crutches, a false leg, porn magazines and sex toys, handbags, keys, belts and ties. Reading glasses are in the top ten most common items left behind. Most items went to charity if not claimed, but if it was an item of value – such as a gold watch or a piece of jewellery – then the member of staff that found it was entitled to have it if the original owner was clearly not going to collect it within six months. The discovery of pornography was common, but sometimes months or even years after the guest had vacated the room. Rather than throw their magazines in the waste-paper bin, where the maids would find them and know who had left them, guests used to hide pornography and sex toys behind a bath panel or at the back of a toilet cistern where they would not be discovered until much later. When royalty or VIPs were due at the hotel and a thorough search had to be made with sniffer dogs, it was then that these things came to light.

Sometimes valuables could be left behind at Grosvenor House for thirty or forty years if guests had secured them in safe-deposit boxes. A facility for guests allowed them to go to the cashier section where they would be given the only key to a deposit box. In it they could store whatever treasures they wanted, and there must have been two or three hundred stainless-steel boxes of varying sizes, stacked six feet high, each with its individual red identity number. The hotel had no way of opening them and, if a guest lost the single key, the only way in was to actually drill through the lock. We then had to charge them for the cost of replacing the box. If a resident died and had not informed their family that they had anything stored with us, then the box remained unopened indefinitely. People who lived in the apartments rarely remembered to include the boxes in their wills.

When the reception area at Grosvenor House was refurbished in the late 1980s – one of my assignments as Projects Manager – the cashier section was moved and five old, long-forgotten safe-deposit boxes were discovered. Steve the Security Manager called me down because there were record cards saying to whom the boxes belonged, though some of them clearly had not been touched for years. The contact details were out of date and the hotel had been unable to track down the owners. A maintenance man drilled through the locks, leaving Steve and me feeling rather like Howard Carter opening Tutankhamen's tomb, as we had absolutely no idea what we might find inside. One contained some jewellery, not particularly spectacular or precious. Others had various documents, a passport, a small amount of cash, a watch, but nothing very exciting. We had the final box to search when Steve's bleeper went off with a call to attend to a security alert.

'I can deal with this, if you like,' I said.

'No, it's OK, we might as well just go through the last box.'

He lifted the lid and inside was half-a-million pounds in cash.

Our eyes must have been out on stalks. It was crammed full of fifty-pound notes in cellophane packets, so many that not another note would have fitted in. It had been left by a wealthy Arab five years earlier, who had simply never returned to collect it. I just looked at all this forgotten money, and I know without a shadow of a doubt that if Steve had not been there I would have helped myself to a few hundred thousand pounds. Nobody would have been any the wiser, and what a difference it would have made to my life. If only I had insisted that Steve had gone to sort out the security problem and had left me alone with the box for five minutes. My jacket would have been stuffed with fifty-pound notes! I was gutted at the thought of it because here was money that had just been left behind and the owner obviously didn't need or care about it. Even today I sometimes think that I should have suggested to Steve that we shared a little of it, but I didn't say a word. He probably feels exactly the same. Half-a-million pounds! We could have been very rich boys. What would you have done?

We tried to contact the owner of the money, but there was just no way of locating him. Even the Saudi Arabian Embassy could not help. We later discovered that he had also left behind two cars in the garage with covers on. When the covers were removed, we found a Ferrari and a Rolls-Royce. Like the half-a-million pounds, the cars were never collected. Forte plc benefitted from the cash and the sale of the cars, as they were found on their property, and we did not see a single penny of it.

Some of the discoveries at Grosvenor House were a little more sinister. A distressed chambermaid once called me up to a suite on the sixth floor after she had gone in to clean the shower, pulled back the curtain, and found a dead sheep inside with its throat cut. There was blood everywhere.

We had received a call from the office of one of King Fahd of Saudi Arabia's seven brothers. The Prince used to roam the world, going from hotel to hotel, as he was an outcast from the Saudi Royal Family. He had been staying at the Hilton on Park Lane, but wanted to transfer to Grosvenor House with his entourage and needed seventy bedrooms for four or five weeks. The bill was paid weekly in cash and it was fantastic business for the hotel, but some of the entourage used to cook food on the floor of their rooms and this sheep was obviously intended for that night's dinner. It gave us all a nasty shock.

The Prince used to employ staff from different parts of the world and one day I received a phone call from the loading-bay staff to say that they had found a Moroccan girl curled up in a ball underneath a desk in their office, frightened and crying. I went down to see what was going on, and recognised the girl as being part of the Saudi household. She spoke poor English, but told me that she had been working for the family for two years and had not been allowed home to see her husband and children. She was running away because she had been beaten with a whip by the King of Saudi Arabia's sister-in-law, and she did not know what to do. She was in great distress and showed me the terrible marks on her back where she had been beaten with a lash.

A few days prior to her escape she had thrown a note out of the hotel window, written on the cardboard lid of a laundry box, saying 'Please help me'. A guest had found it on the pavement with its Grosvenor House logo and handed it in at reception. Police came to investigate, but the situation was covered up by her employer.

At that moment I could see the Saudi Prince's security men from the French Foreign Legion outside, walking up and down Park Street. They had clearly been sent out to find this girl. I asked the loading-bay men to close the eighteen-foot-high electric metal doors to the bay so that nobody could see inside. I then led the girl secretly along the warren of corridors under the hotel, which I knew like the back of my hand, from the Park Street side of the building to Park Lane on the opposite side and helped her escape into a taxi. As soon as I opened the car door she lay immediately on the floor at the back, shaking and sobbing with fear. I gave the taxi driver £20 and told him to drive her straight to the Moroccan Embassy and not to stop for anyone. He shot off at speed and I never saw or heard from the girl again. I just hope that she was able to get back home to the safety of Morocco.

I did not tell a soul at the hotel what had happened for fear of reprisals. The girl told me that she had tried to escape before, but had been caught and beaten as the Saudi Royal Family were frightened about any secrets she might reveal. So much of the ruling family's private life is clouded in

240

mystery and they go to great lengths to hide it. In 2005 there was a bitter dispute between King Fahd and one of his ex-wives, the beautiful Janan Harb, who tried to obtain an increase in maintenance from his £32 billion fortune and threatened to expose what went on behind the scenes. Even then lawyers listed the case as *Maple v Maple* so that nobody would recognise the family involved. Proceedings ended when King Fahd died in July that year.

Prince George, the Sultan of Brunei's nephew, once had a girlfriend whom he kept hidden in a room on a floor below his suite so that his family would not find out. The girl lived a life of luxury and used to order dinner to be taken to her room each evening so that she would not be seen in public. Room service one day set up a table for her meal, and on it she placed a £230,000 diamond-encrusted tennis racquet–shaped brooch in a glass of cleaning solution while she ate. When the table was later cleared by staff, the glass containing the brooch was unintentionally removed with the rest of the crockery and the contents were disposed of with the refuse. Despite a very thorough search, the brooch was never found and is probably now hidden somewhere in a landfill site. When I informed Prince George about the lost jewellery, he simply said to forget all about it. He was unconcerned.

Prince George's father was Prince Geoffrey, who in later life bought the Dorchester Hotel. Brunei protocol stated that only one Prince could stay in a hotel at a time, so if Prince Geoffrey was at the Dorchester, Prince George came to stay at Grosvenor House.

During my valeting years, a delightful couple had apartment 44. I got on very well with them and used to undertake occasional private work for them too. They had houses in Sandwich and London and I used to go there with my fellow valet, Michael, to help with the catering whenever they held large dinner parties. The man was in the insurance business, very rich and lived the life of Riley. Then one day I read in the national newspapers that he had defrauded people out of millions of pounds by siphoning off money and was wanted by the police. The whole family fled to Spain, but were later tracked down. You never can tell.

Controversial heavyweight champion Mike Tyson was someone who caused me problems when he propositioned a young member of my staff in the lift. The pretty Chinese girl worked in the hotel's Health Club and happened to

241

be in the lift when the world famous boxer entered. She should not have been in the guest lift and I later gave her a telling off for it. In those days the Health Club girls wore extremely short skirts, in navy blue with a pleat rather like a school PE kit, and a short-sleeved top. They did look rather sexy and left very little to the imagination. She was obviously impressed at seeing Mike Tyson in the lift, I don't know if she began to flirt with him but he was clearly attracted to her, and he invited her back to his room.

Although he didn't actually lay a finger on her, he had the girl pressed against the lift wall as he tried to chat her up, and held his arm across the door so that she couldn't get out. The girl became extremely distressed by the incident. When he finally let her go after four or five minutes, she came to me in tears, and my immediate thought was to have him thrown out of the hotel. But I feared that it would only bring with it bad publicity, it was her word against his after all, and I did not fancy doing a round with Mike Tyson. If she had not wrongly used the guest lift in the first place, she would not have found herself in that position. Nicknamed 'The Baddest Man on the Planet', Mike Tyson later served three years in prison when convicted of raping a woman in an Indianapolis hotel room.

Other boxers were regular visitors to Grosvenor House, as boxing matches used to be held in the Great Room. I particularly remember Henry Cooper's many visits, as he was a large man, always immaculately dressed, and he was charming to everyone and a gentleman. If guests asked him for an autograph, he always signed his name for them without any quibble. He also came to functions such as the Water Rats Dinner, along with Frank Bruno, and did a lot of charity work. I was less enamoured with Chris Eubank though, who stayed at the hotel a lot. He was world champion for over five years and undefeated middleweight and, although he was pleasant enough, I found him demanding and always trying to cut a deal. Everything had to be the best with him too – the best food, the best room – but if he could get something for nothing, he was happy. I have to say that I never felt comfortable in his presence.

Although there were many old Music Hall jokes about unmarried couples, or people having an extra-marital fling, booking into hotels as Mr and Mrs Smith or Mr and Mrs Jones, it still happens even today. And we can always tell who these couples are, they just stand out a mile. It becomes more difficult though for this kind of deception, as the credit card instantly gives their real names away.

An unwelcome visitor occasionally appeared on the third floor of the hotel; a young lady in her mid-twenties, always in tears. Whether she had previously stayed at Grosvenor House, we never knew, but this ghostly apparition in a white silk dress was seen by many guests over the years. Many of the staff also reported a strange sensation whenever they were on the third floor, although I never saw the ghost myself.

One of the worst situations for any hotel manager is when guests make their final departure through natural causes. Over the years so many people died of old age or over-indulgence at Grosvenor House. Once a doctor had confirmed the death, undertakers used to come in the side door with a metal coffin, and the only way out of the hotel without distressing the guests was to take the coffin down in the staff lift. However, as the coffin would not fit in the lift horizontally, it had to be stood on its end. There were many occasions when I was showing undertakers the way, and we had to go through the rigmarole of tipping up the coffin. As this was done, the body would move with a loud thud and I never knew whether it was the head or the feet. It really made me cringe.

15

An Opportunity in Difficulty

A pessimist sees the difficulty in every opportunity; an optimist sees the opportunity in every difficulty.

Sir Winston Churchill

Although technically I was only appointed caretaker General Manager, I was certain it just a mere formality that the role would become permanently mine. I probably had more experience of that hotel and the workings of each department than any previous General Manager and I loved every minute of it. After twenty-eight years at Grosvenor House I had finally reached the top of the tree.

Rocco Forte called me unexpectedly one day and invited me for a run, which had not happened for a long time.

'You've done a great job at Grosvenor House,' he said, 'but we're going to move you on.'

It was a real bolt from the blue. Only four months in my dream job, which I had waited more than half my life to achieve, and now it was being taken away just as suddenly as it had been given to me. The Forte directors apparently felt that twenty-eight years was far too long for me to remain in the same hotel. I had no other option than to reluctantly agree. I temporarily returned to being number two again, back in my old job as Deputy Manager. I was very frustrated and felt that, somewhere along the line, the knives were out. Someone wanted to get rid of me.

A new General Manager was appointed in my place, who later turned out to be a thief and had to be sacked. He was running up large bills, having champagne parties in his apartment at the hotel's expense, and living the life of a lord. It was discovered that even his wife was stealing paintings from the hotel.

Rocco always supported me and at least had some words of comfort. He had asked the Area Director to give me the position of General Manager at the Berystede Hotel in Ascot, another Forte hotel. Rocco's idea was that I would go there for a couple of years to gain more experience as a General Manager, and then I could return to London in the top position at one of their major hotels, possibly the Waldorf. At least all was not lost.

The Area Director of the Forte hotel chain bought me breakfast at Grosvenor House one morning and revealed that the present General Manager of the Berystede was still there, so I would have to wait. Until that moment I had no idea that I would be stealing another man's job, and nobody had yet broken the news to him either. I had really been offered a position that didn't actually exist at the time. This placed me in limbo. Carrots were being dangled before me, but not the reality of an actual job. At Rocco's instigation I was sent on a period of secondment to the King Edward Hotel in Toronto. It was for two weeks to study the food and beverage side of the operation. I think it was really just to get me out of the way until the job became vacant.

I flew to Canada in December 1994. The General Manager of the King Edward Hotel was a lovely guy, but I think he was nervous about my arrival. He must have wondered why I was there, whether I was a Forte spy, or if I had been sent to steal his job and take over the hotel. Built in 1903, the 'King Eddie' (as it is affectionately known) had been fully restored in 1981 and over the years has seen many celebrity guests, just like Grosvenor House. Film stars such as Rudolph Valentino, Elizabeth Taylor and Richard Burton, politicians including Margaret Thatcher, and pop stars from The Beatles to Britney Spears have all stayed in the hotel at various times.

Although I was there to gain experience, they looked after me extremely well and I was really living like one of the celebrity guests. I ate so much good food that I began to put on a little weight. I went jogging with the General Manager several times to try and keep fit, although the temperature in Toronto at that time of year was absolutely freezing and the ground was treacherously slippery. Although he included me in the regular staff meetings and occasionally asked my advice, I can't say that I learned a great deal from the experience. But it served its purpose of keeping me out of the way while the company decided my fate.

I came back to England laden with toys for our children and, for the first time in years, I was able to spend Christmas and New Year at home with my family. I was thrilled to learn that Rocco had received a knight-hood in the Queen's New Year's Honours List for services to the UK tourism industry, which was certainly well deserved. We toasted Sir Rocco as January 1995 dawned, but the poor General Manager of the Berystede, Peter Astor, still hadn't been told that he was surplus to requirements and my own future was equally uncertain.

I was then unexpectedly sent to the White Horse Hotel in Dorking, ostensibly as an introduction to the Heritage Hotels group, one of around forty-six four-star hotels that Forte owned under this banner. The Berystede at Ascot, my ultimate destination, was also one of these Heritage Hotels. Unlike Grosvenor House, the White Horse had only seventy-eight rooms and was run on very different lines. There were no big budgets of hundreds of thousands of pounds to play around with, profit margins were tight and there were many limitations. I spent six weeks there, bored to tears as I really wanted to start work at the Berystede. I just seemed to be a hanger-on in other people's hotels, with no real position.

I could not understand why it was such a long drawn-out process, until I discovered that it was because the Area Director really did not like the idea of me being sent to the Berystede at Sir Rocco's behest. It meant pushing out Peter Astor, a General Manager that he did not actually want to get rid of. He felt that I was only being given the job because I was Rocco's blue-eyed boy, and that is why he stalled. One day I received a tele-phone call from Peter.

'Is it true that you're coming here as General Manager?' he asked. He had obviously heard rumours.

'I'm sorry, Peter, but I can't say anything about it.'

It put me in such an awkward position, and I felt so sorry for Peter. I had worked with him at Grosvenor House when he was Front Office Manager, and he had deserved his promotion to the Berystede. Now he was being pushed out to make way for me.

Eventually the matter came to a head. Peter was moved on, and I took his place as General Manager, but it clearly rankled with the Area Director and we had a very difficult relationship. The Berystede was a luxurious hotel with ninety bedrooms in Royal Ascot, home of the famous race-course, and, although I was happy to be there at last, I knew that the Area Director was just looking for an excuse to get me out of the Forte group. One day the dishwasher broke down and we had to start washing and drying everything by hand until it could be repaired. It was not ideal, but we had no other option. That very day an Environmental Health Officer turned up at the hotel to do an inspection. It was a huge coincidence that he should arrive at a time when things were not running as efficiently as usual and I was certain that the Area Director had masterminded this visit. The next thing I knew, I was summoned to the Area Director's office.

Rocco and I had stopped running marathons together, but I suddenly got a call from his PA saying that Rocco would like to go for a run. The last time this had happened, he had dropped the bombshell that I was to leave Grosvenor House, so I was curious as to why I had been called on this occasion. As we ran, he started asking me questions about my work at the Berystede. As always, I was perfectly honest with Rocco and explained that I did not get on with the Area Director and that he had summoned me to his office for some reason.

At the appointed time I went to the Area Director's office in Slough, where I unexpectedly received a warning because the dishwasher had not been working when an Environmental Health Officer had visited. As if the dishwasher breaking down had been my fault! I was not happy about that at all and could feel my blood starting to boil. Suddenly a secretary appeared at the door and said that Sir Rocco Forte was on the telephone. As the Area Director went to take the call, she said, 'No, Sir, the call's for Neil Kirby.'

His face was a picture.

I went into an office, where I could take the call privately. That did not go down well at all, I'm sure. Rocco asked me about the meeting, so I described what was going on and that I had just been given a warning by the Area Director.

'Don't worry about him,' Rocco said, 'We're going to get rid of him anyway once all this has died down.'

I put down the receiver and returned to the room, now feeling very confident and cocky.

'I don't know why I'm here really,' I began, 'This is beginning to annoy me now.'

By this time the Area Director was less sure of himself, knowing that Rocco had personally called me and he was completely in the dark, of course, as to the content of our conversation.

'I'm extremely disappointed with this,' I continued, really feeling cocka-hoop. 'If a machine breaks down at the hotel, it is not my fault. We tried to get it repaired, but in the meantime we had to wash everything by hand. The Environmental Health Officer then came in at the very time that the machine had broken down. So, why am I here? All the years I've been in this business . . .'

'Let's forget all about it,' said the Area Director.

He knew that he was scuppered.

While I was at the Berystede, Rocco used to hire the nearby Sunningdale Golf Course for five days at a time for the Forte Hotels Tournament and many veteran professional golfers came and played, such as Arnold Palmer, Tony Jacklin and Jack Nicklaus. A number of celebrity players took part too, including Ronnie Corbett, Bruce Forsyth, Ian St John, Alan Hanson, Mike Reid, Kenny Lynch and Jimmy Tarbuck. I had to organise the catering for the event, so I called on Andrew Coy and my old colleagues at Grosvenor House to help. There had been complaints about the food in the previous year, so I was determined that it was going to be superb quality this time, with no room for complaint. We had a magnificent marquee set out on the lawn, put on exquisite food with a running buffet, and everyone seemed very happy. Sir Rocco came down to the hotel to support me and we hosted a cocktail party together for some of the pro golfers. I took advantage of his presence and pointed out that many of the chairs needed replacing. I knew that Head Office wouldn't sanction the expense, but hoped that Rocco would be able to set the wheels in motion.

'Talk to that Area Director chappie over there,' he said, pointing to my nemesis.

So the next day I approached the Area Director.

'Sir Rocco Forte told me last night that we can replace the chairs in here.'

He just looked at me and said, 'You bastard, Kirby.' He knew that he could not refuse the money if Rocco had agreed, and within six weeks I was able to spend £2,000 on new chairs. That was not the end of it, of course. Later the Area Director came round and told me that I had over-spent by £2,000 on my budget. So I then had £2,000 less to spend on operating costs at the hotel. He really had it in for me.

I was General Manager at the Berystede Hotel for exactly two years and, although the original intention was for me to eventually return to manage a big London hotel, the Forte empire collapsed and I was unexpectedly made redundant after thirty years in the business. Within two years of becoming chairman of Forte plc, Sir Rocco succumbed to a hostile £3.9 billion takeover bid by Granada, the television and leisure group, headed by Charles Allen and Gerry Robinson.

It was a terrific blow to the Forte family, but Rocco typically hosted a farewell party at the Waldorf Hotel in London to go out in style and say thank you to his staff. It was a very sad occasion. Rocco and his sister Olga must have been very bitter about the takeover, but neither let it show. As I said goodbye to them that day, it really seemed like the end of an era. Lord Forte had retired by this time, but I could not help wondering how he must have felt. Forte plc, which he had worked so hard to build up, had gone for ever.

Despite this setback, the Fortes nevertheless netted a reputed £324 million from the deal and Rocco re-established a new business in 1996 based around some of Europe's top hotels – the first being the Balmoral Hotel in Edinburgh. By 2006 the new Forte empire also included the Hotel de Russie in Rome, the Astoria in St Petersburg, the St David's Hotel and Spa in Cardiff, the Hotel Amigo in Brussels, the Hotel Savoy in Florence, the Lowry Hotel in Manchester and Brown's Hotel in London, with further plans for hotels in Frankfurt, Geneva and Munich. Sir Rocco's sister, Olga Polizzi, sat on the board of the family business and held the title of Managing Director, Building and Design, and now has hotels of her own, including the luxurious Hotel Tresanton in Cornwall. Rocco and Olga showed that they had inherited their father's fighting spirit and resolve.

Granada took over the Berystede and decided to 'cluster' their general managers to save money; so a single General Manager became responsible for three or four hotels, and I was told that I was surplus to requirements. For the first time in my life I was unemployed.

Out of the blue I received a telephone called from Giuseppe Pecorelli, a former Managing Director of Trusthouse Forte. He now owned Exclusive Hotels, once part of the Forte group, which included four hotels and two golf clubs. One of these was Pennyhill Park Hotel, at Bagshot in Surrey, and having heard that I was now on the market, Mr Pecorelli offered me a position. Initially he asked me to be a consultant for three months and gave me a list of improvements that needed to be made at Pennyhill, just as a trial to see how we got on. I soon fired the Deputy General Manager and a few chefs, and within ten days Mr Pecorelli asked me if I would accept the job of General Manager.

I was able to move Pennyhill Park Hotel forward as Mr Pecorelli had envisaged, and by 1999 we had been awarded our fifth AA black star, which we were very proud of. We put in extra bedrooms, a new bar, a second restaurant, and continuously refurbished. I had a new £1 million kitchen built, which meant demolishing the original and for an entire year the chefs worked out of sixteen Portakabins as a makeshift kitchen, which was horrendous at the time but worth it in the end.

At Pennyhill I was able to renew acquaintance with Sir Jackie Stewart, whom I had not seen since my leaving party from Grosvenor House in 1994. He was living in nearby Sunningdale by this time. Sir Jackie had taken over Formula One and needed to be in the UK more often, so he did a house swap with pop star Phil Collins. Whenever Sir Jackie needed to be in Sunningdale, he moved into Phil Collins's house, and the Collins family went to stay at the Stewarts' home in Geneva. So it was a good arrangement. Sadly I discovered that life had not treated the Stewarts well, and they had all suffered from cancer in one form or another: his son Paul had bowel cancer, his wife had breast cancer, and Sir Jackie himself had skin cancer.

The England Rugby Team, including Johnny Wilkinson stayed at Pennyhill Park for four years in a row. They would take an entire floor with players sharing twin-bedded rooms, and always propped their doors open with towels so that they could wander in and out of each other's rooms as they pleased. The open doors led to the theft of players' rugby shirts, and boots at £200 a pair, by souvenir hunters. Someone, somewhere has Johnny Wilkinson's boots! Another famous rugby player was found making love to one of the hotel maids over a sink, and I had to take her off that area of duty so that she did not come into contact with any of the players again.

In October 1999 when the All Blacks were playing in the Rugby World Cup, they stayed at Pennyhill. Originally the Rugby Football Union (RFU) had specified which hotels the players should stay in, but eight months before the World Cup, I received a phone call from the All Blacks' management team saying that they did not want the players to stay at the chosen hotel in Slough, and they would prefer them to be with us instead. We had the availability for the dates required, and so the rooms were booked for three weeks. The organisers wanted the best facilities for the All Blacks. Pennyhill was set in 123 acres, and had a suitable training ground at nearby Sandhurst Military Academy, so it was ideal. The RFU sanctioned this, but would pay only a certain amount towards the cost of the rooms and the players agreed to pay the extra. I had everything confirmed in writing, so we all knew exactly where we stood.

Eventually the time of the World Cup arrived, and the team stayed with us for the dates arranged. But when the All Blacks reached the semi-final and were due to play France, their manager became so convinced that they were going to win that he demanded the rooms for an extra week. This situation had never been mentioned before and the rooms had already been pre-booked by other guests, so were no longer available. The day before the semi-final, I had a major row with the manager over this. We were fully booked, and that was that. I rang the RFU and found that they totally supported my position. If the players had stayed in the specified hotel in Slough, this situation would not have arisen. I went to the semi-final, cheered France on, and was secretly delighted when the All Blacks suffered a shock defeat and so did not require the rooms anyway. I was, however, given an All Blacks shirt signed by every single player as a souvenir of the occasion, including the brilliant Jonah Lomu. The next day I sat in the hotel lobby while the manager that I had argued with signed a large cheque to cover the Pennyhill Park bill. A few hours later I heard that he and the entire management team had resigned.

Three years later Clive Woodward came to us and said that he wanted to make Pennyhill the base for the English Rugby squad, and I was invited to a meeting with all the World Cup players. I had to make a short speech, introducing myself and welcoming them to the hotel. Afterwards Clive Woodward spoke and was very strict with them.

'I don't want to see any mobile phones,' he warned the players. 'Anyone seen with a mobile phone will be sent home.' And he proceeded to give them a long list of 'dos and don'ts', as I crept out of the meeting. I had lunch with Clive and his wife in the hotel restaurant and then showed him our facilities. The RFU groundsmen came from Twickenham and cut the grass like a rugby pitch for the boys to train on. I was thrilled when the team actually went on to win the 2003 Rugby World Cup and felt that we had played a small part in it. I proudly received another signed rugby shirt.

The three years that I spent as General Manager of Pennyhill were very demanding, but at the same time very rewarding, yet I missed being in London.

I began to put out feelers for other jobs that would take me back to the capital, and even considered managing the historic Carlton Club, one of the oldest gentlemen's clubs in London. I went for an interview with the committee, but knew that the setup there was not for me. Then Rocco rang me one day and asked me if I would consider managing the new St David's Hotel and Spa in Cardiff, which he had just purchased. I went to Wales, with Wendy and my son David, to stay at the hotel for three days, but I knew that I would feel even more cut off in Cardiff and it was so far away from the family home in Sanderstead, that I declined the offer. Initially I accepted the job and made plans to rent a house, but the more I thought about it the more I knew that it was the wrong move for me. Rocco was not happy when I telephoned him with my decision, but I had to do what was right for me. I wrote to him later to apologise, and he understood my position. He asked if I would consider going to the Lowry Hotel in Manchester instead, but I turned that down as well.

Mr Pecorelli clearly had his ear to the ground and became aware of my restlessness. He invited Wendy and me to a dinner at Marlborough House in London, with Prince Philip as guest of honour, and celebrity chef Gary Rhodes cooked the meal.

'Neil, you're up to something,' said Mr Pecorelli during the dinner.

I told him that I was missing London and hankered after returning. Later, back at Pennyhill Park Hotel, Mr Pecorelli's son Danny invited me for 'a walk around the car park'. This is what I did at Grosvenor House whenever I needed to fire someone, so I felt that I had blown it and was about to be dismissed from Pennyhill. Instead, Danny offered me more money to stay on, plus a good pension bonus scheme. It was unexpected and I agreed to remain. In my heart I knew that it was only on a tempo-rary basis, until a better offer came along.

That better offer came in the year 2000 when I was head-hunted for the job of General Manager at the Royal Horseguards Hotel, 1 Whitehall Place in London. I wanted to be back in London and could not have found anything more central if I had tried, within spitting distance of Downing Street, Trafalgar Square, the Houses of Parliament and Horse Guards Parade. It was a four-star hotel but the Chief Executive, Mr Pratt, told me that they wanted to spend money on it and raise it to a five-star hotel. He knew what I had achieved at Pennyhill and felt that I was the man for the job. At the interview I was asked to undertake an IQ test and came out of it with a very high IQ. What they did not realise was that, when I answered each of the multiple-choice questions, I gave the opposite answer to the one I felt was correct. So if my immediate instinct was that A was the correct answer, I wrote down B. I ended up with a high score, but if I had given what I thought were the right answers, my score would have been very low. It proved to me how thick I am!

The money offered was good, so I gave in my notice to Mr Pecorelli and began work at the Royal Horseguards. I pinched a few of his staff when I left Pennyhill, and it was not long before the telephone rang in my office.

'Neil? It's Mr Pecorelli.'

'Good morning, Mr Pecorelli.'

'You've taken my Maintenance Manager. You've taken my Sales Person. Even my Personnel Manager. Please, no more.'

'OK, Mr Pecorelli.' And I didn't poach any more from Pennyhill, although I did take on Andrew Coy, my former Banqueting Director at Grosvenor House. We had worked well together, and I knew that Andrew could help me move the Royal Horseguards forward in the food and beverage area.

Because of its location, the hotel became the regular haunt of many politicians, particularly the bar and lounge. Others came to the Liberal Club, which was part of the building. In the nineteenth century a Tory politician called Frederick Edwin Smith, 1st Earl of Birkenhead, used to visit the Liberal Club just to use the toilet. He was obviously not a member, and when he was challenged one day he said, 'I didn't know that it was a club as well as a lavatory.' John Prescott, while still Deputy Prime Minister, was once due at the Royal Horseguards officially to meet an African dignitary. We stood waiting for Mr Prescott to travel the short distance from Downing Street, and he eventually arrived half an hour late without a word of apology.

'Hello, Mr Prescott. I'm Neil Kirby, the General Manager . . .'

He had no interest in me whatsoever and just brushed past me. I thought it was the height of bad manners, and was very tempted to punch him under the chin.

The position of the Royal Horseguards in Whitehall meant that the road outside was always being closed off for various events, such as Trooping the Colour, the State Opening of Parliament and the annual Remembrance Sunday Parade. We regularly had to tell guests that a particular entrance couldn't be used. In June 2000 the Queen unveiled a statue for the tank regiment right outside. The road was closed again, but we had a fantastic view of Her Majesty. It was a beautiful statue too. The London Marathon saw many streets closed around us and I loved to be able to watch it, even if I wasn't running myself.

Inevitably not everything went smoothly. On Christmas Eve there was a power failure at the hotel. I received a call at home to say that a circuit box had burnt out. The train journey took me around four hours because it was Christmas, and I finally arrived to find that everything electrical was out of action. The lifts couldn't be used, so everyone and everything had to go up and down endless flights of stairs. The hotel boasts that it has the largest marble spiral staircase in Europe, but nobody cared about that under these circumstances. There was a SAGA party of elderly guests staying with us who just couldn't manage steps at all, and some had to be moved down the road to the Piccadilly Hotel. People were arriving off the *QE2* at Southampton and when they reached the hotel, of course, their luggage had to be manhandled up to the floors. Even worse, the kitchens were severely disabled and we could do nothing but serve salads. It was a disastrous way to begin the Christmas celebrations, but fortunately all was fixed in time to roast the turkeys on Christmas Day and boil the puddings.

Giuseppe Pecorelli and his wife came to London one evening to see a West End show, and stayed overnight at the Royal Horseguards Hotel. I saw them next morning at breakfast and he called me over to his table.

'Neil, this hotel is not for you,' he said emphatically, 'It is just not you.'

I was a little suspicious and knew that something was going on in his mind. A few weeks later his son, Danny Pecorelli, came to see me and said that they were looking for a General Manager at their country hotel in West Sussex called South Lodge, and asked if I would consider taking the job.

'Not really, Danny,' I said, 'This hotel's got 280 bedrooms, South Lodge only has forty. It's just not busy enough for me. That's why I came here in the first place. I don't really want to go back to the country. Plus the money here is very good, I couldn't take a drop in salary.'

'I'll match the money,' he said, 'and I'll give you a bonus of £15,000 every year, plus £6,000 a year towards your pension.'

It was not an offer to turn down lightly. My relationship with Mr Pratt, the Chief Executive at Royal Horseguards, had just taken a downturn too. He had originally asked me to raise the standard from a four-star to a five-star hotel, but he pulled the rug from under my feet every time I needed to spend money on improvements. Instead of employing one receptionist, who simply couldn't cope with the amount of work, especially in the mornings with hundreds of people checking out at the same time, I took on three. But Mr Pratt said that we couldn't afford it. He even forced me to get rid of Andrew Coy to save money. All Mr Pratt saw was a temporary reduction in profits, because money had to be spent on upgrading, and he did not seem to realise that once the necessary changes were in place, the profits would increase accordingly.

'The wages bill has gone up by £10,000 a month,' he grumbled to me one day.

'You told me that you wanted to make this hotel five-star,' I fought back. 'Once it's five-star, you can increase the average room rate, and we will start getting in some of the people who usually stay at the Savoy and the other big hotels in this area. It's only by improving the quality of the service, that you will attract the high spenders.'

When he forced me to dispense with Andrew Coy because the food costs had risen, I was within an inch of pushing Mr Pratt across a table. Andrew was absolutely brilliant at his job and it was total madness to lose him. At heart Mr Pratt was just an accountant by trade and could not see the relevance of staff efficiency, of high-quality food, and the importance of offering a first-class standard of service.

'The only reason that you will *never* do well in this company,' I told him, 'is because you don't understand five-star. It's very short-sighted.' I was pleased when I read in the *Caterer & Hotelkeeper* magazine a little while later that Mr Pratt had been fired.

I decided to accept Danny Pecorelli's offer and moved to South Lodge. Although it was a smaller, quieter hotel, there were many projects to keep me busy. I was asked to oversee the building of a new £5 million conference centre, and so was able to put into practice all that I had learned from the Fortes. It consisted of twelve meeting rooms, which took just under two years to complete, and I placed great emphasis on attention to detail and the importance of quality. Everything in the centre was of the highest possible standard, with the latest drop-down screens and back-projections, and I put in an audio-visual room with up-to-the-minute technology for clients. In March 2009 the Centre was used by the G20 Finance Ministers' Summit and the hotel received a personal letter of thanks from the Chancellor of the Exchequer, praising the facilities. Using my design skills acquired from Olga Polizzi, I refurbished the hotel's bedrooms and raised the score from seventy-two to eighty-six per cent in the AA inspection. Today the hotel has eighty-nine bedrooms instead of the original forty. I was able to take it from a £2-million-a-year turnover to £5 million.

I started my first Ladies' Lunch Club at South Lodge, and 145 ladies came every couple of months to hear a guest speaker and enjoy a superb lunch. I loved hosting it and we soon had a waiting list for people, desperate to get in. I began having events in the grounds such as garden parties on the lawn, an annual Big Band Concert, and open-air Shakespeare, which all raised the profile of South Lodge and increased the flow of non-residents. Some hotels cater mainly for their resident guests, but I feel it is essential to be at the hub of the community and encourage the facilities to be regularly used by non-residents in the area. We had our share of celebrity guests too. Rock legend Ozzy Osbourne came and brought his own keep-fit bicycle with him. He tried to avoid the other guests and never once ate in the restaurant. We speculated that he was probably drying out from drink or drugs.

Although the Mannings Heath Golf Club at South Lodge with two 18-hole championship courses was a separate entity, after three years the Pecorellis asked me if I would manage the facilities there as well. I was able to get the Golf Club under control by tightening expenditure. It was difficult to make a profit, but at least it broke even, which kept everyone happy.

I enjoyed working for the Pecorelli family. They were good employers and cared about their staff and customers alike. They had very high standards, and I learned a lot from Giueseppe Pecorelli. I spent over four years at South Lodge and loved it. With so many challenges and projects, the boredom that I feared after leaving London never actually materialised. There was just no time to be bored. I was proud of what I was able to achieve there, I made many lifelong friends, and am still involved with the Chase Children's Hospice, which is the hotel's chosen charity. By 2005, though, I began to get restless again. Not because I was unhappy at South Lodge, but at the back of my mind I had been mulling over the idea of buying a hotel of my own. Sometimes the thought seemed ludicrous. The financial outlay was almost too great to even contemplate. It was a huge leap from being General Manager to hotel owner, and yet I felt that the knowledge I had acquired after almost forty years in the business put me in good stead. I was inspired by Charles Forte's rise from owning one small milk bar to becoming head of the world's largest hotel chain, and that alone encouraged me to press on with my dream.

I was now financially secure. The mortgage was paid off. Wendy and I were settled in our respective jobs. It was madness really to even think of turning our world upside down by buying a hotel. It would mean insecurity and debt until we could make a success of it, and there was the real possibility of it all going disastrously wrong. We could end up losing everything.

In 2004 we had bought ourselves a flat on the Sussex coast at Eastbourne marina, really as a bolthole; somewhere to relax when we had time to ourselves. When I shared my dream with Wendy, she thought I was totally mad. Yet the more I thought about it, the more I realised that I did not want to reach retirement without having invested in my own business. It was all new to me, but I put out feelers about borrowing money and began to obtain details of hotels that had come on the market. One morning I was reading the latest edition of *Caterer & Hotelkeeper* magazine when I saw a photograph of a hotel for sale in Eastbourne, called The Langham Hotel.

The Langham was privately owned, had eighty-five bedrooms, and was on the market for £1,950,000. It was in an absolutely fantastic location on the seafront, looking out over Eastbourne Pier in one direction, and across the bay towards Hastings in the other. I could see that it needed some redecoration outside, and the white plastic chairs on the terrace by the bar would have to go, but this was purely cosmetic and easily changed. The Victorian building itself was attractive, reminding me of the Fortes' home in London and some of those elegant houses in Eaton Square. I could see that it had enormous potential.

I started sitting outside on Mondays, Wednesdays and Saturdays to get an idea of the visitor numbers and the passing trade at various times of day. There was a pedestrian crossing opposite, from the hotel to the promenade, and I saw that thousands of people a day crossed at that point and so came directly towards the Langham. Hundreds of cars stopped at the crossing each day too, and while they waited for pedestrians to cross they looked at the Langham. It was a fabulous position to be noticed and certainly not a hotel that you could ignore. It even had a clock at the front, which I loved, and people wishing to know the time turned towards the Langham.

By speaking to local people I learned that the hotel was not as good as it used to be, simply because the owners planned to sell it and so had lost the enthusiasm for marketing the business in the right way. I knew that this could work to my advantage from a purchasing point of view and would enable me to knock down the price. Wendy and I ventured inside one afternoon and found a young lad behind the bar, reading a book. I looked at the menu and asked him if we could have two coffees and some sandwiches.

'Sorry, the chef's off duty,' he said, 'there's nobody in the kitchen.'

I had been used to hotels that offered 24-hour service, so it was a shock not to be able to get a simple sandwich.

'This is going to change,' I whispered to Wendy. In my mind the Langham Hotel was already mine.

I looked at a few other hotels that were on the market, but I knew that the Langham was for me. Wendy began to worry and was very sceptical about the whole idea, as it was a gigantic leap for us to make, but she supported me throughout. She never once said that we shouldn't go ahead and I knew that she would back whatever decision I made. Before going any further I sent some 'mystery guests' to stay at the Langham, four couples, just to check it out properly and report back to me about their overnight stay.

'I don't care about holes in the carpet, or any dust you might find,' I told them. 'I don't even need you to come back and say that the food's crap. Any of those things can be changed. What I want to know is the attitude of the staff, from the reception through to the Duty Manager. That will show me how the hotel is being run.'

There was a large sign outside saying that the hotel was licensed for weddings, so one of my mystery guests enquired about having his at the Langham.

'Oh, we don't do weddings,' he was told.

'But there's a big sign outside. My girlfriend and I would like to get married here.'

'When are you planning to get married?'

'July.'

'Sorry, we're full.'

It was clear that, as the hotel was on the market, the staff had lost all interest. Possibly they felt that they would soon be out of a job, so why bother.

Another of my mystery guests stayed up late in the bar, consuming only soft drinks. He chatted to staff members as they drank alcohol and became loose-tongued, revealing some of the Langham's secrets. He noticed that none of the money for the drinks was going into the till either. This all gave me a picture of the situation and put me in a position of strength. I made an offer of £1.8 million, and eventually succeeded in buying the hotel for £1.85 million, having knocked them down £100,000 on the asking price. The Langham Hotel was mine.

I telephoned Sir Rocco Forte to tell him my good news.

'Welcome to the club!' he said.

16

You're Doin' Quite Well

Is that Mr Reilly, can anyone tell?
Is that Mr Reilly who runs the hotel?
Well, if that's Mr Reilly they speak of so often,
Upon me soul, Reilly, you're doin' quite well.
Anonymous, 'Is that Mr Reilly?', a popular music-hall chorus, 1882

On 1 July 2005 my dream came true. Wendy and I signed the contract and we now officially owned the 85-bedroom, AA three-star Langham Hotel in Eastbourne, in a prime position on the seafront. Although champagne corks popped and I grinned from ear to ear in public, my nights were sleepless with worry. I had remortgaged the family home in Sanderstead for £400,000, even though it was worth £525,000 at the time; I also remortgaged our flat at Eastbourne marina; I cashed in a pension, put in all my savings, and borrowed £1.3 million from the bank.

Wendy and I spent days drawing up a feasibility study and, despite the heavy burden of debt, I just knew in my heart that I could make a success of the venture. For the first time in my life I would have no bosses to answer to. How the Langham Hotel was run was entirely up to us.

On 2 July I went to see Danny Pecorelli at South Lodge to tell him that I had bought my own hotel. I had said nothing sooner because I knew that his father would try and get me to change my mind. Fortunately Danny was very pleased for me and wished us well, although he asked me to work out three months' notice. I agreed that it was unfair to leave him in the lurch, so I remained at South Lodge five days a week until October. I owned a hotel, but was still working for someone else!

On Friday afternoons at 4 p.m., I used to leave South Lodge and head back to the coast and the Langham Hotel. During the week poor Wendy was left in sole charge as General Manager, something she had never done before in her life. Her working background had always been in administration and she was totally out of her comfort zone. She had no experience of hiring and firing staff, and problems came at her from all directions. By the end of each day she would often be in tears through the strain of it all. She worked from 7 a.m. to 9 p.m. seven days a week, overseeing housekeeping, dealing with the reception, handling the guests' requirements, managing the staff, signing cheques, and tried to jump all the hurdles placed in front of her. There were debts to be chased, new accounts with suppliers to open, the staff wages to be organised. The lift broke down, the ovens kept going out, and every day there was another situation to deal with. Some mornings she would have a few more tears before facing another long day. We decided to live at the hotel initially, just to show the staff our authority and to get to know the building ourselves, but it meant that Wendy was never able to get away from the place. Every night we would have a meeting to discuss the events of that day, and usually didn't sit down to eat until 11 p.m. We both lost around eight pounds in weight during the first month.

Unexpected problems arose right from the start. There was no computerisation, the accounts were still written in pencil, and often there was a lack of coordination between departments. Wendy had to face the wrath of guests who arrived, only to find that they had not been booked in.

'But we made the reservation six months ago!' they would argue, quite justifiably. It was not Wendy's fault if no record of the booking could be found, but we were the owners and the buck stopped with us. I'm sure that Wendy must have had regrets in those early days.

Taking over the hotel, complete with around forty staff, inevitably meant that changes needed to be made to move the business forward. Although I couldn't be there all the time during those first months, it did not prevent me from firing staff in all areas of the hotel that were either not pulling their weight or had the wrong attitude. Some had just been there too long and were far too set in their ways. We gave them the opportunity to change to our ways, but a few were dinosaurs and I knew that we had to replace them with fresh blood. I admit that I was tough with some of them, and many handed in their resignations without me having to fire them, which suited me fine. Some decided to gang up on us, and that was their downfall. It took time, but eventually I was able to build a good team of people that were happy, professional and worked well together.

After I left South Lodge, I decided to become the General Manager of the Langham myself so that I could be on-site all the time with the staff and guests. My daughter Nicola agreed to come and take over the accounts, my son David became a chef, and Wendy took over housekeeping for a while, and now concentrates on the administrative side of the hotel, which is her area of expertise and a role she enjoys. I had a vision as to how I wanted the Langham to be, and knew that I could use my experience from all the other hotels that I had worked in to bring those plans to fruition. It meant that Wendy and I each worked 130 hours a week at first, but there was a lot to be done.

I began by tackling the lobby area in January 2006, as the reception is the hub of any hotel and the first place that people see when they walk through the door. The carpet was frayed, the reception desk was outdated, and it really called out for a total makeover. We gutted the lobby completely, raised the ceiling by two feet, and knocked out the old reception desk – which had been constructed out of concrete breeze blocks and wire mesh. My son-in-law James was over-enthusiastic with the demolition, and a piece of concrete missed my head by just a fraction of an inch and smashed on to my arm. I fell to the floor, with blood pouring everywhere, and had to be rushed to hospital for eight stitches. I now have a long scar as a permanent reminder of the lobby refurbishment.

Using Olga Polizzi's edict of only having the best, I had a solid-oak reception desk constructed, put in beautiful cornicing and crystal chandeliers, wood panelling to dado height was installed throughout, new carpeting was laid, and chairs and sofas were custom-made to my designs. A lot of the work was carried out by a wonderful craftsman called Bob Prodger, and his wife, Rita, was also a great help when it came to buying paintings at galleries and auctions. We selected table lamps and shades, chose the wallpaper, and made sure that the rich colour scheme came together as I had envisaged. Olga had taught me that deep red and dark wood go well together, and it is a combination that I love. I also learned a great deal from Giuseppe Pecorelli, who had a great eye for detail. Everything he did was the height of luxury and he would think nothing of spending £70,000 on refurbishing a bedroom. To complete the look Bob carved a magnificent wooden key-rack for behind the reception desk, with pigeon holes for each room number, and finally I ordered a bust of my hero Sir Winston Churchill from the Imperial War Museum to keep a reassuring lookout over my guests as they arrive and depart.

The bar had to become a temporary reception for a while, but I kept the customers informed throughout and they seemed to like my hands-on approach. Even if they felt that their bedroom was a little old-fashioned, they accepted it because they could see that changes were underway. I had a scheme board set up to display samples of carpet, wallpaper, wood panelling, and a section of the cornice. There were photographs of the chandelier and pictures of how the completed reception would look, which not only kept the customers involved, but made them want to come back and see the finished project.

I then moved on to the main restaurant and had it redecorated and recarpeted. Because of the large area, the carpet alone took five days to lay. Wendy and I designed stained-glass panels for some of the windows, which were handmade and depict local scenes. Chairs were made to the height, depth and comfort that we required. We purchased new china, glasses, cutlery and table linen. Then we moved on to do the same for the attached Portico Restaurant, where a new oak floor was laid, elegant lighting was installed, and chic black blinds put up at the windows. I renamed it The Conservatory, as it is all glass and has outstanding views across the sea, and soon turned it into an à la carte restaurant. Once Michael Titherington was employed as Head Chef, the Langham quickly began to establish a reputation for its food. In September 2008 Michael was awarded his first AA Rosette, and again in 2009. In Eastbourne, only the Grand Hotel and the Langham have AA Rosettes, so I was chuffed about that accolade. Michael's wife, Claire, also became our Head Receptionist, and the couple actually got married at the hotel.

Wanting to re-establish the Langham as a wedding venue, we created a honeymoon suite by knocking a single room and a twin room into one, to make a large space. Situated on the first floor at the front of the hotel, it has stunning views across the bay from the windows. We had a huge four-poster bed made, as I wanted it to be one of the most luxurious hotel rooms in town. It took eight weeks to complete and I am very proud of that suite, with its red carpet, superb chandelier and elegant Zoffany wallpaper. When brides and grooms come to discuss their wedding arrangements, they all say that it has the 'wow factor' as soon as they walk in. The refurbished restaurant and the honeymoon suite together gave me the facilities I wanted, and the wedding diary soon filled up as a result.

Next the kitchens received attention, with the latest ovens and equipment, including walk-in fridge-freezers. In January 2007 the bar received a total makeover too. It was completely gutted, walls were knocked down, the ceiling height was raised, and once again I had an exquisite hand-made cornice put up from a design chosen by Wendy and made for us by a specialist firm of craftsmen in Sheffield. Solid wood panelling was instated, which not only looks splendid but is extremely practical. If knocked or scratched it can easily be sanded and made to look as good as new. Zoffany wallpaper was hung above the panelling, all new furni-ture was put in place on the luxurious red carpet, and striking black-and-white photographs completed the look, along with unusual black-crystal chandeliers. The bar itself was made from black granite, and an office behind was turned into a still room. Outside the bar, new silver-and-black chairs and tables were set up on the terrace to replace the white plastic chairs that I had disliked on my first visit. With black umbrellas and a canopy saying 'Langham's Bar', it is absolutely the look that I had in my mind from the moment I knew that the hotel was going to be mine.

Improvements to the hotel saw the balance of customers change from ninety-five per cent coach parties to many more private guests. As the income increased as a result, I ploughed it all back into the business so that the upgrading and development could continue. And it is ongoing, of course: in 2008 I had a new fire-alarm system installed at a cost of £40,000, recar-peted all the corridors, installed new lighting, bought new washing machines and tumble dryers, and developed the basement area into three conference rooms with an additional bar. It is a never-ending process.

Although I have been able to see much of my vision come to fruition, some areas are dependent upon finance before they can proceed and the hotel continually evolves as I strive to develop to improve standards. My next major project is the building of a one-million-pound ballroom, which will be 89 feet long with a grand porticoed entrance, so that larger func-tions and dances can be held. Planning permission is already in place. I am determined that the Langham will eventually become a four-star hotel. And, who knows, maybe one day I will be the owner of a five-star estab-lishment!

Every three weeks I stand on the seafront and study the Langham from the outside. I want to see what the customers see as they walk past, es-pecially in the evening. So I put myself in their position and look to see if the chandeliers in the bar and restaurant stand out, if the candles can be seen flickering on the dining tables, if any of the stucco needs painting or a window frame should be replaced. I want it to look impressive, with its predominantly white façade and black detail in the blinds and canopies. The Union Jack flies proudly at the front, too, and every summer I bring out the genuine Victorian bathing machine that I purchased with the hotel and which has become a real tourist attraction.

The staff continue to evolve as well and they are just as important to me as my customers. I promote employees whenever I can, so that they have the opportunity to progress within the business. Where would I be today if Lord Forte had not enabled me to work my way up at Grosvenor House? Maybe I'd be a bitter kitchen porter, still washing dishes after forty years. I was given chances to make something of my life, so I like to give other people an opening to advance in their careers too. I notice that my staff often receive 'thank you' gifts from the guests, and I feel that is a great compliment. I have never seen a box of chocolates being left for staff at any of the big London hotels.

Not for the first time in my career, I poached Andrew Coy and in September 2008 he became General Manager at the Langham. I knew that I could not continue to work a 130-hour week, and so my strategy for our third year at the hotel was to employ a General Manager to take off some of the pressure. My father warned me that I was going to wear myself out if I carried on as I was. After working for me at Royal Horseguards, Andrew had gone to Woburn Abbey to run the estate for the Duke of Bedford. I called Andrew out of the blue and discovered that he had eventually moved on to work four days a week for a recruitment agency and one day selling high-quality silverware. I could tell that he was not totally happy. His great expertise was in hotels.

'Why don't you think about coming to work for us?' I asked. 'I need a General Manager here, and you would be the best man for the job.'

I met up with him in London, we discussed terms, and so my former Banqueting Director at Grosvenor House became General Manager of the Langham Hotel. It was great to be reunited – Coy and Kirby back working together again – and I knew that I could trust Andrew to move the business forward. His boast has always been that, wherever he is, he can increase business by twenty per cent, and he certainly proved that to be true. As I had hoped, Andrew Coy took the pressure off me by taking charge of all the functions, including weddings, and his fantastic eye for detail ensured that everything ran like clockwork. The fact that Andrew had previously worked at the Savoy, the Ritz, the Café Royal, Grosvenor House, Royal Horseguards and Woburn Abbey meant that he had a reputation before he even started.

'I hear you've got a new General Manager from London,' other local hoteliers would say jealously. Andrew Coy has been called one of the best Banqueting Managers in Europe, and I am proud to have him at the hotel.

Once the main refurbishments were completed, and I had a reliable team in place including a good chef, I decided to continue the approach I had taken at South Lodge and began to develop the non-resident trade. I started a ladies' lunch club in 2006 and had forty-three ladies at the first one. This number doubled for the second lunch, and by the third occasion the dining room was full and I had to start a waiting list. It has gone from strength to strength, and now I frequently put on two lunches on consecutive days each time just to fit everybody in. At less than half the price of similar lunch clubs in competitors' hotels, word soon got around that mine was good value for money, with a glass of champagne on arrival, an excellent three-course lunch with wine, and a top-class speaker in elegant surroundings. This had the knock-on effect that many of the ladies from the local community came back for lunches and dinners at other times, booked their children's weddings at the hotel, and used it as a venue for a variety of functions, even just calling in with their friends for morning coffee or afternoon tea on a regular basis. Many come to the restaurant for important anniversaries and birthday parties, so the lunch club really helped build up the non-resident business. To judge how a business has grown, in the trade we look at the Rev-Par (revenue per available room). This is where you add up all the money taken, divide it by the number of people actually staying at the hotel, and you are able to calculate the income per head. Our target was to reach £50. When we bought the hotel it was £23, and today it has gone up to £56. In 2008 the hotel was valued at £3.5 million, a large increase on the price I paid. My mother often used to say to me when I was young that one day I would be a millionaire. I am just sad that she did not live to see it.

In 2009 I began a Gentlemen's Lunch Club, so that husbands did not feel left out. I started hosting a Pudding Club and literary lunches, and we put on regular chef demonstrations, which are a great asset. Themed dinners are always an attraction and the Langham has been the venue for a sixties night when pop star Wayne Fontana and The Dakotas performed, and a very successful opera evening. The Masonic trade built up too, as did the graduation ball season, and a whole host of private business from writers' groups to social clubs. We bought our own blackjack and roulette tables, which is a great draw for party nights and Christmas when people enjoy having a Las Vegas–style flutter. Eastbourne is the venue for the International Ladies' Tennis Championship every June, just prior to Wimbledon, which attracts the top players from around the world and inevitably boosts our business. The feedback I get is that customers like the personal touch, as I try to be at every event and speak to as many people as possible and get to know them. Having the owners on-site seems to be a great crowd-puller too, and has helped grow the business.

'Oh, I know Neil and Wendy,' is a frequent comment from customers, and it gives them that little bit of kudos. 'Let's eat at the Langham, I know the owners . . .' It's a silly little thing, yet it brings customers back.

One thing I have noticed about many of my guests today is that they seem generally to be larger in size. An indication of this trend was brought home to me in 2009 when we had health and safety instructions to take down our 'Maximum 8 persons' sign in the lift and replace it with 'Maximum 6 persons'. At the Langham today the biggest single maintenance expense is replacing toilet seats, broken by overweight guests. They are nearly always people under the age of thirty, as obesity appears to be an increasing problem in the young. I have genuinely considered designing a larger lavatory seat so that hotels can cater for modern trends. The second expense is replacing toilet-roll holders which have been pulled from the wall as guests use them to lever themselves from the seat. In the end we have had to install disabled handrails beside toilets, simply to assist able-bodied but overweight guests. One girl even wrenched a washbasin from the wall in her efforts to stand up. Forty years ago this kind of situation would simply not have arisen.

I had one overweight guest who literally got stuck on the toilet, with her backside wedged into the seat. That was very embarrassing for all concerned as we tried to release her. Another large lady fell in the shower and could not get out as she was wedged in so tightly. We had to call the fire brigade to come and cut the shower cubicle down around her. That was the only way to get her out.

Bathrooms can be a hazardous place at the best of times, and hotels are no exception. A woman once accidentally dropped a drinking glass in the bath and cut her hand very badly when she tried to pick up the pieces. I was horrified at the sight – there was just so much blood everywhere – and she needed eight stitches in her hand. With accidents being a common occurrence, we have one member of staff trained in first aid for every fifty guests at the hotel.

When a guest at the Langham needed a light bulb replaced in his bathroom, it seemed like a very simple task. I took a tall stepladder with me and climbed up to undo the glass light fitting. It was tricky trying to manoeuvre the ladder between the bath and the washbasin and, when I reached the top step, I found that I was facing the wrong direction. I turned awkwardly to detach the glass shade and, as I unclipped it, it slipped from my grasp. Not wanting the glass to shatter into the bath, I tried to catch it and felt myself plummet from the top step. I grabbed the top of the shower curtain in an attempt save myself, and the rail snapped as I fell to the floor, smashing my hip on the edge of the bath.

'Oh my God, oh my God!' the guest started to panic and tried to lift me up, as I lay winded between the bath and the stepladder.

'No, I'm all right,' I groaned. 'Don't move me. Just press zero on the telephone and ask my wife Wendy to come up.' I was convinced that my hip was broken and thought it best to remain still.

Wendy came running and between them they helped me out of the bathroom, by which time my ankle was throbbing like crazy and began to swell to more than twice its normal size. I was rushed to hospital, where X-rays showed that nothing was actually broken. I was very lucky, but the guest must have thought he was staying at *Fawlty Towers*.

Injuries seem to be an occupational hazard of the trade. At Christmas 2007 I burned my hand very badly while helping to serve 140 breakfasts from the hotplate. There was a large saucepan of boiling water on my left, ready for poaching eggs, and I accidentally thrust my hand into it. The pain was indescribable. The very next day one of the waitresses was about to take a teapot out to a guest, when I noticed that the lid wasn't down properly. I pushed the lid to secure it, the hinge broke, and my hand plunged straight into the boiling tea. The same hand, of course, and this time all the skin began to peel off. I was hopping around like a dervish.

Wendy covered my hand with antiseptic cream and bandaged it up.

269

Three days later one of the waitresses was feeling unwell, took too many painkillers and suddenly collapsed. An ambulance was called and I travelled with her to the hospital.

'What's happened to your hand?' one of the paramedics asked.

'I scalded it in boiling water,' I told her.

'Well, you can check into the hospital as well!' she said as soon as she looked at the bad state of my skin, which by this time had become even more painful and infected. I was at the hospital until 3.30 a.m. receiving treatment, and will always have the scar.

No matter how closely health and safety regulations are followed, accidents are unavoidable. I've lost count of the number of guests at the Langham that have walked straight into glass doors. Sometimes they injure themselves – one man cut his knee badly by not looking where he was going – and occasionally the glass is smashed too. One of my pet hates is finger marks on windows, and maybe we keep the glass too clean. We have lines in place now as a precaution, but it still doesn't stop some guests bumping into doors.

We've had cracked ribs, broken shoulders, and the inevitable sickness and diarrhoea bugs, which are no fun for staff to deal with. One lady felt dizzy on the stairs and fell backwards. A man hit his head very badly by not looking where he was going as he descended the stairs. 'I seem to be bleeding,' he said to the receptionist, as half the skin on his head was torn back. Two elderly ladies got their walking sticks entangled and toppled over; one of them broke her hip as she hit the floor.

The Langham, of course, is not exempt from theft. I had a coach driver staying on the second floor who noticed a man loitering in the corridor, standing round a dead corner that led nowhere, hidden partly by a maid's cupboard. The coach driver later found that his credit card and some cash had been stolen.

During some refurbishment in the winter of 2005 we had one unseen visitor who, without my knowledge, was climbing up some scaffolding every day and was making use of an empty guest room. The chambermaids discovered that someone had been in the room, had a shower, used the coffee-making facilities, slept on the bed, and yet no guest was actually booked in. The window was locked, but the next day it happened again. I suddenly received a phone call from reception and was told that a chambermaid had confronted an intruder in the room and had been punched.

As I went to investigate, I saw a 'hoodie' just running out of the main door. I followed in hot pursuit and as a runner I quickly caught up with him. He suddenly turned and hit me straight in the mouth. I grabbed the hood and punched him back, and as he fell to the ground I saw that it was not a 'he' at all but a 'she'. At that precise moment a car pulled up, having seen what must have appeared to be me attacking a girl.

'I saw you hit her!' the driver shouted. 'I'm an off-duty policeman.'

I could not believe it. I was only trying to protect my property, but now I looked like the villain. I was furious.

'If you're really a policeman, you need to know what's been going on here,' I shouted back. 'Now sort this girl out.'

He got out his mobile phone to call for back-up. The next thing I knew, the girl was coming at me with a plank of wood with nails sticking out, shouting all manner of abuse, and she began hitting the hotel door ferociously. My blood was boiling by this time and I wrestled the wood away from her, while the policeman just stood there doing absolutely nothing to help.

'Bloody well come and do something!' I screamed at him. 'You're supposed to be a policeman!' and finally he came to my rescue and grabbed the girl around the throat. Although she was arrested, there was a suggestion that I could be prosecuted for GBH. Unbelievable, when I was the injured party. Fortunately they found the hotel room key in the girl's pocket, and she was charged with burglary. The charges against me were dropped.

Another time I was less lucky and ended up in a police cell. I was in my office when a call came through from reception that a man was complaining because his room hadn't got a sea view. His was a last-minute booking for a single room, although he arrived with a friend who he was clearly hoping would be able to share the room without paying. When he was shown the room the man said that he didn't like it and demanded another with a sea view.

'That's fine,' the receptionist told him. 'Rooms with a sea view have a £12 supplement.'

'I don't want to pay a supplement,' he said, 'I just want a sea view.'

He then became very stroppy, and so the receptionist called me.

The man was around fifty years of age, and I could see that he was the belligerent type before he even opened his mouth.

'How can I help you, Sir?' I asked cheerily, although I just knew that he was going to be trouble.

'Who are you?' He looked at me menacingly.

'I'm the owner of the hotel.'

'I want a room with a sea view.'

'No problem, Sir. We have one available, but as the lady said, it's a £12 supplement for a sea view. That's standard for everybody.'

'I don't want to pay it.'

'Well, you have a choice. Either you stay where you are, or pay the supplement for a room with a sea view. It's as simple as that.'

'I don't want to stay where I am.'

'You've got three choices now . . .' I was beginning to get irritated by this time. ' . . .Stay where you are. Upgrade to a sea view. Or you go.'

'Don't you talk to me like that!'

'I'll talk to you how I like.' His attitude was really making me angry now. 'I tell you what, just give me the key and bugger off.'

'I'm not going to give you the key.'

'Don't be so stupid. Just grow up, and give me the key.'

He adamantly refused to hand back the room key, so in the end I telephoned the police. I was not going to have this idiot stealing my property.

'I want you to put in writing that you're not going to charge me for the room,' he shouted.

'I'm not going to charge you. I just want you to give me the key and leave. I don't want you in my hotel.'

Before the police arrived, the man decided that it was time to depart. He ran out of the door with his friend and down the steps, still holding on to the room key. I was not having that, so I ran after him and blocked his way.

'What is your problem?' I yelled. 'You're not going anywhere until you give me back my property. Now pack this up.'

I stood outside in the freezing cold of a December night, praying that the police would turn up. But there was no sign. It was 9.45 p.m. and an hour later I was still keeping the man at bay. As midnight approached, the Night Manager came out with a mug of tea to warm me up. Taking advantage of my momentary distraction with the tea, the man saw his chance to get past me, so I quickly grabbed his suitcase.

'What are you doing?' He tried to wrench the case from my hand.

'Don't you touch me!' I warned. 'That's the last thing you want to be doing. You've got my key, now I've got your bag. If you want to leave, give me back the key, or you're going nowhere.'

It was a Saturday night and the police clearly had other priorities. So we waited. And we waited. It was total stalemate. The man continued to hurl abuse at me and I was determined not to give in. At 11.45 p.m. Wendy had telephoned from home as she was wondering why I was so late getting back, and now she pulled up in the car.

'You're the one that started all this,' I was shouting at the man. 'Just give me the key and bugger off!'

'Oh, who's this then?' he sneered as Wendy approached.

'It's my wife, why?'

'You're married to *this*?' he goaded her.

That was too much. I was not going to have him insult me. I so desperately wanted to give him a right hook under the chin and knock him out, as my father had taught me, but instead I threw the mug of tea in his face.

'That's it!' he screamed. 'I'll have you for GBH. You're in trouble now!'

'Oh shut up, you big drip,' I'd really had enough of him. 'You're lucky I didn't whack you one.'

At this moment, a police car came along Royal Parade outside the hotel. Thinking it was heading for the Langham, the man ran straight out into the road, right in front of the vehicle. Unfortunately the driver was heading elsewhere, knew nothing whatsoever about our incident, and nearly knocked the man over. Screeching to a halt, a female police officer got out of the car and screamed at the man for running in front of her. She really tore him apart, as he was within an inch of being killed or badly injured.

'He threw a cup of tea over me!' The man pointed angrily in my direction. I just could not believe what was going on.

'Did you throw a cup of tea over him?' the police officer asked.

'No, officer,' I lied. 'I tripped on his bag and the tea went over him accidentally.'

I'm not sure that she was convinced.

'He's stolen my key,' I continued, 'He's *not* having my key. It's my key, my property, I paid for it, and I want it back.'

We went inside the hotel where she took a statement, and finally the key was returned. As I signed a paper to confirm that I had it back, she warned me that the man might decide to take the matter further.

'I'm sorry about that, Mr Kirby, but he could press charges for assault.'

'I understand that, but I was not prepared to have my property stolen.'

To my utter astonishment, the man did decide to take it further and the following afternoon I was asked to visit the local police station. I stood in front of an unnecessarily high reception desk, with a constable looking down on me as he took my name and details. We happened to be doing the Police Christmas Ball at the hotel that year and the Duty Sergeant recognised me.

'Oh, hello, Mr Kirby, you're the owner of the Langham, aren't you?' he grinned, turning to his constable, 'So what's been going on?'

'Mr Kirby's been accused of throwing a cup of tea.'

'A cup of tea? *A cup of tea!*' The Duty Sergeant looked bemused. 'No stabbing, no shooting, no fighting, no murdering? A cup of tea!' It could have been a scene from *Dixon of Dock Green*. They had no option but to take my fingerprints and a mouth swab, and photograph me, before I was taken to an interview room to give my version of the story. Then I was led down to a police cell.

An hour later I was sitting on the edge of a concrete slab, with my legs dangling over the side. They had taken away my ring and watch, the belt from my trousers and my tie, presumably so that I couldn't hang myself. Suddenly a voice from nowhere asked, 'Mr Kirby, would you like a cup of tea?'

I thought someone was taking the mickey! I knew that I shouldn't have thrown a cup of tea over someone, but this was farcical. I then realised that there was a speaker and camera in the corner, so it was a genuine request.

'No, I'm all right, thank you.'

After speaking to Wendy, the receptionist, and the Night Manager at the Langham to confirm how abusive the man had been, the police dropped all charges.

In 2008 we were approached about holding a workshop at the Langham and a function room was duly booked for a date in October, in the name of Dr Philip Nitschke. It is not our business to interrogate customers as to the content of their meetings, but in this instance I had a shock to turn on the television and see the Langham Hotel featured on the news. Philip Nitschke, known as 'Dr Death', was apparently planning a workshop at the Langham on the controversial subject of euthanasia. He was the first doctor in the world to give a legal, lethal injection. Police and politicians expressed concerns that he might be committing a criminal offence, and members of the public spoke out against the workshop, feeling that 'Dr Death' could encourage vulnerable people to commit suicide. We immediately cancelled the booking and the depth of public reaction made it clear that 'Dr Death' was not welcome in Eastbourne. When Dr Nitschke planned a UK tour in May 2009, I told a journalist: 'If he tries to come in the back door, as he did last time by not explaining what he was doing, he will get a right foot shoved up his backside.' She printed it too. That same month I was photographed outside the Langham with a prospective candidate for the County Council, prior to the local elections. This picture featured prominently on a leaflet pushed through every door in the constituency. Soon afterwards he was on the front page of the papers, with the headline: 'BIGAMY SHOCK OF CANDIDATE'. Oh well, you can't win them all.

The hotel and leisure industry has certainly changed in the twenty-first century. Today technology plays a greater part than it has ever done. Even when I purchased the Langham in 2005, we used to only get two or three occasional bookings from the internet. Now the internet plays an enormous role, especially when people are looking for a room at the last minute, and forty per cent of our business comes that way. The Langham website suddenly became crucial.

In 2008 Wendy and I were staying at the Dorchester Hotel in London, a near neighbour of the Grosvenor House in Park Lane. When we arrived, we were greeted by the Guests' Relations Officer. She acknowledged us in a genial way and just seemed to brush her face as we passed by. As soon as we entered the hotel lobby, a receptionist that I had never met before in my life welcomed us with, 'Good evening, Mr and Mrs Kirby.' Later I discovered that the 'doorman' had a microphone up her sleeve and, when she appeared to brush her face, she was actually alerting reception to our arrival. It certainly makes guests feel special when they are greeted by name.

In many industries modern technology is impersonal, but in five-star hospitality it is actually leading to an even more personal service. Through computers, hotels can now keep a record of regular guests' individual requirements. So a barman can seemingly remember a guest's favourite tipple, a waitress will automatically give a non-meat-eating guest the vegetarian menu without having to be asked, and we can alert guests by email of special promotions that will be of particular interest. When I first worked in hotels we simply had to learn the guests' names by rote, and it was always so much easier to remember the ones that gave the largest tips, but today's technology has made life easier for both staff and residents alike. Not surprisingly, the most recent addition to the list of employees is the E-Butler, who guides guests through the systems in their rooms, from demonstrating the infrared cordless keyboard to showing them how to select some of the 5,000 music tracks available on demand.

I have lived through four recessions in the hotel business and with the world financial crisis in 2009 we had to make economies. We sold our flat at the marina and moved back into the hotel, and downsized our car. Wendy and I worked behind reception occasionally to save money. I sometimes found myself serving behind the bar and am still doing 100 hours a week. So nothing gets any easier as the years go by. I'm working harder than I did forty years ago at Grosvenor House, but I am proud that the Langham has been such a success. Strangely, sales gradually began to increase as a result of the recession. Many couples, for example, found that they could no longer afford to have their wedding at some of Eastbourne's four- or five-star hotels, and so they came to the Langham instead. It's an ill wind, as they say.

I love being in the hospitality business, and enjoy meeting clients and guests, and dealing with staff. The only people I have never really liked are hotel inspectors. In five- and four-star hotels AA inspectors arrive unannounced for an overnight stay, scrutinise various aspects of the hotel, and only reveal their identity when they check out at reception the following morning. They then meet with the General Manager and give a verbal report of their stay, followed by a walk around the hotel to point out where improvements can be made. Later a written document is sent, giving an AA grading as a percentage.

Before we bought the Langham and I was still in management, if a guest was suspected of being an AA inspector, and they were invariably easy to spot, we waited until they came down for tea and then someone would have a glance at their room. If an AA business card was found, then we knew for certain that they were an inspector and the service improved dramatically. Inspectors nearly always arrived in the same type of car, usually a Vauxhall, which gave an early clue to their identity. This was because the AA rented the same vehicles for all their inspectors. The person was always alone, smartly dressed, carried a briefcase or a laptop, and, if I thought that he or she might be an inspector, I immediately went outside to see what type of car they were driving. Just a glance through the car window at papers or maps on the seat would often be enough to confirm my suspicions. I was once certain that a particular woman was an inspector, rather than a regular guest, so I searched her room when she had gone into dinner to look for proof of an AA card inside her suitcase. Later she came to me at the reception desk and complained that somebody had been in her room.

'How do you know?' I asked, trying not to blush.

'Because I always pack my suitcase very neatly, and now something is hanging out of it.'

I did not dare confess that I was the culprit, but she received wonderful service throughout the rest of her stay. In the end, it turned out that she was not an inspector at all.

Having had many years' experience of hotel inspectors, I am irritated by the inconsistencies amongst them. I appreciate that it is not an easy job to do, but their conclusions after a stay are purely a personal opinion. So what might be praised by one inspector can be criticised by another. One year an inspector may perhaps say that all bathroom accessories need to be stainless-steel if you want to increase the rating, so the hotel will invest in stainless-steel accessories. The following year's inspector might then penalise the hotel for having stainless-steel, because in his or her opinion all the accessories should be made of white porcelain. So recommendations from one assessor can be overturned by another. I've known inspectors tell a small hotel that they must invest in a particular brand of tumble dryer to make their towels fluffy, then a year later the hotel loses points for not being environmentally friendly because they are using that make of tumble dryer. It is also ridiculous to try and impose the same standards on a country house hotel as a modern boutique hotel, so allowances ought to be made for individuality too. If an inspector at the Langham today says that he doesn't like a new black-and-white marble floor in an en-suite bathroom, I find that irritating. If I like it and my guests like it, what does it really matter if a hotel inspector doesn't?

One of my biggest gripes is that a lot of younger hotel inspectors are relatively inexperienced within the hospitality trade. Sometimes during an inspection they have begun to tell me how I should change my restaurant.

'Can I just stop you there,' I will say calmly. 'Where have you come from within the industry?'

'Oh, I used to be a housekeeper.'

'A housekeeper. And so how do you know about food?'

That always floors them, and the tables are turned. Even when we achieved two AA rosettes for our food at the Berystede Hotel, inspectors could still be unnecessarily critical. I don't mind constructive criticism in the least, and it is helpful, for example, to know that the lighting over a particular bedroom mirror needs to be improved. But I do object to pointless fault-finding just for the sake of it.

'You don't have tea and coffee-making facilities in the bedroom,' one inspector complained at Grosvenor House.

'That's because this is a five-star hotel,' I said. 'If guests want tea or coffee, they ring down for it.'

Hotel inspectors invariably carry out the same ploys. Before they arrive, they send themselves a message to the hotel reception. This is to check on our efficiency.

'There's a message for you, Mr Smith,' reception would say as the inspector checked in. That was a good sign, because it showed that the hotel staff were on the ball. If they forgot to pass the message on, that meant points lost. How the message was delivered was taken into account too. It had to be taken down accurately in clear handwriting, and placed in a sealed envelope.

'Do you have a guest called Mr Smith staying with you?' a telephone caller might have asked earlier in the day.

'Yes, Sir.'

'Can you tell him that I'll meet him in the bar at 7.30 p.m. for dinner this evening? My name is Mr Jones.'

'Certainly, Sir.'

I used to tell my staff that if such a message awaited a guest's arrival, the chances were that the guest was actually a hotel inspector. It is very unusual for an ordinary guest to have a message waiting for them like that, so this was an early indication. We became very wise to them and could almost recognise an inspector from the moment the initial reservation was made.

The inspectors nearly always used to come down to the lounge and order afternoon tea soon after their arrival, and just seemed to stand out a mile. They used to not only follow the tea with a large dinner, but they would also order a room-service meal as well. This was to check out all aspects of the food and service. They could not eat all the food, of course, as they would have been ill or obese, so it must have ended up being flushed down the toilet. We made sure that inspectors received the best possible service throughout their stay, and even ironed their newspapers.

'Did you know that I was an AA inspector?' they would generally ask, once they had revealed their identity.

'I hadn't got a clue,' I would say innocently. 'You've caught us well and good here. None of us knew at all.'

We always got high scores. Once the inspector had gone, we then rang or emailed fellow hotel owners to warn them that inspectors were in the area and to be on their guard.

At one time we had AA, RAC and Michelin Guide inspectors turning up – and had to pay for the privilege too. The RAC inspections were less efficient in my opinion and now no longer exist. The Michelin inspections were annoying, simply because the hotel received no feedback whatsoever and you had to wait for the results to be published. Environmental health inspectors are far more important, because cleanliness is paramount in a hotel, and they give good, practical advice. It is all part and parcel of running a hotel.

In June 2009 I was delighted to be able to help the next generation of hoteliers get a foot on the ladder. I joined former England footballer Graeme Le Saux, athletes including Iwan Thomas and Roger Black, chef Michel Roux junior, and a number of celebrities, hoteliers and chefs, in a 4.5-kilometre run around the Serpentine in Hyde Park, ending with an exhausting climb up twenty-eight floors to the Windows Restaurant at the top of the Hilton Hotel on Park Lane. The last part was punishing, but I at least managed to come fortieth out of 120 runners. The event raised around £30,000 towards a project, initiated by the Hilton, which offers apprenticeships in some of London's top hotels to disadvantaged young people between the ages of eighteen and twenty-four. Youngsters who could previously only ever dream of working 'front of house' in a five-star hotel can now see that dream become a reality, and the best possible training will equip them with the skills that they will need to succeed. Council-estate kids, as I had once been, might one day have a hotel of their own. How could I not support such a project?

After the race, that evening Wendy and I ate at Michel Roux junior's restaurant Le Gavroche in Upper Brook Street, just yards from Grosvenor House. Michel was absolutely charming, gave us a free drink, and we discussed the importance of staff having a good attitude and working together as a team. I was thrilled that he and I shared the same views about the key to running a successful business.

'The food was better than Gordon Ramsay's,' I joked as we said goodbye.

'Don't swear in here!' he grinned.

Recently I returned to Grosvenor House for a lunch, back to where my career began so long ago. It was odd, sitting on the other side of the fence, being served in the rooms where I had once served. There was the lounge area that I had designed with Olga Polizzi, almost unchanged. The famous 1933 painting of the Prince of Wales and Mrs Wallis Simpson, still hanging where I had hung it. I watched the Great Room being set up for a major award ceremony that night, some of my former employees suddenly looking up, taken aback at the sight of me watching over them once again as if time had momentarily reversed. It was a world that all seemed so familiar, and yet strangely so very far away.

The doorman still knew me by name, and as he hailed a taxi for us when we departed, asked:

'Who do you work for now, Mr Kirby?'

'Oh, I've bought my own hotel,' I answered and, as the car swept out of the forecourt and into Park Lane, it suddenly hit me for the first time just how far I had really travelled.

It was a journey worth making. I returned to Eastbourne's Royal Parade that evening, inhaled the fresh sea air deeply into my lungs, and stood motionless for a moment just looking at the Langham Hotel. She seemed to be almost glowing in the reflection of the setting summer sun. The Union Jack fluttered lazily on its pole, holidaymakers were sitting out on the terrace enjoying a cool beer, and I could see diners in The Conservatory restaurant, their faces highlighted by the candles flickering softly between them. It was a scene of calm contentment. This was my hotel, and I knew then without a shadow of doubt that I had no regrets.

'Welcome home, Mr Kirby. Good trip to London? The sink's blocked again in 216, eight guests got stuck in the lift this morning, and the meat delivery hasn't arrived. Oh, and chef's cut his finger . . .'

Acknowledgements

Having now spent more than four decades working in various hotels, many thousands of people have been 'guests' in my life. Some have made only a short stay, but have left a lasting impression. Others have been long-term inhabitants who still influence me today. A few have taken up permanent residence in my life, and for that I am truly grateful.

I cherish the memory of the late Lord Forte for his inspiration and for giving me opportunities to progress in my career. I am grateful to Sir Rocco Forte, for our many years together as employer and employee, as running partners, and, I hope, friends. I have always valued his faith in me. I am indebted also to Sir Rocco's sister, Olga Polizzi Shawcross, for teaching me so much about interior design.

Thanks go to my darling wife Wendy, who (despite raising her eyes to heaven each time I told people that I was one day going to write a book) has not only given invaluable advice on grammar, syntax, spelling, and jogged my sometimes failing memory, but has been the most wonderful friend and partner for more than thirty-five years. Words cannot express how grateful I am for her constant support.

I would like in addition to thank the following for their practical help and encouragement: Tony Murkett, now Managing Director of the Sloane Club in London, who was once my direct boss as General Manager of Grosvenor House and saw the potential in me to progress, and promoted me to Deputy General Manager – without him I might still be a kitchen porter or valet; Giuseppe Pecorelli, who employed me at Pennyhill Park and South Lodge, and who was a real inspiration and taught me a great deal about the refurbishment of hotels; Giuseppe's son, Danny Pecorelli; Dennis Hearn, the Deputy Chief Executive of Trusthouse Forte, who gave me many opportunities and supported me in my career; Paul Harvey, former

Chief Accountant at Grosvenor House, the best accountant I ever worked with and for whom nothing was too much trouble; Andrew Coy, who worked with me at Grosvenor House and Royal Horseguards, and who is now General Manager of the Langham Hotel – he has been a great teacher and his attention to detail is second to none.

I worked with some wonderful people at Grosvenor House and here pay tribute to them. John Salmon was employed there for over fifty years. He began originally as a pageboy and later became Head Valet. We worked together for many years and both played for the Grosvenor House football team – he gave great service to the hospitality industry. David Jones worked at Grosvenor House even longer, clocking up more than fifty-one years. He also started as a pageboy and ended up as number- two Concierge. He has reminded me of things that happened to us, which I had long forgotten, and I thank him for nudging my memory. Willy Bauer was my General Manager at Grosvenor House in the early 1980s, and taught me a lot about the importance of paying attention to detail. David Abbott was the Apartments Manager and was the first man to interview me, giving me my first job at Grosvenor House. Linda Woodhouse was Human Resources Manager during my time at Grosvenor House and taught me a great deal about understanding the rules and regulations within the industry. Colin Thorn was Head Waiter and coach of the Grosvenor House football team, while brothers Mel and Alan Trundley of the Grosvenor House Maintenance Department were great footballers with whom I shared a fantastic time as the Hotel and Catering League Champions. Brothers Charlie and Michael Wiggins, valets in the apartment block, were wonderful to work with. Dickie Elms, Karl Edmunds and Lewis Hamblett were all very talented chefs, from whom many of today's celebrity chefs could learn a great deal. Mark Mitten worked for me in the Laundry Room when I was Back of House Manager, and John Patterson was in charge of the Laundry Room. They were both brilliant employees.

Other colleagues and friends I should mention include: John Beecroft, General Manager of the Royal Horseguards Hotel; Magdi Restum, my Front of House Manager at Grosvenor House; my PAs at Grosvenor House, Susan and Marianne, and Pam Smith my PA at Pennyhill; Harry Murray MBE, former Hotelier of the Year, a great all-rounder in the hospitality industry; Alan Gomm, who was Head of Security at Grosvenor House and did such an important and difficult job; Simon Brown, who I employed at Pennyhill Park, Royal Horseguards and South Lodge; my mate Stuart

Portlock, with whom I have worked in several hotels including the Langham; Debbie Guy, Sales Manager at the Berystede Hotel and later Pennyhill; Louise Wilmott, who first worked for me as a receptionist at Grosvenor House and the Berystede, and later in sales at Pennyhill and Royal Horseguards; Janice Covington, my former Housekeeper at the Berystede and Pennyhill; Peter Carter, my Deputy Manager at Pennyhill; John Josey, my decorator at Pennyhill, South Lodge and the Langham, who works from my designs and always manages to achieve the result I have visualised; Christine Davies, who has been a fantastic financial advisor; also the linen manufacturers and suppliers Sylvie and Nick Van Gelderen, and their son Derreck, not only for their superb merchandise but also their valued friendship. Not forgetting one of my oldest friends, David O'Keeffe, with such happy memories of our footballing years.

I am indebted to some former colleagues who have sadly now passed away: Dick Smith, the Head Valet who taught me so much about the job; the Guests' Relations Manager, Jimmy Welsh, who was yet another who worked at Grosvenor House for more than half a century, and from whom I learned a great deal about customer service; Tony Preston, a chef at Grosvenor House, who sadly broke his neck in a holiday accident and died all too young – he taught me that not all chefs are bad; George Lehrian, once General Manager at Grosvenor House before becoming Managing Director of Exclusive Hotels, another who taught me so much and who gave me a gift – an original Grosvenor House tie with its gates emblem – which I still have to this day.

I must thank the wonderful team of employees that I have at the Langham Hotel, with particular gratitude to my Head Chef, Michael Titherington; Head Receptionist, Claire Titherington; Restaurant Manager, Aliona Sertvytyte; and Head Housekeeper, Zdenka Zakova. Not forgetting Rita and Bob Prodger, who have given us so much practical help and support since we bought the hotel.

I would also like to thank the many friends, past and present colleagues, hotel patrons, and members of the South Lodge and Langham Hotel ladies' lunch clubs, who have all proffered support and encouragement. I am grateful also to Carol Biss and her team at the Book Guild for their help and enthusiasm.

Last, but certainly not least, I am indebted to the author and broadcaster Paul James, without whom this book simply would not have been written. He has coped admirably with my dyslexic handwriting and spent many hours listening patiently to my stories, to put my words and thoughts into print. We have laughed ourselves silly in the process, drank gallons of coffee, and consumed enough chocolate biscuits, cakes and flapjacks to feed a small hotel.

Any book of this nature inevitably relies heavily on memories of events that have taken place over a long period of time. Occasionally the chronology can be hard to remember, but we have tried to verify information wherever possible. In certain circumstances names of employers, employees and guests have been changed for the sake of confidentiality. Any opinions expressed in the book are my own, as are any unwitting errors or omissions.

NEIL KIRBY
Langham Hotel, Eastbourne
April 2010

www.langhamhotel.co.uk

Index